The Law and the Expanding Nursing Role

The Law and the Expanding Nursing Role

Second Edition

edited by

Bonnie Bullough, R.N., Ph.D.
Dean, School of Nursing
State University of New York at Buffalo
Buffalo, New York

APPLETON-CENTURY-CROFTS/New York

Copyright © 1980 by APPLETON-CENTURY-CROFTS
A Publishing Division of Prentice-Hall, Inc.

All rights reserved. This book, or any parts thereof, may not be used or reproduced in any manner without written permission. For information, address Appleton-Century-Crofts, 292 Madison Avenue, New York, N.Y. 10017.

80 81 82 83 84 10 9 8 7 6 5 4 3 2 1

Prentice-Hall International, Inc., London
Prentice-Hall of Australia, Pty. Ltd., Sydney
Prentice-Hall of India Private Limited, New Delhi
Prentice-Hall of Japan, Inc., Tokyo
Prentice-Hall of Southeast Asia (Pte.) Ltd., Singapore
Whitehall Books Ltd., Wellington, New Zealand

Library of Congress Cataloging in Publication Data

Main entry under title:

The Law and the expanding nursing role.

   Bibliography: p. 213
   Includes index.
   1. Nursing—Law and legislation—United States.
I. Bullough, Bonnie.
KF2915.N8L3 1980   344.73′0414   80-10322
ISBN 0-8385-5632-X

Text design: Doug Jones
Cover design: Myrna Sharp

PRINTED IN THE UNITED STATES OF AMERICA

Contents

Contributors	vii
Preface	ix

Section One: Nursing Practice Law 1

1 The Law: History and Basic Concepts 3
  Vern L. Bullough

2 Licensure and the Medical Monopoly 14
  Vern L. Bullough

3 The First Two Phases in Nursing Licensure 23
  Bonnie Bullough

4 Role Expansion: The Driving and Restraining Forces 36
  Bonnie Bullough

5 The Third Phase in Nursing Licensure: 47
  The Current Nurse Practice Acts
  Bonnie Bullough

6 Avoiding Legal Liability 67
  Joan P. Randall

Section Two: Changing the Law 85
and the Law as an Instrument of Change

7 The Political Process or the Power and the Glory 87
  Donna F. Ver Steeg

8 The Washington State Success Story 100
  Joan P. Whinihan

9	Institutional Licensure—Panic or Panacea? *Lucie Young Kelly*	109
10	Denver: A Case Study *Craig S. Barnes*	125

Section Three: Nurse Practitioners, Clinical Specialists, and Physician's Assistants   139

11	Nursing Functions in Other Countries: Insights for the United States *Ruth Roemer*	141
12	Nurses in Private Practice *Patricia J. Lewis*	156
13	The Evolving Mental Health Clinical Nurse Specialist in Private Practice *Corrine L. Hatton*	164
14	Physician's Assistants and the Law *Bonnie Bullough and Carol Ann Winter*	170
15	Constructing and Adapting Protocols *Martha A. Siegel and Bonnie Bullough*	179
16	Protocols as Analogs to Standing Orders *Sheldon Greenfield*	186
17	Emerging Trends in Nursing Practice and Law *Bonnie Bullough*	203
	Bibliography	213
	Index	229

Contributors

Craig S. Barnes
Attorney at Law
Denver, Colorado

Vern L. Bullough, R.N., Ph.D.
Dean, Faculty of Natural and Social Sciences
State University of New York College at Buffalo
Buffalo, New York

Sheldon Greenfield, M.D.
Associate Professor, School of Public Health
University of California
Los Angeles, California

Corrine L. Hatton, R.N., M.N.
Mental Health Clinical Nurse Specialist in private practice
Santa Monica, California

Lucie Young Kelly, R.N., Ph.D., F.A.A.N.
Professor of Nursing in Public Health
School of Public Health and School of Nursing
Columbia University
New York, New York

Patricia J. Lewis, R.N., M.N.
Founder, Health Care Professionals
Merton, Wisconsin

Joan P. Randall, R.N.
Nurse Consultant
Long Beach, California

Ruth Roemer, J.D.
Researcher in Health Law
School of Public Health
University of California
Los Angeles, California

Martha A. Siegel, R.N., M.S.
Associate Professor of Nursing
California State University
Long Beach, California

Donna F. Ver Steeg, R.N., Ph.D.
Assistant Dean, School of Nursing
University of California
Los Angeles, California

Joan P. Whinihan
Director of Communications
Washington State Nurses Association
Seattle, Washington

Carol Ann Winter, B.S.N.
Obstetric-Gynecologic Nurse Practitioner
Los Angeles, California

Preface

A second edition of *The Law and the Expanding Nursing Role* seemed necessary for several reasons. First, the state nurse practice acts and the regulations governing nursing practice have been changing at a rapid rate as nurses expand their roles in diagnosis and patient care. This book gives an update on the significant changes that have occurred and suggested trends that may create further changes.

Second, much additional material on the basic structure and function of law, particularly as it relates to malpractice, has been added to this edition in response to suggestions from nursing professors who wanted to use the book as a text in courses on law for nurses. They explained that students need to be armed with this type of information before they can practice safely.

Third, several of the authors who wrote chapters for the first edition of the book have revised and updated their offerings in light of the changing situation or changes in their point of view. One of these authors, Ruth Roemer, has even decided that she is opposed to the further development of nurse practitioners. This puts her in direct ideological opposition to the editor, who favors all types of role expansion for nurses. Roemer's reasons are interesting and they certainly add a note of controversy to this edition. Nurses will need to think through this important issue, and the contrasting opinions should help with this task.

Fourth, included in this edition is a chapter on what may become a landmark law suit, *Lemons et al. v. City and County of Denver*. Although this case has been decided in favor of the City and County of Denver and against the nurse plaintiffs, the decision is being challenged. Win or lose, this case marks the beginning of an important struggle for equitable pay, not only for nurses, but as well for women generally.

The interaction between the changing scope of function for nurses and the changing laws governing nursing make this an exciting but somewhat difficult era for nurses. I hope that this edition will further illuminate this changing picture.

One other new development with this edition should also be noted. The editor's favorite co-author, Vern Bullough, has added the title of nurse to that of historian.

BONNIE BULLOUGH

The Law and the Expanding Nursing Role

SECTION ONE

Nursing Practice Law

1 The Law: History and Basic Concepts

VERN L. BULLOUGH

While most nurses will never end up in court, ours is becoming an ever more litigious society, and there is always the possibility that even the most innocent of actions will be taken by someone as grounds for a lawsuit.

Nurses may come into contact with criminal law not only as everyone else does but also through their unique circumstances. For example, theft of drugs is a criminal activity regarding which people with access to drugs, such as nurses, have unique temptations. When negligence leads to the death of a patient, it is possible for a nurse to be charged with manslaughter or even murder. Here as in other legal areas, however, there have been changes. A few years ago any nurse assisting with an abortion was engaged in a criminal act, but after the 1973 Supreme Court decision recognizing abortion as a constitutional right, it could become part of a nurse's assigned duty to assist in or to give abortions.[1] Nurses who still believed that abortions were immoral, could request other assignments.

Some understanding of the history and procedures of law is therefore not only helpful but essential in an age when nurses are increasingly being held legally accountable for their practice.

The term *law* is derived from the Anglo-Saxon *lagu*, meaning that which is laid down or fixed. In simple terms, law includes all the rules of conduct established and enforced by the authority, custom, or legislative action of a given community, state, or nation. This means that laws vary from one community to another and the differences become greater as we move to larger units such as states or countries. Within a nation such as the United States, however, there are some binding ties which foster similarities between the laws of various localities or states. Some of these ties predate the formation of the United States and can be traced back to England, whose legal traditions are part of our history since we use what is known as English common law as a basis for our law. Law in Europe, Latin America, and many other parts of the world is based on Roman law which has different precedents and assumptions than common law.

The American Constitution, legislation by Congress, and interpretations of law by the United States Supreme Court are other unifying forces shaping American law. There is greater uniformity of law among communities within any one state than with those outside because of enactments of state legislative bodies, legal decisions of the state supreme court, and the binding force of the state constitution. Still, each city and county has some limited right to make laws governing its own area of jurisdiction.

THE HISTORY OF LAW

Precedents for current laws can be traced far back in history. Moses, the Jewish prophet, was a lawgiver, and the Ten Commandments which the Bible says he received from Jehovah are a primitive form of law, still holding great meaning for many Americans. Some prohibitions of the Mosaic law still appear in various criminal codes in the United States; for example, the provision of penalties for violating the commandment *Thou shalt not kill*. But the law now recognizes various levels of killing, some of which are not punished; we tend to distinguish murder from manslaughter, and to indicate degrees of each, and sometimes we say that killing is justified. At times we even give medals to those who kill others (as in war). What was once a simple prohibition has become quite complex. Other actions prohibited by the Mosaic Code—such as adultery—are not now regarded as criminal activities or even as violations of the law; in such cases the code is seen as providing moral guidelines for society.

Some of the earliest surviving written documents are laws, such as the laws of Sargon from ancient Mesopotamia—evidence that every society of any size had or has laws. Not all laws, however, are written down; many derive from local customs which in many ways achieve the force of law. Inculcation of what a particular society regards as acceptable as distinguished from what it regards as unacceptable begins with the childhood socialization process. Children are punished or rewarded for doing certain things, and grow up learning to accept the rules of society. Not surprisingly, most individuals conform to what is expected, so that adherence to laws and awareness of laws seems to become almost intuitive. Most of us stop at stop signs, pay our income tax, avoid the temptation to steal, and in general are law-abiding citizens. Society, in fact, is based upon the assumption that most citizens will obey the laws. We have police and other law enforcement officials to act as sort of reminder, and courts to punish us if we are caught ignoring the laws, but without majority support, laws are not ordinarily effective. A historical example of the failure of a society to enforce an unpopular law is the Eighteenth Amendment to the Constitution, ratified January 29, 1919, which made the manufacture, sale, and transportation of intoxicating liquors illegal. Americans ultimately came to ignore this prohibition in such numbers that there was a mass breakdown in law enforcement, with an accompanying widespread corruption of police and city governments. Ultimately the amendment was repealed by the Twenty-first Amendment, which was declared ratified on December 5, 1933.

At times laws seem to be an unnecessary and complicating fact of life. Consequently individuals or groups known as philosophical anarchists have from time to time appeared, urging the existence of an open society without laws, or rather without overt enforcement of the customs of the society. Periodically, small utopian societies have been established based on anarchical principles, but ultimately in order to survive they have had to adopt rules and regulations of their own which were equivalent to laws. Even dedicated religious communities, such as monasteries and convents, have found that they needed rules and regulations to function effectively. This evidence has led scholars to conclude that laws are essential to the functioning of societies.

E. A. Hoebel, an anthropologist who studied law among primitive peoples, concluded that law performed certain essential functions necessary for the maintenance of all but the most simple societies:

1. The first is to define relationships among the members of a society, to assert what activities are permitted and what are ruled out, so as to maintain at least minimal integration between the activities of individuals and groups within the society.
2. The second is derived from the necessity of taming naked force and directing force to the maintenance of order. It is the allocation of authority and the determination of who may exercise physical coercion as a socially recognized privilege-right, along with the selection of the most effective forms of physical sanction to achieve the social ends which law serves.
3. The third is the disposition of trouble cases as they arise so that social harmony may be reestablished.
4. The fourth is to redefine the relations between individuals and groups as the conditions of life change.[2]

In the earliest primitive societies the rules for conduct were a part of the oral tradition which was passed on from one generation to the next. At a later date they were written down. As society became more complex, the laws became more complex. When Moses issued his code of laws they were understood by all of his followers; if the laws were violated Moses or the Council of Elders could meet and judge the situation. As society grew and its laws became more numerous, some people were recognized as having particular skill in interpreting the law, and they came to be called judges, a term derived from the Latin and meaning one who declares what the law is. Such an official was almost a necessity, since no matter how clearly a law is written, it cannot cover all circumstances which might lead to its violation. Thus a judge is called in to interpret the meaning of the law as it applies in a specific case.

Nominally, kings or rulers were the final arbitrators of what the meaning of the law should be, but in most cases the rulers preferred to rely upon trusted councillors or judges, and themselves acted only as a final court of appeal, as the President of the United States or the governor of a state now does in commuting sentences or pardoning individuals. Officials surrounding the king who acted as his advisers were known as his court; in addition to the large court there were specialty courts, and it is from these that our own judicial courts developed.*

Once it became apparent that laws could be interpreted in various and conflicting ways, it became important for those accused of violating the law to have an advocate urging the interpretation most favorable to them. Thus the concept of the attorney developed. This term derives from Old French and means to commit one's business to another. The courts, however, did not want just any advocate appearing before them, but one over whom they also had some control. Thus an attorney at law is an attorney recognized by the court, one who has been admitted to the bar. The term *bar* comes from the railing that separated the judge and the defendant from the public, and which attorneys, as officials of the court, could pass through.

If the accused could have advocates urging their cases, then accusers, whether individuals or government entities, could also have advocates urging their side. The result was the emergence of the principle basic to the American system of judicial advocacy: the adversary system. Each side in a case tries to make its side appear to be the side of rightness and virtue and the other side to be wrong and sinful. Theoretically, such a conflict is the best way to reveal which side has the greater amount of justified claim, as determined by either a judge or a jury.

The jury does not usually decide law, but only the evidence in the case. It is derived from the English custom of calling upon twelve men in the community to determine the truth or falsity of certain statements of fact. The jury was eventually called upon to determine innocence or guilt, after which the judge passed sentence.

Although truth and rightness will, in theory, prevail in a trial, the only thing the court can guarantee is that the judicial process will be carried out. That is, the judge and the officials of the court will promise to listen more or less impartially and render a judgment based on their perception of the facts, which might or might not agree with that of others. In any particular case, what the judge determines are the law and the penalties to be imposed. Since there are so many grounds for error, and even judges are occasionally prejudiced, decisions can usually be appealed to higher courts on the state or the federal level if a defendant has sufficient money or support to carry out an appeal. In some cases, such as the imposition of the death penalty, review has come to be almost automatic, even for those who cannot afford to appeal their sentences.

It is apparent that laws have varied over time. In fact, to be effective laws must change with the times, to meet the needs of a changing society. At one time certain cities required the new horseless carriages to be preceded by a runner, who would alert carriage drivers that an automobile was approaching. As

---

*The word *court*, however, still retains some of its other meanings: beauty queens have their court; so does the ruler of England, while the military sometimes have courts of honor, and a young man might court (pay attention to) a young woman.

automobiles became ubiquitous, such a law simply had no place. In the United States laws are changed both by statute (statutory law) and by court decision (case law). The reasons for this are discussed below.

COMMON STATUTORY LAW

Basic to American law is "common law," a term used to distinguish the legal systems of the English-speaking countries (with few exceptions) from the civil law systems which are current in European countries and their former colonies (such as Latin America). Civil law systems are based upon Roman law, especially as codified by the Emperor Justinian in the sixth century A.D. The common law originates in judicial decisions rendered in the English royal courts established by Henry II in the twelfth century. Common law is essentially judge-made law, the aggregate of decisions in thousands of individual cases, and it originally was called "common law" because all the king's subjects were ultimately subject to such decisions. The common law is nowhere explicitly set forth in writing, but rather is the accumulation of legal decisions that have been handed down, first in England and now in various other common-law countries. American common law differs from English common law because after the Revolution, when the American states had severed their connection with England, decisions of the English courts were not necessarily regarded as authorative for American courts.

Still, some English decisions made in the nineteenth century were incorporated into American common law. A good example is the concept of insanity. When is a person insane? While insanity might be a medical diagnosis, for all practical purposes in the past it has been a legal definition. To be committed to an institution, a person had to be declared insane. The issue is complicated by the fact that a person committing an offense can sometimes escape punishment by claiming insanity at the time the act was committed. All states except New Hampshire based their legal definitions of insanity on the McNaghten case, which was decided in England in 1843.[3] Daniel McNaghten failed in an attempt to assassinate the Prime Minister of Great Britian in 1843, but did succeed in killing his private secretary. At his trial McNaghten was ruled insane at the time of the act on the basis of medical evidence and was acquitted. The acquittal resulted in an inquiry into the case by the House of Lords, out of which the so-called McNaghten rules emerged.

> Each individual was presumed to be sane, and to possess a sufficient degree of reason to be responsible for his crime, until the contrary was proved . . . and . . . to establish a defense on the ground of insanity, it must be clearly proved that, at the time of committing of the act, the party accused was labouring under such a defect of reason, from the disease of the mind, as not to know the nature and quality of the act he was doing; or if he did know it, that he did not know he was doing what was wrong.[4]

Thus the issue of criminal responsibility was determined by whether a person knew what was right or wrong. Obviously this was a legal fiction without relation to the real world of insanity, and in fact is contrary to much of the psychiatric and psychological evidence of the twentieth century. It was not until 1954 that a prominent federal judge, in a rather lengthy opinion,[5] reviewed much of the relevant psychiatric literature and determined that the test as an "exclusive criterion" of rightness or wrongness was inadequate because it did not take into account psychic realities and scientific knowledge. It was based upon one symptom and could not validly be applied in all circumstances. But if this is the case, what standards can be used? Increasingly the courts are turning to the American Law Institute's *Model Penal Code,* * which states

> (1) a person is not responsible for criminal conduct if at the time of such conduct as a result of mental disease or defect he lacks substantial capacity either to appreciate the criminality of his conduct or to conform his conduct to the requirement of law and (2) the terms "mental disease or defect" do not include an abnormality manifested only by repeated criminal or otherwise anti-social conduct.[6]

Gradually the law, at least in this respect, has been changing. Oliver Wendel Holmes, Jr., one of the most famous of United States Supreme Court justices, known during much of his term as the Great Dissenter, wrote about common law:

> The life of the law has not been logic: it has been experience. The felt necessities of the time, the prevalent moral and political theories, intuitions of public policy, avowed or unconscious, even the prejudices which judges share with their fellow-men, have had a good deal more to do than the syllogism in determining the rules by which men should be governed. The law embodies the story of a nation's development through many centuries, and it cannot be dealt with as if it contained only the axioms and corollaries of a book of mathematics. In order to know what it is, we must know what it has been, and what it tends to become.[7]

Laws not only can be reinterpreted by the courts, but their actual content can be changed by statute. Statutes are acts by legislative bodies declaring, commanding, or prohibiting something. Generally in the past neither English nor American lawyers looked favorably upon statutory law, and for a long time such laws were regarded as exceptions to the familiar rules of the common law and were subjected to rather restricted interpretation by the courts unless they regulated an entirely new matter or were largely remedial. Only two states as of this writing have more or less completely codified (statutory) laws: Louisiana and

---

*The American Law Institute is a private organization including all branches of the legal profession: bench, bar, and law schools. One of its major publications is the *Model Penal Code.*

California. Louisiana is a special case since much of its original law was based upon the French or civil law code rather than on English common law. Five other states—Montana, North and South Dakota, Idaho, and Oklahoma—are known as *code states,* since most of their laws are codified or statute law. Other states have codes in particular fields—usually criminal law, criminal procedures, and to a lesser extent civil law. New fields such as taxation, labor, and occupational licensure are almost exclusively statutory, while others are mainly common-law tradition even in statutory states.

American law, however, is unique since all laws, whether common or statutory, must conform to the Constitution of the United States. This is true not only of federal law but of state law since 1807, when the United States Supreme Court decided that state law in contravention of the Constitution was invalid even if it had been passed by the state legislature. Certain laws are more or less prohibited from being passed—namely laws restricting freedom of religion, freedom of speech, and other freedoms mentioned in the Constitution and the Bill of Rights. The ultimate decision about whether a given law contravenes these constitutional provisions is the United States Supreme Court.

In arriving at their decisions, judges rely on precedents, that is, what has been decided before. In legal terms this is called *stare decisis* (or as the full Latin phrase reads, *stare decisis et non quieta movere,* "to uphold precedents and not disturb settled things"). The decision in one case will control the decision of like cases in the same court or in subordinate courts of the same jurisdiction, unless and until the prior decision is overruled by a higher court or by the court from which the precedent emanated. A lower court will not disregard a precedent by a higher court except in rare cases where the lower court concludes that the trend of other decisions by the higher court is such that it would overrule its own earlier decisions if again faced with the same legal problem. The Supreme Court does in fact sometimes change its opinion. This happened, for example, regarding segregated facilities. In 1896 the Court allowed the state of Louisiana to segregate railway cars, and ultimately allowed segregated educational facilities, commercial districts, and even drinking fountains.[8] In 1954 the Court determined that segregation in schools, and ultimately elsewhere, could not in itself give the equal protection set forth in the Fourteenth Amendment to the Constitution, since separate was not equal.[9] In essence the system which the Court had allowed to be established in 1896 was undone by it 58 years later.

CRIMINAL AND CIVIL LAW

The two major divisions of law are criminal law and civil law. Criminal laws deal with crimes or offenses against the state; they are designed to protect all members of society from undesirable and detrimental forms of conduct. Civil laws regulate private disputes or attempt to establish ways to regulate controversies.

Criminal laws attempt to deter crime by indicating to potential violators that penalties or sanctions will be imposed. Theoretically, criminal law is also supposed to involve rehabilitation, and the assumption is that a criminal who is apprehended, tried, convicted, and punished can reenter society as a useful member. There is considerable debate about the rehabilitative function of punishment for criminals, but criminal law is also supposed to give society collectively a kind of revenge, which it more clearly does. In the past, before the state intervened, individuals or families imposed their own punishment on people who injured a clan member or violated a clan tradition. This led to feuding, sometimes to near anarchy, and the state was forced to intervene.

The second major division of law, civil law, involves disputes between private persons, ranging from business contracts to divorce. An important division of civil law is that known as torts. The term "tort" comes from the Latin word meaning twisted and involves a wrongful act resulting in an injury, loss, or damage, for which the injured party can bring civil action. The overriding objective of the tort law is to provide a means for compensating those injured by the wrongful conduct of another. Its purpose is not so much to punish or penalize as to compensate the injured party. A nurse, for example, can be accused by a patient or the patient's heirs or family of negligence for failing to read the warning wrapper on a new drug or of wrongfully applying a restraining device. After a formal charge is made, the case goes to court, where a judge or jury renders a decision based on the evidence and awards appropriate damages. Since the assumption behind tort law is that someone is at fault, it is necessary to prove fault, although most of these cases involve negligence rather than an attempt to commit a deliberate wrong. Negligence in the medical and nursing field has been labeled malpractice, and so malpractice is one area of tort law. Originally the field of torts was more rigidly confined, but recent decisions granting damages for wrongful causation of mental pain without physical injury or for prenatal injuries have expanded the field. A complicating factor in the field of malpractice law has been the development of malpractice insurance. While the insured is protected from paying the large damage claims now in vogue, the knowledge that insurance coverage exists undoubtedly encourages suits. As the economic status of nurses improves, and as nurses become more independent in decision making, they will be the target of more malpractice litigation simply because suing them is economically feasible. This in turn will raise their malpractice insurance premiums.

Nurses are also subject to another kind of statutory law: the regulatory statutes dealing with nursing as an occupation. Medicine, as the most powerful and historically the most organized of the health professions, has long been the subject of special regulation, a topic which is covered in Chapter 2. From the beginning of the twentieth century, nursing practice has also fallen under state control. Nurse practice acts are examined in detail in Chapters 3, 4, and 5.

THE COURTS

The key to the enforcement of the law, whether criminal, civil, or regulatory, ultimately is the courts, and so it becomes important to understand the nature of the courts; their names vary somewhat from state to state but they have a great similarity. The two major divisions are courts created by state action and those created by federal action. Overseeing both of these court systems through its review ability is the Supreme Court of the United States. Generally, federal courts administer laws promulgated by the Congress of the United States, and their jurisdiction is derived from Article III of the Constitution. Unless there is a particular federal interest or federal law involved in a dispute, the federal courts have no power to hear it. Most citizens therefore turn to their state courts to settle legal issues between themselves; federal courts are available for civil controversies between antagonists from different states. Once a decision has been made by a judge, the loser usually can appeal to a higher court. Ultimately the final decision is by the state supreme court, unless there are federal issues involved (including basic constitutional questions); in such cases the U.S. Supreme Court serves as the court of last appeal. There are also special courts created by Congress to handle specific problems; among these are the Court of Customs and Patent Appeals, the Tax Court, and the Court of Claims.

State courts, set up either the state constitutions or by legislative action, handle all types of civil disputes between private citizens as well as criminal cases that arise from violations of the state criminal statutes. Most states have established a number of different courts, including municipal courts which handle minor traffic violations, probate courts which handle the administration of wills and estates, juvenile courts, and small claims courts. States also usually have one or more appellate courts sitting in review of the decisions of their subsidiary courts.

Since criminal actions are regarded as acts against society, not simply against an individual, there is no such thing as a private criminal action. For this reason it is always the state, acting through the office of the public prosecutor, which institutes a criminal proceeding. Except for a few cases of extreme abuse, the decision of whether to prosecute is within the discretion of the prosecutor and ordinarily is not reviewable by the judiciary. In cases involving borderline criminality, such as questionable business dealings or improper family conduct or failure to properly discharge family or business obligations, the prosecutor often tries to encourage the settlement of the dispute without resort to the criminal process.

Usually, after the prosecutor has heard the complaining witness and a sworn complaint has been submitted by either a police officer or a private person, the prosecutor will order the arrest of the suspect. This means that a suspect might escape prosecution if the injured party can be persuaded to refrain from making a complaint. A suspect who has been charged and arrested is supposed to be brought before a magistrate in order to establish a formal record. Often the arrest and detention last only long enough to fingerprint and photograph the suspect and complete the necessary records. Suspects may then be released on their personal bond (their word that they will return), or in the custody of their attorney, or sometimes at a nominal bail. Theoretically bail should be only high enough to assure that the defendant will reappear when required. For more serious crimes, release on bail may be denied. Once a suspect is arrested, the judge must conclude that there is probable cause to believe that the suspect has committed the offense charged. A suspect can request a preliminary examination, at which the state must prove that there is probable cause in order to hold the suspect for trial. This is sometimes requested so that the defense counsel can learn something about the state's case, although the state need only show enough of its evidence at such time to indicate the existence of probable cause for prosecution.

In some states, in order to secure an indictment, the prosecutor presents evidence to a grand jury, a specially empaneled body of citizens, usually 23 in number, from the county having jurisdiction in the case, 16 of whom constitute a quorum, and 12 of whose votes are required to return an indictment. Such procedures are normally required for the more serious offenses, and in federal courts the Fifth Amendment to the Constitution requires indictment by grand jury unless the accused waives such a procedure. After a preliminary examination before either the magistrate or the grand jury, the suspect must be arraigned before the trial court and enter a plea of guilty, not guilty, or not guilty by reason of insanity. The suspect may, with the permission of the judge, also plead *nolo contendere* (I do not wish to deny), which is like a plea of guilty but may not be used in subsequent civil litigation as an admission of guilt. If the defendant stands mute, that is, refuses to plead, the court enters a plea of not guilty, since American law and common law in general assume that a defendant is innocent until proven guilty. (This is one of the major differences it has from those civil law systems based upon Roman law.) If the defendant pleads guilty, the court must be satisfied that the plea is voluntary, or it will not be accepted. Occasionally a judge might even require the prosecution to present evidence to justify the plea of guilty. The judge also has to make certain that the defendant realizes the consequences of the plea and what the sentence might be.

If the defendant pleads not guilty, the judge sets a date for the case to go to trial. Except for those petty offenses which at common law were tried without a jury, the accused has a right to trial by jury, although a defendant can also waive this right. In capital cases a defendant who does not have counsel will be furnished a lawyer by the state; in lesser offenses the defendant has a right to counsel at state expense, but this right is still not always given without great difficulty. Decisions can be appealed either on procedural grounds or for other technicalities.

In civil cases the procedure is different. (1) The plaintiff—the injured party—has to file a complaint alleging that his or her legal rights have been infringed upon by the conduct of another. (2) The defendant or the accused has the right to file an answer. (3) There are pretrial activities engaged in by both parties, designed to elicit all the facts in a situation, a device known as discovery. (4) The case goes to trial, where all the relevant facts are presented to the judge or jury for decision, and a decision is made. (5) There is the possibility of appeal from a decision by a party who contends that the decision was wrongly made.

During the trial the plaintiff must show by the preponderance of the evidence that he or she has a right to recover from the defendant, or the district attorney must show by the preponderance of evidence that the accused is guilty. The burden of proof rests on the plaintiff or the prosecuting attorney. Many civil cases, however, never go to trial but are settled out of court. Trials are costly and time-consuming, and often delayed, and it may be advantageous to both sides to settle matters without a trial.

REFERENCES

1. *See* V. L. Bullough and B. Bullough, SIN, SICKNESS AND SANITY 91–117 (1977).
2. E. A. Hoebel, MAN IN THE PRIMITIVE WORLD 482 (1958).
3. Clark & Fin. 200, 210, 8 Eng. Rep. 718, 722 (1843).
4. *Ibid.*
5. Durham v. United States, 214 F. 2d 862, 874 (D.C. Cir. 1954).
6. American Law Institute, MODEL PENAL CODE (1955).
7. O. W. Holmes, Jr. THE COMMON LAW 1 (1881).
8. Plessy v. Ferguson, 163 U.S. 537 (1896).
9. Brown v. Board of Education, 347 U.S. 483 (1954).

2 Licensure and the Medical Monopoly

VERN L. BULLOUGH

Discussion of change in nursing roles cannot be undertaken without considering modification in the roles of physicians. Since both roles are regulated by the state, the problem becomes a legal as well as an interoccupational one. The difficulty is compounded because medicine, by law as well as by custom, has been given control over the whole health field; other health occupational groups, such as nurses, dentists, pharmacists, therapists, technicians, and even psychologists, have only been able to assume certain delegated or specified responsibilities and duties. In effect, by exercise of the state licensure powers a medical monopoly has been created, and this monopoly has both good and bad effects.

On the one hand it has been argued that medical licensure raised the level of medical practice by setting a high standard. Licensure eliminated the quacks and incompetents, and provided some guarantee to the patient that the physician consulted was qualified. Thus, medical licensure was a successful effort by the state to protect the public against unqualified practitioners.[1] Conversely, it can be claimed that medical licensure handicapped the effective delivery of health care by giving a monopoly to a small self-regulated group, whose interests were not necessarily in better medical care but rather in bettering the standing of their profession. By restricting the number of practitioners, licensure allowed physicians to raise their economic standards and achieve a much higher social status than might otherwise have been warranted. The state, rather than acting to protect its citizens by licensure, gave a monopoly to a few to exploit the public; further increased such exploitation by giving one segment, the physician, control over all other health fields and specialists. In sum, the state thwarted the public interest by creating a pyramid of medical practitioners, which guaranteed wealth and power to those at the top and then gave them the means of perpetuating their power.

Probably the truth, if there is such a thing, lies somewhere between these two extreme points of view. Regardless of view, however, it is clear that physicians dominate the field, and this domination tends to prevent the other health professions from asserting complete control over their own areas.

Perhaps the best way to deal with the problem of licensing is to understand why we have licensing at all. The answer is not as simple as it might seem. Opposition has often existed to giving any professional group a monopoly over a field. One of the most ardent opponents was Adam Smith, often looked upon as the intellectual founder of capitalism. Smith was consulted in 1774 for advice about giving university-trained physicians an exclusive monopoly on the practice of medicine—a monopoly that they enjoyed in many of the continental countries but did not then have in England. Smith opposed the granting of any such monopoly by the government because, he claimed, the universities would abuse their right, and no examination or degree that they awarded could "give any tolerable security that the person upon whom it had been conferred was fit to practice physic" (an eighteenth-century term for medicine). Indeed, he argued that if the Royal College was given a medical monopoly the price of medical care would rise to double or triple the sum it then cost, and there would be ever-continuing attempts to limit the number of practitioners in order to keep medical fees high.[2]

Smith was not the only one concerned with the dangers of a state monopoly through licensure, and over the years writers and critics both within and without medicine have been concerned. Some opposed licensure for conservative reasons, others for more liberal reasons. William Osler, for example, one of the greats of modern medicine, felt that licensure as practiced in the United States and Canada was "provincialism run riot."[3] Henry Sigerist, the founding father of medical history in this country, opposed the administration of state tests or examinations to determine qualifications for medical practice.[4] In spite of such opposition various governmental units, encouraged by the organized medical profession, decided that the guarantee of some minimum standards was essential to the public interest. In the process of establishing these standards they severely curtailed the number of physicians, raised the cost of medical care, and helped create some of the difficulties that other health professionals face today. Moreover, since physicians were the first to be licensed they achieved a monopoly over the medical care field, and other health occupations could be licensed only with their permission. Other practice acts originally were more or less amendments to the medical practice act, although this no longer is always the case.

The controversy among various allied health groups is an old one. In fact, the basis for the medical monopoly can be traced back to the Middle Ages, when medicine was just beginning to emerge as a profession. At that time, physicians in the newly emerging universities argued that in the best interests of the public welfare they ought to be allowed to control the practice of medicine, because they were better educated than other would-be practitioners—barbers, surgeons, pharmacists, midwives, and so forth.[5] Though the physicians never quite achieved an absolute monopoly, they did force other groups of medical practitioners to define their roles vis-à-vis the university-trained physician; by achieving the dominant position in the pyramid of health care, they managed to eliminate many groups of practitioners altogether—primarily and most notably Jews and women.

One of the reasons for the physicians' failure to achieve absolute control in the medieval period was their own status demands, which made them unwilling to do certain medical procedures (particularly surgical ones) that they considered beneath their dignity. Another reason was the lack of sufficient numbers of university graduates to serve all segments of the population. The university-trained physicians tended to be concentrated in the larger cities and to serve the richer clients, while the lesser-trained practitioners served in the villages or market towns. Providing that the latter group did not threaten the former, its members were allowed to practice. In England the issue was complicated by the fact that London, the largest city and the nation's capital, lacked a university until the nineteenth century. To remedy this the London physicians organized into a college, which was given a charter as the Royal College of Physicians in 1518. By 1522, the Royal College controlled examination and licensing throughout England. Similar authority was given to the London Company of Barber-Surgeons in 1540, to the London Society of Apothecaries in 1617, and to the Surgeons' Company in 1745; but effective control of such groups was usually limited to the London area. Further adding to the difficulties was the failure of the medical schools at Oxford and Cambridge to keep up with developments in curriculum or medical expertise in the seventeenth and eighteenth centuries. When the kingdoms of England and Scotland were merged under the rule of James I, at the beginning of the seventeenth century, large numbers of Scottish university physicians began to move to London. In many cases university degrees in medicine were worth little more than the parchment on which they were printed, and the real training in London took place in the various hospitals. Outside of London most people were treated by village surgeons or apothecaries, who were trained through an apprenticeship system.[6]

Neither the British Crown nor the British Parliament extended professional regulations to any of the overseas provinces. Here the practice differed from that of Spain, which established the medical code of Castile in the Spanish-American colonies in the sixteenth century. Because physicians, like the upper classes in general, did not migrate overseas, and because for a long period no American city was large enough to maintain a medical college, American medical practitioners at first were rather free-enterprise types. Clergymen often practiced medicine on the side. In other cases individuals simply set themselves up as practitioners. A few went to Europe, particularly to Edinburgh, for some training, before attempting to practice. Generally, would-be medical practitioners served a brief period of apprenticeship under other practitioners before setting out on their own. Regardless of training, most quickly claimed to be doctors of medicine—a term that the Americans applied with egalitarian abandon to all types of practitioners. In Great Britain and continental Europe, the term *doctor* had been reserved to those who graduated from the higher faculties of the university, primarily those who intended to teach. Admission to these faculties came only after earning a baccalaureate degree. In America, however, all medical practitioners, whether surgeons, barbers, physicians, or apothecaries, called themselves or were called *doctor*; a term that originally meant "to teach" (from the Latin *docere,* to teach) became a euphemism for all medical practitioners.

The first American medical school was founded in Philadelphia in 1765. Its founders hoped to control the issuance of licenses in the colonies, but this plan was thwarted by the opposition of the Royal College of Physicians in London. In order to bring about some regulation New York City enacted its own licensing procedures, followed by New Jersey, but the initial governmental efforts in this direction collapsed during the American Revolution. Following the Revolution medical societies were organized in the newly independent states, and these societies began to advocate state tests and licensing, usually in order to protect themselves against their would-be rivals. Legislatures usually granted the requests for licensing acts, although the specifics varied widely from state to state. In some states a state examining board was created; in others medical societies were granted the power to test and license; in still others, various regions had permission to do their own testing. Regardless of procedures, however, the medical societies had control of licensing. The result was a kind of self-policing, the purpose of which was not so much to protect the public as to protect the profession.

This system failed, largely because graduates of medical schools (as distinguished from those trained by apprenticeship) did not have to undergo the same licensing procedures as others, and in effect were licensed by the colleges from which they graduated. In the nineteenth century there was a rapid proliferation of medical schools, many of them adherents of particular medical philosophies. Since most of the schools were proprietary ones run for profit, the number of licensed medical practitioners increased rapidly and standards dropped just as rapidly. So did the cost of medical care, since the competition drove fees down. Just how well educated a physician might be was indicated by an 1850 survey of practitioners in eastern Tennessee, which found that of the 201 physicians in the area (for a population of 164,000 people), 35 (17 percent) were graduates of some sort of regular medical school; 42 (20 percent) had taken a course of lectures but never graduated; and 27 (13 percent) were botanic or natural healing practitioners. The others (almost 50 percent) generally had received no instruction other than their own reading, and even this had been limited.[7]

Even a diploma from a medical school was no guarantee of competence. Most schools depended upon student fees for their operation, and it was to the advantage of the proprietors to take in as many students as possible and graduate them as quickly as they could. It was not until the last part of the nineteenth century, when a few of the leading universities began paying medical professors salaries, that some of the incentive for awarding medical degrees was lost. Concern with the university's right to proclaim anyone a physician led to the founding of the American Medical Association in 1847. The call for the organizing meeting was made in 1846 by the New York State Medical Society in an effort to raise the level of professional competence and status, and the Society tried to restrict its appeal to those who were members of "regular" societies and "approved schools." Gradually, certain standards were adopted that eventually led to better premedical training, minimum periods for medical schooling, stronger state boards of licensing, and stronger professional societies. In 1873 Texas became the first state to pass a modern registration act requiring state examination and registration. In 1881 a West Virginia statute was challenged by opponents, and not until 1889 did the Supreme Court decide that this type of licensure was a valid exercise of the police power of the state. The result was further encouragement of state licensing, and by 1895 all the states had passed registration laws for physicians.[8] In almost every state the boards of licensing worked in collaboration with the state medical societies, which were also usually cooperating with the AMA.

This collaboration proved a handicap because efforts by the physicians to raise standards further met with fear that the cost of medical care would also increase and a suspicion of the motives of the medical profession. The AMA felt that to go further it strongly needed outside support. This support came from the Carnegie Foundation for the Advancement of Teaching, which commissioned a survey of medical education under the direction of Abraham Flexner, a nonphysician. His report, published in 1910, had great effect on public opinion and on state licensing.[9] The almost immediate result was the establishment of ever-stricter licensing standards, elimination of the worst of the so-called diploma mills, and a gradual decline in the number of medical graduates. Typically in most states the governor appointed a Board of Medical Examiners, selected from a list of practicing physicians recommended by the state medical association. These boards operated, and continue to operate, with considerable autonomy in determining the qualifications of applications for licensure, although certain statutory requirements must be kept in mind.

Medical licensing, however, did not solve all the problems affecting the medical profession, and it has created problems for other members of the health-care field. One of the difficulties with licensing as it has existed in the past is that there has been little effective check on the continued competence of the physician who continues to practice for decades after being licensed. Physicians at the beginning of their careers might well have been aware of most of the developments in medicine, but licensing guarantees their competence for life without any effort to ascertain if they still retain competence. An incompetent could continue to practice with little fear of being denounced by the organized medical profession. In the United States, medical licensure gave physicians the right to practice in all fields of medicine, even though they might know little or nothing about most of them. Gradually, volunteer boards have developed to certify specialists, although in order to gain support these boards have had to "grandfather" in a number whose background was dubious. Although many hospitals insist on board certification for their staff members, even present American medical practice goes on the assumption that a physician is competent in all areas of medicine.

Still another difficulty is the control the physician has over all other medical groups, caused by the general claims of the medical practitioner and the political backing these claims have through the state licensing board. Though there are large numbers of disinterested physicians, it is probably asking far too much of any profession that it give away any of its powers or even claims of powers without a struggle, or deal with other health professionals without keeping its own interests in mind. Some states have attempted to insist that at least one member of the Board of Medical Examiners represent the general public, but this tokenism is particularly ineffective. Medical examiners generally look upon the health field as their own preserve and resent any encroachment, however slight. This control is like leaving direction of colleges and universities entirely in the hands of the professors, doing away with state lay boards of education or boards of regents and consultation with students. The problem in education is to harmonize professional needs with public welfare, and this kind of give-and-take is lacking in medicine except through direct appeal to the legislature. Inevitably, when any segment of the health-care pyramid attempts to extend or modify its role, the legislature must be appealed to for support. This is the only direct way of modifying or checking the medical dominance.

Further complicating the problem is that the Board of Medical Examiners in most states does not necessarily represent the latest trends in medicine or even the majority of medical opinion. This is the result not of any kind of conscious conservatism, but rather of the nature and demands of medicine and the political process. Most beginning physicians are not particularly interested in the political arena either of their profession or of state government; the most interested physicians tend to represent the older, often even semiretired, members of the profession, and much too often their interests reflect the concerns of a few decades ago rather than the needs of the present or the future.[10] Thus, medical boards today are often dominated by general practitioners, because they are the most common medical practitioners of the past. This means that far too many physicians in a position of power are basically unaware of current demands—or, if aware, tend to dismiss them. Obviously this is a generalization with many exceptions, but it helps to explain why both the AMA and the various Boards of Medical Examiners often seem to be fighting the battles of the last generation rather than those of the present.

This history helps to explain why there is so much difficulty in modifying the traditional nursing role. It also explains why there are so many mixed feelings in the nursing profession itself about a change in the nursing role. The same theories that apply to the medical establishment tend to apply to the nursing establishment, although nurses, lacking the power of physicians, have always been more subject to public and legislative pressure. Licensure in nursing was about a generation behind that in medicine.[11] This delay meant that the primary power position in the health field had been preempted by the physician, forcing nurses to define their role in terms of the physician even more than did dentists and pharmacists, who were earlier on the scene. From the first, the nursing role has been defined as more limiting than it really was because nursing was considered a women's profession while medicine generally was restricted to men. Therefore nurses, even before they became nurses, learned to play the male–female game; because the role of women was very narrowly and strictly defined, the role of nurses (one of the largest women's occupations) also was very narrowly and strictly defined. The rigid definition of theory, however, was not carried out in practice because female nurses pretended to leave most of the decisions to male physicians while in effect quietly making decisions of their own or manipulating the physicians to make the desired decisions.[12] Thus, though nurses lacked formal power, they had a great deal of informal power if they were able to mask their power and decision making. This ability to masquerade as innocent also protected them from any responsibility for their decisions. Many male physicians never did catch on to the game, and still hark back to this model. But the world keeps changing; developments in medicine and nursing, as well as rising consciousness among women, led to a demand for change. Increasingly, the strains of the game have begun to show, although both sides have been slow to rethink the old rules. Such rethinking as has been done has more likely come from the nurses than from the physicians, because in any pyramid of power it is those at the bottom who are most likely to demand change. Nurses have been encouraged in their new demands by the demands of other women who have been at the bottom of the pyramid of power and prestige in a variety of occupations.[13]

The importance of specialization of hospital medicine has added to the difficulties. As physicians have become more and more specialized they have become more and more part of an institution, whether it be a health maintenance organization, a hospital, or simply a group practice. Nursing became institutionalized somewhat earlier than medicine, but specialization came later. In any case there has been a growing vacuum in primary patient care, if only because specialization tends to increase fragmentation. Though there have been and continue to be attempts in medical schools to encourage students to enter general practice (often renamed family practice), the rewards in medicine today go to the specialist—not only monetary rewards, but also prestige and, perhaps more important, the ability to deal with many of the real illnesses afflicting patients. Though the general practitioner can diagnose cancer (so for that matter can the nurse practitioner), its treatment in today's medicine is most effectively carried out by an oncologist.

The result has been to confuse the rhetoric of the family practitioner with the reality of medical practice. General practice, while it is in theory an emotionally satisfying ideal to many physicians, often means turning many patients most in need of medical services over to a specialist while the general practitioners end up doing physical examinations and treating common human miseries, a job for which they were not prepared by their medical school training. Inevitably, many turn increasingly to specialty medicine.

The alternatives are either to give the same kind of financial rewards to the family practitioner as is given to the specialist—a rather unrealistic and costly alternative—or to develop a multilevel medical education and certification program in which the standards for the general practitioner are different from those for the specialist. We now implement this second program on an informal basis by importing foreign medical graduates to do much of the general practice in this country, and making it more difficult for them to become specialists because of their allegedly inferior medical education.[14] In the long run, this practice can only undermine the medical profession, and it goes contrary to the tradition built up over the past few decades. Moreover, any attempt to raise the standards for foreign practitioners in the United States (many of whom lack clinical experience and enter medical school without collegiate education) only creates a greater problem in the delivery of primary care. The third alternative is to move up another category of the health team, namely nurses, to give official recognition to what they have been doing in the past and to allow them to further expand their role. Of the options available, this seems the most logical to assure quality medical care, but the problem lies in dealing with boards of medical examiners who feel their position threatened by any but the first alternative. Thus, the solution in most states is a political one, with the legislatures acting to modify traditional roles and meet changing needs by changing nurse practice acts. That task is complicated by the fact that the medical practice acts were written first and most often were written as if medicine was the only health profession. Nurses are thus faced with moving into territory that has already been pre-empted by medicine.

REFERENCES

1. This traditional view is effectively summarized by E. Fogotson, R. Roemer, & R. Newman, *Legal Regulation of Health Personnel in the United States,* in REPORT OF THE NATIONAL ADVISORY COMMISSION ON HEALTH MANPOWER II, Appendix VII, 279–541 (1967); *see also* R.Roemer, *Legal Systems Regulating Health Personnel: A Comparative Analysis,* 46 MILBANK MEM. FUND Q., 431–71 (October 1968); *see also* H. E. Sigerist, *The History of Medical Licensure,* in HENRY E. SIGERIST ON THE

SOCIOLOGY OF MEDICINE, M. Roemer ed. (1960); the article originally appeared in 104 J. AM. MED. ASSOC., 1060 (1935); R.H. Shryock, MEDICAL LICENSING IN AMERICA, 1650–1965 (1967); R. Derbyshire, MEDICAL LICENSURE AND DISCIPLINE IN THE UNITED STATES (1969) for historical background to the American situation.
2. The letter which Smith wrote on this subject is perhaps most readily available in John Rae, LIFE OF ADAM SMITH 372–80 (1895, reprinted 1965).
3. W. Osler, AEQUANIMITAS 276 (1944). Osler, however, was not opposed to licensure *per se*.
4. Sigerist, *supra*.
5. For a lengthy discussion of this see V. L. Bullough, THE DEVELOPMENT OF MEDICINE AS A PROFESSION (1966).
6. See F. N. L. Poynter, THE EVOLUTION OF MEDICAL PRACTICE IN BRITAIN (1961).
7. Shryock, *supra*, 31–32.
8. Derbyshire, *supra*, 1–8.
9. A. Flexner, MEDICAL EDUCATION IN THE UNITED STATES AND CANADA, Carnegie Foundation for the Advancement of Teaching, Bulletin No. 4 (1910).
10. Derbyshire, *supra*, 40–41.
11. V. L. Bullough and B. Bullough, THE CARE OF THE SICK: THE EMERGENCE OF MODERN NURSING 98–100, 136–38 (1978).
12. See, for example, L. Stein, *The Doctor-Nurse Game*, 16 ARCH. GEN. PSYCHIATRY 699–703 (1967).
13. See V. L. Bullough, THE SUBORDINATE SEX (1973), with a final chapter by B. Bullough.
14. See, for example, Institute of International Education, OPEN DOORS REPORT ON INTERNATIONAL EXCHANGE (1966); D. M. Greely, AMERICAN FOREIGN MEDICAL GRADUATES, 41. J. MED. EDUC. 641–50 (1966); T. D. Dublin, *Foreign Physicians: Their Impact on U.S. Health Care*, 185 SCIENCE 407–14 (August 2, 1974).

3 The First Two Phases in Nursing Licensure

BONNIE BULLOUGH

The history of nursing licensure in the United States can be divided into three major phases. The goals of the nurses who sought legislation, and the types of laws that were passed in response to their efforts, differed in each of these periods. The first phase coincided with the beginning of the twentieth century, when nurses began actively to campaign for state laws to register trained nurses. By 1923, nurses had succeeded in obtaining some type of licensing act in each of the states, although later amendments were sought to raise educational standards and facilitate the work of the state boards.

The second phase began in 1938, when New York, which tends to be a bellwether state in the field of nursing licensure, passed a mandatory act defining the scope of functions of registered and practical nurses. Following this precedent, the goal for the next three decades of nurses in other states was to seek definitions of nursing practice, to differentiate the roles of registered and practical nurses, and to make it illegal for unlicensed persons to work as nurses. The definitions of nursing developed in this period carefully differentiated between medical and nursing practice, particularly after 1955 when the American Nurses' Association approved a model definition that specifically disclaimed any independent role for nurses in diagnosis or treatment.

Phase three is the current phase. Its roots can be found in the decade of the sixties, with the development of intensive and primary care nursing, but the phase became overt in 1971, with the passage of amendments to the Idaho nurse practice act authorizing acts of diagnosis and treatment under rules and regulations to be drafted jointly by the boards of medicine and nursing.[1] The New York act, signed in 1972, allowed nurses to diagnose and treat in terms of a nursing regime.[2] Forty-three other states have now moved to amend their nurse practice acts to allow diagnosis and treatment; but the changes are not taking place without social upheaval and great effort on the part of nurses.

This chapter traces the first two phases in some detail in order to set the background for an understanding of the current revolutionary phase in licensure.

PHASE I: THE NURSE REGISTRATION ACTS

The year 1873 is usually thought of as the beginning of the modern era in American nursing because three "Nightingale" schools were opened that year: Bellevue, Connecticut, and Massachusetts General hospitals. Although several earlier attempts had been made to establish training for nurses, these were the first schools to remain open for any significant length of time. These three schools, and the many that followed (using the same model), were successful partly because of the publicity that had been given the English nursing school started by Florence Nightingale and partly because of a growing awareness that the establishment of apprenticeship education led not only to better patient care but also to significant savings in the cost of running a hospital.[3] The movement to establish nurses' training schools rapidly gained momentum. In 1880 there were 15 schools; in 1890 there were 35; in 1900 there were 432; and in 1910 the number reached 1,023.[4] To put these figures in perspective, it is necessary to realize that in 1972 there were only 1,372 schools preparing registered nurses.[5]

The rapid growth of hospital training programs, particularly in the period between 1890 and 1900, created a problem for the new graduates. Because the hospitals were staffed primarily by students, most of the graduating nurses were forced to seek employment as private duty nurses, and as such they often worked in the homes of their patients. Here it was necessary to compete with untrained nurses, correspondence school graduates, or ex-classmates who had failed or dropped out of the arduous two-year courses. Moreover, the traditional linkage of the nursing role with that of the wife and mother or the domestic servant had prevented the growth of the image of the nurse as an educated practitioner. The popular literature of the period still referred to the "born" nurse, or intimated that the requisite skills of the nursing role could be acquired intuitively.

Within the ranks of trained nurses, and particularly among nursing educators, there was, however, a growing sense of self-identity. A few leaders were ready to take the beginning steps toward the professionalization of nursing. The precursor to the National League for Nursing (at first called the Society for Superintendents of Training Schools in United States and Canada) was founded in 1894, and in 1896 the organization that was to become the American Nurses' Association (originally the Nurses' Associated Alumnae of United States and Canada) was established. Primary objectives in the formation of both these organizations was to gain control over the profession and to stem the untrammeled growth of substandard nursing schools.[6]

As soon as the initial work of organizing was completed, members of both groups turned their attention to seeking state licensure as a mechanism for accomplishing their goals. Sophia Palmer, one of the founders of both organizations and first editor of the *American Journal of Nursing,* made the first public statement supporting licensure in a paper read before the New York State

Federation of Women's Clubs in 1899. She argued that nursing's greatest need was for a law that would control the schools. She asked that the schools be placed under the supervision of the Regents of the University of the State of New York, the pattern for other types of professional licensure in the state. The Regents would then be responsible for appointing a board to examine and register nurses.[7] Lavinia Dock, the superintendent who was the driving force behind the establishment of the Nurses' Associated Alumnae,[8] wrote an article for the first issue of the *American Journal of Nursing* favoring licensure, although she pointed out that it could not solve all of the problems of the profession.[9] In her presidential address before the third annual meeting of the Nurses' Associated Alumnae, Isabel Hampton Robb outlined the two priorities of nursing as the support of the growth of the professional organizations and the campaign for registration for nurses in each of the states.[10]

Although the process of professionalization was also beginning among nurses in other countries, there were no extant governmental registration programs for those nurses at the time American nurses started to consider the idea. Most European countries did not institute any type of nursing licensure until about 1920.[11] Although the medicine and pharmacy act of the Cape Colony, passed in 1891, had mentioned nurses, the first nurse registration act was enacted in New Zealand in 1901. This act encouraged American nurses to push forward, but it also came at a time when they were already committed to the goal of registration.

It is interesting to note that although the English experience was used as a model for nursing education in this country, England did not furnish a model for nurse registration. This was because the British scene was dominated by the strong figure of Florence Nightingale, who did not approve of individual licensure for nurses. In 1886 a proposal was made by a committee of the Hospitals' Association to create a body of examiners, not connected with the training schools, to test nurses and to keep a list of those who qualified. The objective was to create a standard of excellence in nursing and to protect the hospitals and public against employing incompetent nurses. Nightingale fought against this proposal because she felt that technical competence should be secondary to good character. Although she agreed that training programs should include instructions in how to carry out nursing procedures, in her estimation the primary goal of training and related experiences (such as the requirement that students live in closely supervised nurses' homes) was to build character.[12] She felt that she had "raised nursing from the sink" by emphasizing culture and moral standards, and that the new focus on competence rather than character would destroy her life's work.[13] Nightingale felt that the then current model, in which the former student was kept closely tied to the training school, or affiliated with some other institution, so that the matron could give ongoing surveillance and thus be able to vouch not only for the technical competence of the nurse but also for the character, was a better one for protecting the public. This Nightingale system was in many ways the precursor to what is now being called a "new" proposal for institutional licensure.

In 1888 the British nurses organized an association, and tried several times to obtain a royal charter that would allow them to test and register nurses. They were defeated because of Nightingale's influence, however, and nurse registration did not become a reality until 1919.[14]

American nurses were not unaware of the controversy that raged over licensure in England. Florence Nightingale was revered, and most of her tenets were followed. But, Ethel Gordon Bedford Fenwick, one of the leaders of the proregistration forces in England, was the more influential figure on the issues of organization and registration. She visited this country in 1892 to prepare an exhibit for the Chicago World's Fair, and apparently spent much of her time visiting with Isabel Hampton Robb and other American nurses to urge them to organize and to later seek registration.[15] Her arguments seemed most reasonable to American nurses. There is little evidence in any of their writings that they were particularly concerned about any negative consequences that might follow from a possible shift in emphasis from character to technical competence, and so the objections of Florence Nightingale and her followers were of little influence.

In looking for a model for the type of registration they wanted, nurses necessarily turned to other professions. Dock, in her article for the *American Journal of Nursing*, cited the example of medicine, although she also noted that dentistry had been able to control educational standards through the efforts of the schools rather than the state.[16] Palmer mentioned physicians, pharmacists, dentists, and teachers.[17] Because of the close association of medicine to nursing, medicine undoubtedly furnished the major model as well as the major barrier to nurses in their search for professional status. As outlined in Chapter 2, state medical practice acts had been enacted in all the states by 1895. A Supreme Court decision in 1889 had held that occupational licensing laws were a valid exercise of the police powers of the states, so the way was open for the nurses to proceed.

The 1889 decision also pointed up the fact that licensure could not be conceived on a national basis, as it was and is in most countries. The federal government has only those powers listed in the constitution which were granted to it by the original colonies or added by amendments, and these powers do not include the right to regulate occupational groups. As a result, the drive for registration had to be carried out separately in each of the states. To facilitate this effort the Nurses' Associated Alumnae moved to set up constituent state organizations so that the local membership could do the necessary work for lobbying for the registration acts.[18]

The North Carolina nurses were the first to succeed.[19] A nurse registration act was passed there in March 1903. Three other registration acts were passed that same year in New Jersey, New York, and Virginia. The North Carolina act allowed for licensure by waiver for the rest of that year. Anyone from a "reputable training school," or anyone who could produce a certificate signed by three registered physicians stating that she or he had been working for at least two years as a nurse, was entitled to be listed by the county clerk as a registered nurse. Starting in 1904, only those persons who were certified by the Board of Examiners could be listed as registered nurses. The board was instructed by the law to examine the applicants to make sure they were of good character, knowledgeable in anatomy, physiology, invalid cookery, household hygiene, and medical, surgical, obstetric, and practical nursing. Certification by the board allowed the applicant to use the initials "R.N." and to have her or his name entered on the registry kept by the county clerk.[20]

The campaign in New Jersey met with so much opposition that the statute which passed was weaker than the one in North Carolina. The term *trained* nurse was used, rather than *registered* nurse. Applicants were required to have completed two years of practical and theoretical training before applying, but no examination was required and no board of examiners was set up. New Jersey also included provisions for nurses from "foreign states," if their training was comparable to that offered by New Jersey schools. The New York law created a Board of Examiners, appointed by the Regents of the State University of New York from a list of names supplied by the State Nurses' Association.[21] The provisions of the law matched those proposed by the members of the nursing organization. Nurses were particularly pleased with the all-nurse board, which was felt to be preferable to the mixed nurse and physician board mandated in North Carolina.

One by one the other states followed suit: by 1910 twenty-seven states had passed nurse registration acts, and by 1923 all the states then in the Union, plus the District of Columbia and Hawaii, had licensure for nurses on their books. The Alaskan and Puerto Rican acts came later.[22] Although state governments had the constitutional right to pass these acts, this does not mean that legislation was ordinarily planned by or initiated by members of the legislatures. Rather, the first steps usually were taken by nurses who contacted friendly representatives for their assistance. Programs of local, state, and national nurses' associations often featured "how-to" seminars to help nurses with the lobbying process.[23] This pattern is not unusual. In fact, even though the professions often speak of public control by means of state licensure, the professions themselves have participated and continue to participate significantly in the licensing process.[24]

What little opposition there was to early nursing licensure tended to come from hospital administrators, people who ran correspondence courses to prepare nurses, mental hospitals, and occasionally charitable organizations that sponsored home nursing programs. Physician opposition came usually from doctors who administered hospitals or nursing homes, rather than from active practitioners.[25] Such opposition was sufficient to cause nurses to lower their sights, from their original goal of protection of the term "nurse" to the term "registered nurse," although it was not sufficient to stop the movement in any state. Often, nurses could marshall enough lobbying power to pass a nurse registration act in a single session of the legislature; but if that was not possible they would try again and again until the bill passed. Sometimes they settled for a weak bill and planned their strategy for revision. One of the most common compromises that had to be made was to settle for a board of examiners that included one or more physicians. When the efforts of these early nurse activists are evaluated, it is important to remember that the first round of nurse registration acts were achieved by nurses at a time when women did not yet have the vote. Their achievements are truly monumental.

As the original registration acts went through successive revisions, other goals emerged. Nurses worked actively to obtain legislative sanction to close schools connected with small or highly specialized hospitals, including mental hospitals, and to make high-school graduation a pre-entry requirement for nursing education.

None of the original registration acts included a definition of nursing in terms of the scope of practice of the profession. They might more accurately be called nurse *registration* acts rather than nurse *practice* acts. The term *registered nurse* was defined as a person who had attended an acceptable nursing program and passed a board examination, rather than a person who engaged in a specific type of practice. This definition placed the emphasis on the educational process, and early reform efforts tended to be focused on improving training. Some of the laws became quite elaborate in their requirements for specific theoretical or clinical content. A comparative study of six professions done in 1938 indicated that the educational process in nursing was more regulated than that of the other five professions analyzed.[26]

PHASE II: THE DEVELOPMENT OF DEFINITIONS OF PRACTICE AND MANDATORY LICENSURE

The second phase in the development of nursing licensure stated in 1938, when the first mandatory practice act was passed in New York. This law established two levels of nurses, registered and practical, and restricted nursing functions to members of these two groups.[27] This event marked the beginning of a new drive among nurse activists. Although there was unfinished business, with 19 states still not requiring high-school graduation for registration and 17 states still including one or more physicians on their boards,[28] the primary goal for reform became mandatory licensure. By 1939 there were three national nursing organizations: the American Nurses' Association, the National League for Nursing Education, and the National Organization of Public Health Nurses. The boards of directors of these three groups met in January of that year to celebrate the success of the New York nurses and to approve a recommendation favoring "licensure for all those who nurse for hire."[29] This became the rallying slogan for the second phase of nursing licensure.

Although mandatory licensure can be thought of as a long-time aspiration from the beginning of the century when abortive attempts were made to restrict the title "nurse," the goal did not seem realistic until the New York nurses broke the barrier. Their efforts, and those of nurses in several states that followed the precedent, were facilitated by the development of licensure for practical nurses. The employment patterns for nurses were changing in this period from private duty to hospital nursing, and hospital administrators argued with some justification that all nursing functions did not require the standard three-year training period that was by then the norm. The development of the practical nurse as the basic bedside practitioner allowed registered nurses to argue more successfully for licensure for all practitioners.

In 1918, Virginia had passed an act regulating attendants.[30] A few other states had followed suit, but most of the early legislation was aimed at attendants in mental hospitals rather than practical nurses in general hospitals. In 1944 15 states had provisions for some type of auxiliary personnel.[31] However, the major impact of the New York precedent of full recognition for practical nurses was not felt until the period immediately after World War II, when the shortage of nurses created pressure for the stratification of the nursing role and the concept of team nursing developed.[32] By 1960 all the states and territories had licensure for practical nurses, although in two states the title is "vocational" nurse.[33,35]

Besides its connection with the stratification of the nursing role, mandatory licensure also had another interesting ramification. In order to pass a mandatory act of any kind, it was necessary to spell out the scope of practice of the occupation that was being protected against encroachment. The older nursing laws made it illegal for an unauthorized person to use the title "registered nurse," but not illegal for such a person to practice nursing. Once the new mandatory laws made it illegal for an unauthorized person to practice nursing, a definition of the scope of practice had to be written into these laws. The 1938 New York act indicated that:

> A person practices nursing within the meaning of this article who for compensation or personal profit (a) performs any professional service requiring the applications of principles of nursing based on biological, physical and social sciences, such as responsible supervision of a patient requiring skill in observation of symptoms and reactions and the accurate recording of the facts and carrying out of treatments and medications as prescribed by a licensed physician, and the application of such nursing procedures as involve understanding of cause and effect in order to safeguard life and health of a patient and others; or (b) performs such duties as are required in the physical care of a patient and in carrying out of medical orders as prescribed by a licensed physician, requiring an understanding of nursing but not requiring the professional service as outlined in (a).[34]

This definition of nursing became the model for other legislation, with Louisiana, Arkansas, and West Virginia adopting the same language and other states using modifications. By 1946, ten states and Hawaii had adopted some sort of a definition of nursing.[35] Thus, a statement about the scope of practice became inexorably tied to the movement to gain mandatory licensure, and even came to be thought of as a goal in and of itself. Nurses and the legal advisors of the day advocated that the scope of practice be defined in nurse practice acts.[36]

The process of defining nursing and passing mandatory nurse practice acts was facilitated in 1955 when the Board of Directors of the American Nurses' Association adopted a model definition of nursing. Professional and practical nursing practice were defined as follows:

> The term "practice of professional" nursing means the performance, for compensation, of any acts in the observation, care and counsel of the ill, injured or infirm or in the maintenance of health or prevention of illness of others, or in the supervision and teaching of other personnel or the administration of medications and treatments as prescribed by a licensed physician or a licensed dentist; requiring substantial specialized judgment and skill and based on knowledge and application of principles of biological, physical and social science. The foregoing shall not be deemed to include any acts of diagnosis or prescription of therapeutic or corrective measures.
>
> The practice of practical nursing means the performance for compensation of selected acts in the care of the ill, injured, or infirm under the direction of a registered professional nurse or a licensed physician or a licensed dentist; and not requiring the substantial specialized skill, judgment, and knowledge required in professional nursing.[37]

This definition became the new model for changing nurse practice acts. By 1967 15 states had incorporated the language of this model into their state laws and 6 states had used the model with only slight modifications.[38] A notable aspect of this model act, as well as of the other similar definitions of practice that were used, is the disclaimer, which clearly spells out the fact that nursing did not include any acts of diagnosis or the prescription of therapeutic measures. Before the era of mandatory licensure, nurse registration acts did not define nursing. As a result, they did not include any such disclaimer. The fascinating thing about the disclaimer is that it was made not by the American Medical Association, but by the American Nurses' Association. Although a reasonable assumption might be that the nurses felt the disclaimer necessary to avoid medical opposition to the new practice acts, there is little evidence of overt pressure by medical people. In effect, organized nursing surrendered before any battle over boundaries could occur.

The reasons for this collective behavior by nurses are complex and involve some speculation. Some nurses, particularly those in university settings, were beginning to evolve an ideological position calling for a separation of the function of nurses from that of physicians. They naturally supported such disclaimers, because they felt that the nursing role should emphasize psychological support rather than medical diagnosis or treatment.[39] Others welcomed the protection of the pretense that they did not make decisions.[40] However, probably the major reason for support of the disclaimer in the model practice act and the various state acts was a type of alienation, or anticipatory self-discrimination. Rather than risk a rebuff or a possible boundary dispute with medicine, nurses almost unconsciously decided to avoid admitting their role in the patient care decision-making process. Similar patterns of anticipatory self-discrimination are a fairly common phenomenon among minority groups; the ghetto walls are often as well-policed from the inside as from the outside. Feelings of powerlessness and fear prevent people from challenging discriminatory practices.[41]

Actually, by 1955, when the model act was formulated by the ANA, nurses were a fairly well-educated group of workers. Although there were still a few states that did not require high-school graduation for licensure, this requirement had become a dead issue because the schools themselves, aided by standards developed by the National League for Nursing, had moved to uphold the standard. A trend to move educational programs into colleges and universities was developing, and although only about 15 percent of the schools were collegiate, the movement was already a significant factor in motivating the diploma schools to improve their programs and move away from the old apprencticeship model.[42] National pool examinations had been developed to upgrade state board examinations and to facilitate the movement of nurses between jurisdictions.[43] The standard training period was three years, and with the improved academic content a substantial body of knowledge could be imparted to the student nurses in that length of time.

With this background, nurses in 1955 were observing patients, collecting data about their conditions, arriving at decisions, and acting on those decisions to care for their patients. They were, in short, making diagnostic and therapeutic decisions. Although recent developments in intensive and primary care have greatly expanded the role of nurses in medical decision making, the scope-of-practice statements enacted in this period were outdated at the time they were written.

Various coping mechanisms evolved to attempt to deal with this situation of immediate obsolescence; one of these was the joint statement. The first joint statement was promulgated in California in 1957. Representatives of the California Nurses' Association met with representatives of the medical and hospital associations to draw up a statement regarding nurses doing vena punctures. The statement they adopted authorized agencies to allow nurses with proper preparation to start intravenous fluids.[44] Following this precedent, similar statements were made by joint committees in Ohio and Pennsylvania; in California, subsequent conferences of the three original organizations supported nurses performing other procedures. As the nursing role was extended in the intensive care units, new kinds of statements emerged. In 1966, the Michigan Heart Association passed a resolution approving the use of defibrillators by coronary care nurses. Reporting this resolution, Harvey Sarner pointed out that the Michigan Heart Association was in fact improperly taking on the role of the Michigan legislature.[45] Although his argument would probably hold true also for the joint statements, position papers by the professional organizations and other groups continued. In 1968, the Hawaii Nursing, Medical and Hospital Association approved nurses' performing cardiopulmonary resuscitation.[46] The joint statements were given further support when permanent joint practice commissions were set up in various states in response to recommendations by the National Commission for the Study of Nursing and Nursing Education.[47] These joint practice commissions have continued to draft statements supporting expanded functions for nurses.

The joint statements were apparently effective to some degree in preventing legal problems for nurses. In 1967, ten years after the first joint statement was made, the California Nurses' Association reported that not a single nurse who had followed criteria set up under one of the statements had been indicted.[48] Of course, the truth of the matter is that nurses in this period were not often cited or sued for exceeding their scope of practice unless negligence was in some way involved. Moreover, the best known cases of this type involved practical rather than registered nurses. For example, in the often cited case of *Barber* v. *Reiking* (Washington: 411 P.2d 861 [1966]), a practical nurse who was employed in a physician's office was found negligent for exceeding her scope of practice. She was giving an injection to a child who moved, and the needle broke off in his buttock. Surgical removal of the needle proved difficult and was not accomplished for nine months. The family sued both the physician and the nurse, and after a lengthy court battle both were found negligent because the mandatory nurse practice act of the State of Washington at that time reserved injections to registered nurses.[49]

In a more clearly negligent case, a practical nurse was charged with a violation of the medical practice act for going into a New York bar and grill during the 1947 smallpox scare and injecting some 500 people with water, claiming it was smallpox vaccine.[50] Neither of these cases would have emerged had negligence not been involved, and in the second case the fraudulent actions of the nurse are more noteworthy than her violations of the scope-of-practice rules. Medical boards have been unwilling to indict nurses for practicing medicine as long as they were working under physicians' directions. The traditional attitude of medical people has been that nurses are permitted to perform any function that physicians care to delegate to them.[51] These functions have of course included acts of diagnosis, in spite of the legal prohibitions that existed in the medical and nurse practice acts. On the other hand, in at least one case an occupational health nurse was found negligent because she failed to refer a patient with basal cell carcinoma to an appropriate source of treatment. While the court acknowledged that only a pathologist could diagnose basal cell carcinoma, it held that the occupational health nurse should have been able to diagnose sufficiently well to know whether she could appropriately treat the patient or whether he should have been referred to a physician. Thus diagnosis, albeit limited, was clearly called for in this case (*Cooper v. National Motor Bearing Company* 136 Cal App 2d 229, 288 P.2d 581 [1955]).[52]

The legal crisis was escalated by the rapid development of the new roles of nurses in acute and primary care. In 1971 a special committee appointed by the Secretary of the Department of Health, Education and Welfare announced that it saw no legal barriers to role expansion for nurses.[53] This statement merely caused confusion. The Attorneys General of Arizona and California added to the uncertainty when they issued statements, based on the statutes of their respective states, that nurses could neither diagnose nor treat patients.[54] The feeling, particularly among nurses working in expanded roles, was one of confusion and concern, although few of them actually suffered any negative legal sanctions.

Phase II in the development of nursing licensure might be described as ending on this growing note of concern over the legality of much of nursing practice. Still, most of the other goals of the past had been accomplished. Nurses in all states were registered, and educational standards were reasonably high. Mandatory licensing acts had been passed in 42 states for registered nurses and in 28 states for practical nurses.[55] There were still a few physicians sitting on boards of nursing, but a new element of consumer representation was adding a different flavor to the boards and helping to dilute the power of the remaining physicians.[56]

Phase III began when the first new nurse practice acts were passed—acts that honestly admitted that selected nurses or all nurses could diagnose and treat patients. Probably the starting date for Phase III is 1971, when Idaho amended its nurse practice act to authorize acts of diagnosis and treatment.[57] Nurse practice act revisions followed in New York, South Dakota, and Tennessee in 1972. Since then the pace has been increasing as society—and nurses themselves— reassess the role of the nurse in the health-care team. These changes in the role and in the legal status of nurses are probably the most significant developments in nursing in this century. They will be examined in more detail in the next two chapters.

REFERENCES

1. IDAHO CODE, § 54-1413.
2. NEW YORK EDUCATION LAW, § § 6901, 6902 (Supp. 1972).
3. V. L. Bullough & B. Bullough, THE EMERGENCE OF MODERN NURSING 120–49 (2d ed. 1969).
4. L. L. Dock, A HISTORY OF NURSING, Vol. III 141 (1912).
5. *Educational Preparation for Nursing, 1977,* NURSING OUTLOOK 26 (September 1977), 568–73.

6. M. M. Roberts, AMERICAN NURSING: HISTORY AND INTERPRETATION 20–30 (1961). See also Bullough & Bullough, supra.
7. Dock, supra, 44.
8. H. E. Marshall, MARY ADELAIDE NUTTING: PIONEER OF MODERN NURSING 79 (1972).
9. L. Dock, What We May Expect from the Law, AM. J. NURS. 8–12 (October 1900).
10. Address of the President, Isabel Hampton Robb, before the Third Annual Convention of the Associated Alumnae of Trained Nurses of United States, 1 AM. J. NURS. 97–104 (November 1600).
11. L. R. Seymer, A GENERAL HISTORY OF NURSING, 248–52 (1933).
12. C. Woodham-Smith, FLORENCE NIGHTINGALE, 1820-1910 351–54 (1951).
13. Ibid, 352.
14. Seymer, supra, 251.
15. Dock, HISTORY, supra, 125, 142.
16. Dock, What We May Expect, supra.
17. Dock, HISTORY, supra, 144.
18. R. M. West, HISTORY OF NURSING IN PENNSYLVANIA 41–59 (1933).
19. V. Robinson, WHITE CAPS: THE STORY OF NURSING 282–83 (1946).
20. M. J. Lesnik & B. E. Anderson, LEGAL ASPECTS OF NURSING (1947).
21. Ibid., 312–14.
22. Ibid., pp. 306–07.
23. The Biennial, 34 AM. J. NURS. 603–27 (June 1934). See also West, supra, 97–108.
24. R. C. Derbyshire, MEDICAL LICENSURE IN THE UNITED STATES (1969).
25. West, supra, 98; Nursing Legislation, 1939: What the State Nurses' Associations Accomplished, 39 AM. J. NURS. 947–81 (September 1939).
26. Statutory Status of Six Professions, 16 RES. BULL. NAT'L EDUC. ASS'N 184–223 (September 1938).
27. Editorial, 39 AM. J. NURS. 275–77 (March 1939); Trained Attendants and Practical Nurses, 44 AM. J. NURS. 7–8 (January 1944).
28. Statutory Status . . ., supra.
29. Editorial, AM. J. NURS., supra; E. M. Jamieson & M. Sewell, TRENDS IN NURSING HISTORY 533–34 (1944).
30. 18 AM. J. NURS. 929 (July 1918).
31. Trained Attendants . . ., supra.
32. Bullough & Bullough, supra, 182–215.
33. N. Stevenson, Curriculum Development in Practical Nurse Education, 64 AM. J. NURS. 81–86 (December 1964); National Center for Health Statistics, U. S. Dept. of Health, Education and Welfare, Public Health Service Pub. 1758, STATE LICENSING OF HEALTH OCCUPATIONS 9–10 (1968).
34. Lesnik & Anderson, supra, 316.
35. Lesnik & Anderson, supra, 315–18.
36. M. Jacobsen, Nursing Laws and What Every Nurse Should Know about Them, 40 AM. J. NURS. 1221–26 (November 1940); Lesnick & Anderson, supra, 47.
37. ANA Board Approves a Definition of Nursing Practice, 55 AM. J. NURS. 1474 (December 1955).
38. E. H. Fogotson, R. Roemer, R. W. Newman, & J. L. Cook, Licensure of Other Medical Personnel, in REPORT OF THE NATIONAL ADVISORY COMMISSION ON HEALTH MANPOWER, Vol II 407–92 (1967).
39. F. R. Kreuter, What Is Good Nursing Care? 5 NURS. OUTLOOK 302–04 (May 1957); D. E. Johnson, A Philosophy of Nursing, 7 NURS. OUTLOOK 198–200 (April 1959); M. Rogers, REVEILLE IN NURSING (1964); American Nurses' Association's First Position on Education for Nursing, 65 AM. J. NURS. 106–11 (December 1965).

40. L. Stein, *The Doctor-Nurse Game*, 16 ARCH. GEN. PSYCHIATRY 699–703 (June 1967).
41. B. Bullough, *Alienation in the Ghetto*, 72 AM. J. SOCIOL. 469–78 (March 1967); B. Bullough, SOCIAL-PSYCHOLOGICAL BARRIERS TO HOUSING DESEGREGATION, UNIV. OF CALIF. HOUSING, REAL ESTATE & URBAN LAND STUDIES PROGRAM (1969).
42. American Nurses' Association, FACTS ABOUT NURSING: A STATISTICAL SUMMARY, 1955–1956 76 (1956).
43. B. E. Anderson, THE FACILITATION OF INTERSTATE MOVEMENT OF REGISTERED NURSES (1950).
44. G. C. Barbee, *Special Procedures: I.V.s, Blood Transfusions and Skin Testing*, in PROCEEDINGS: INSTITUTE ON THE MEDICO-LEGAL ASPECTS OF NURSING PRACTICE 41–44 (1961).
45. H. Sarner, THE NURSE AND THE LAW 89–90 (1968).
46. N. Hershey, *Legal Issues in Nursing Practice*, in PROFESSIONAL NURSING: FOUNDATIONS, PERSPECTIVES AND RELATIONSHIPS, ed. E.K. Spalding & L. E. Notter 110–27 (1970).
47. NATIONAL COMMISSION FOR THE STUDY OF NURSING AND NURSING EDUCATION, AN ABSTRACT FOR ACTION (1970).
48. S. H. Willig, THE NURSES' GUIDE TO THE LAW 75 (1970).
49. Hershey, *supra*, 114; H. Creighton, LAW EVERY NURSE SHOULD KNOW 19 (1970).
50. N. Hershey, *Nurses' Medical Practice Problems, Part I*, 62 AM. J. NURS 82–83 (July 1962).
51. Sarner, *supra*, 16–17.
52. I. A. Murchison & T. S. Nichols, LEGAL FOUNDATION OF NURSING PRACTICE, 91, 109–11 (1970).
53. EXTENDING THE SCOPE OF NURSING PRACTICE: A REPORT OF THE SECRETARY'S COMMITTEE TO STUDY EXTENDED ROLES FOR NURSES 6 (November 1971).
54. 71 OP. Ariz. Att'y Gen. 30 (August 6, 1971), cited in A. M. Sadler, Jr. & B. L. Sadler, *Recent Developments in the Law Relating to Physicians' Assistants* 24 VAND. L. REV. 1,205 (November 1971); CV 72 OP. CALIF. ATT'Y GEN. 187 (1973); indexed letter from Calif. Att'y Gen. (October 4, 1972).
55. STATE LICENSING . . . , *supra*, 65, 73.
56. L. Y. Kelly, *Nursing Practice Acts*, 74 AM. J. NURS. 1310–19 (July 1974).
57. IDAHO CODE, § 54–1413.

4 Role Expansion: The Driving and Restraining Forces

BONNIE BULLOUGH

The decade of the seventies has been marked by a rapid expansion in the role and scope of function of registered nurses. The trends and events related to these developments are examined in this chapter.

One way to view these changes is to use the theoretical approach of change theorists such as Kurt Lewin, who have conceptualized the collective behavior of people in groups as a dynamic balance between driving and restraining forces, with change occurring when the equilibrium between the two breaks down.[1] Benne and Birnbaum illustrated this theory by using as an example a factory where the production level fluctuates only slightly each day. The pattern looks stable, but that stability is actually a function of two sets of nearly equal forces. The forces which tend to raise production include the pressures by supervisors to increase output, the desire of the workers to please management, and the payment incentive plan in the plant. The forces keeping production down include the group norms against "rate busting," the reluctance of the workers to accept advice and training from supervisors, and the feeling of the workers that their jobs are not important.[2] What looks like a stable situation is actually a balance between the driving and restraining forces (Figure 1). The production rate could change if the driving forces were increased by higher incentive payments or if one of the negative restraining forces could be lessened.

Unlike the straight production level in the factory, the equilibrium line which describes the role and scope of function of registered nurses during the last hundred years is characterized by a gradual upward slope as the need for more complex health care has emerged and the science and technology of nursing has expanded to fill that need. The slow steady upward pace of that trajectory has been broken during the last decade, and the line moved more sharply up to reflect the current expansion in the nursing role (Figure 2).

DRIVING FORCES STIMULATING ROLE EXPANSION

Educational Improvements

Probably the major long-range driving force in expanding nursing functions has been the changes that have taken place in the nursing educational system. Before 1873 efforts to establish permanent schools of nursing in this country had failed,

Role Expansion: Driving and Restraining Forces   37

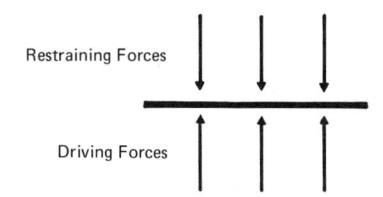

Figure 1. Lewin's theory of equilibrium and change.

so most recruits to nursing learned as they worked. In that year the first three "Nightingale" schools were established—in New York, New Haven, and Boston—setting a new pattern and demonstrating the feasibility of training nurses. Though the schools were new, in general they made no sharp break with the past. They merely formalized and upgraded the existing apprenticeship model. Simple skills were well taught, but the scientific understanding of health-care delivery was left to physicians.[3] Consequently, a second educational reform movement occurred in the twentieth century, when the nursing educational system was converted to a collegiate model. This second reform movement has been slow to take hold, and at times the struggle has been bitter.

Finally, in 1972, a watershed was reached. For the first time in the history of American nursing there were more nurses graduated from collegiate than from diploma schools: 21 percent of the new graduates were awarded baccalaureate degrees; 37 percent earned Associate in Arts degrees, and 42 percent received diplomas from hospital programs. This movement toward collegiate education has continued to gain momentum:[4] in 1978, 31 percent of the new graduates were from baccalaureate schools, 47 percent from community colleges, and only 22 percent from diploma schools.[5]

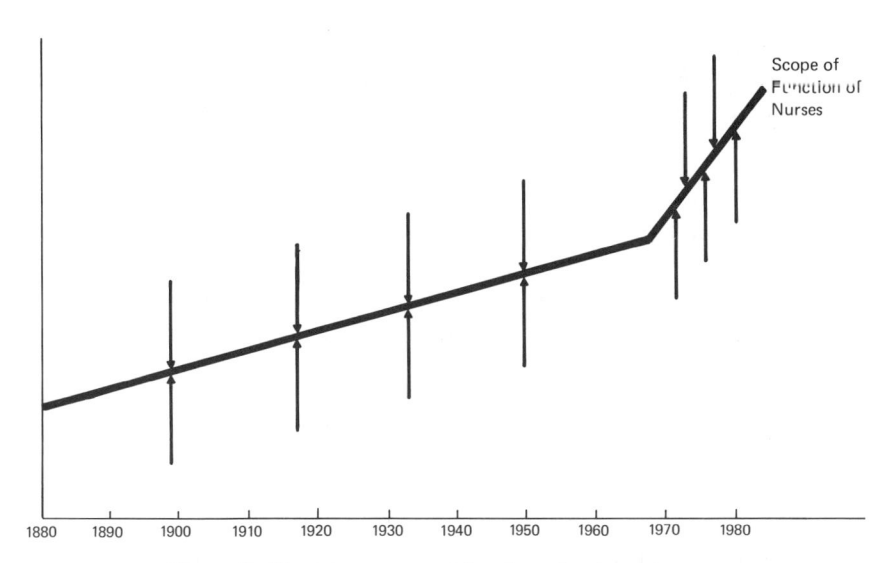

Figure 2. The role or scope of function of registered nurses.

Moreover, the competition from the college-based schools and the rising expectations of student nurses has forced the existing hospital schools to upgrade their programs by hiring more and better prepared instructors and to stop exploiting students in clinical assignments. Although these changes have improved the quality of education in the diploma schools, the cost tends to be prohibitive and continues to surface as a major factor in the closing of diploma programs.

The fact that the current move toward collegiate education is primarily at the associate rather than the baccalaureate level is distressing to some educators. They see this trend as a divisive force which prevents nurses from achieving full power and status within the health-care system. A resolution originating in New York State expresses this concern by calling for legislation to make the baccalaureate degree a requirement for entry into professional nursing by 1985.[6] This resolution was endorsed by the Council of Baccalaureate and Higher Degrees of the National League for Nursing in 1977 and by the American Nurses Association in 1978.[7]

Still, even the limited move into colleges at the associate degree level is having a leavening effect on the profession, since associate-degree nurses are able to continue their education more easily than diploma nurses can. Thirty years ago some colleges gave blanket credits to diploma nurses for their hospital education, but this practice was discontinued because it was thought to be educationally unsound. Consequently, few diploma nurses were willing to return to school to start over, without any credit for the three years they spent in nursing school. As the diploma programs are replaced by associate degree programs, the door is again open for upward mobility, because associate degree nurses have two years of bona fide college credit. For a time the university nursing schools resisted accepting these students because the founder of the community college movement, Mildred Montag, had stated that the associate programs should be terminal.[8] But since that argument was contrary to prevailing practice in community colleges, it is being heard less and less. Special career-ladder baccalaureate programs are now opening up to meet the needs of this growing student population. In a recent study of a sample of 641 southern California Associate in Arts nursing students, 76 percent indicated they intended to go on for further education.[9]

This trend toward continued education can also be seen at the national level. In 1970 there were 2,413 registered nurses who went on to finish baccalaureate programs.[10] In 1977 there were 5,445 previously licensed registered nurses who were awarded baccalaureate degrees.[11] This represents a significant increase, and it is a trend which will undoubtedly continue. As universities face declining enrollments of 18-year-old students, the registered nurse student population will probably be more welcome than it has been in the past.

The number of nurses attaining master's degrees is also increasing rapidly; the number in 1970 was 1,988,[12] while the 1978 figure was 4,271.[13] Since both the career-ladder baccalaureate and the master's degree programs emphasize advanced clinical specialties, including critical care and practitioner specialties, these developments are a significant factor in the recent more rapid expansion of the roles and functions of registered nurses.

Nurse Practitioners

A second driving force for role expansion comes from outside nursing. Throughout the last century the science and technology of medicine expanded at a rapid rate. As medicine became more complex, physicians needed more skilled assistants, including nurses, so they encouraged nurses to learn new procedures and take on new functions.

More recently the shortage of primary-care physicians has served as a major driving force stimulating the nurse practitioner movement. This shortage can be traced to two factors. The first was the long-range limitation on the number of medical trainees. In the years preceding and following the famous Flexner report, which came out in 1910, medical schools were upgraded and many substandard schools were closed. Although this reform actually decreased slightly the number of physicians relative to the population, it also caused the number to stay almost stable at the level of 150 per 100,000 for the next half-century.[14] It is only in the last two decades that the number of physicians has increased sufficiently to reach the current ratio of approximately 180 per 100,000 population. The second factor is that medicine itself has changed, and since the time of Flexner's report the increase in medical knowledge and the growing demand by consumers for better health care has driven the demand for medical services up to outstrip the supply. This has significantly increased the incomes of physicians and contributed to the escalation in the cost of health care. In 1950 Americans spent 4.6 percent of their income on health care; that figure had risen to 7.8 percent by 1973.[15]

Even more important to the nurse practitioner movement than the shortage of doctors has been the trend toward specialization in medicine. In 1910 most doctors were general practitioners; now specialists outnumber generalists by nearly four to one.[16] Thus, the two trends converge to produce a serious gap at the primary-care level where there is a shortage of providers who can treat common episodic and chronic illnesses at a price that ordinary people and government third-party payers can afford.

Nurse practitioners are not the only group that responded to this shortage. Within medicine the specialty of family medicine developed after the Millis Commission reported to the American Medical Association and the Willard Commission reported to the Council on Medical Education outlining the problem of overspecialization.[17] The first family practice residencies were established in 1969 and there are now approximately 500 such slots available for trainees.

Physician's Assistants

Physician's assistants, described in greater detail in Chapter 14, comprise another response to the need for more primary-care providers. In fact, for a time it seemed to many people that physician's assistants were the only answer to the shortage. Their development did not actually predate the development of nurse practitioners since there were public-health nurses working in an expanded role in northern California as early as 1962 and probably in informal types of primary-care situations much earlier.[18] In the out-patient setting nurses also were responsible for the management of patients with long-term illnesses at Massachusetts General Hospital in 1962.[19] Moreover, the Colorado program to train nurse practitioners was established by Henry Silver and others in 1965,[20,21] the same year the first physician's assistant program was started at Duke.[22] Yet it seemed to the public that physician's assistants were the first on the scene. The media no doubt played a significant role here. Physician's assistants were new and newsworthy, but it cannot be denied that the highly visible physician's assistant movement was an important factor in the development of nurse practitioners. It demonstrated publicly that the delegation of a significant number of medical tasks was possible. Once this became apparent, some physicians remembered that nurses existed and thought about them as perhaps better-prepared assistants, probably more tractable, and certainly more plentiful than former independent duty corpsmen, who were the first candidates for physician's-assistant training.[23] The American Academy of Pediatrics furnished leadership in this area, sponsoring conferences, research, and pronouncements supporting practitioners whom they termed nurse associates.[24] In 1971, after a series of negotiations, the Academy issued a joint statement with the American Nurses' Association suggesting guidelines for short-term courses for the preparation of the associates.[25] Although these negotiations were broken off for a year, in 1974 the Academy remained supportive of the idea of nurse associates.[26] The American Medical Association followed the lead of the Academy, and in 1970 issued an official statement supporting the expansion of the role of the nurse.[27]

The physician's assistant movement also gave courage to nurses to rethink their own traditional avoidance of overt expansion of their functions onto the medical turf of diagnosis and treatment.

Clinical Specialties

Inside the hospital the doctor shortage was a less important factor in the expansion of the nursing role. Rather the expanding health-care technology furnished the major impetus for the development of specialized nursing units. New monitoring devices and life-saving techniques require on-the-spot experts who can make diagnostic decisions and treat patients appropriately without delaying to consult a physician.

Coronary care units, the model for many of these nursing wards, evolved during the 1960s when it was realized that most post-myocardial infarction deaths were due to cardiac arrythmias, and that a significant number of lives could be saved if the aberrant rhythms could be converted back to normal rhythms. Staffing coronary care units with full-time physicians was briefly considered, because diagnosing and treating an arrhythmia is clearly a complex medical function, but it was simply not economically feasible. Nurses were given advanced preparation and they now staff all of the units.[28]

The success of the specialized coronary care units in cutting the death rate due to heart attacks has encouraged other special nursing wards. Comparable developments in other areas of the hospital include special units to care for patients suffering from trauma, renal problems, and respiratory problems. The sociological importance of these units for the expansion of the nursing role should not be overlooked. Because the units are growing at such a rapid pace, the nurse clinicians who staff them are probably more important than the ambulatory nurse practitioners in changing the scope of function, power, and income of nurses. The functions of the specialized intensive care nurses are complex, their knowledge base is intensive, and their level of autonomy is greater than that of most other nurses. They represent a significant incursion into what was formerly considered medical territory. Moreover, the specialized units are developing faster than nurses can be educated to staff them. In many areas hospitals bid for the services of such nurses. Certain hospitals in southern California pay a "bounty" to employees who recruit a coronary care nurse. Thus the intensive care nurses are also serving as a catalyst to raise the salary of nurses.

Role Expansion in the Care of Chronic Illnesses: Demographic Changes

The bacteriological revolution of the late nineteenth century has allowed twentieth-century health professionals to control most infectious diseases. This has in some cases almost doubled the life expectancy of populations living in affluent industrialized countries such as the United States. But this happy situation brings with it some negative consequences. We now have an aging population, many of whom must live for long periods with either chronic illness or the infirmities of old age. These patients need the concerned attention of a practitioner who is prepared in the social as well as medical sciences, who is willing to spend time, and whose services are not so expensive that the agency or third-party provider cannot afford that time. Consequently, nurse practitioners are moving into the care of chronic illnesses such as hypertension, diabetes, and arthritis in growing numbers, starting a trend which will probably escalate in the future. The practitioners are influenced by the shortage of physicians in primary care outlined earlier, but the demographic changes are an additional factor influencing the development of this field.

These then are the major driving forces which caused the role of the nurse to expand slowly during the last ninety years and more rapidly during the last decade. The fact that the progress was so slow and that the role is still restricted is partly explained by the restraining forces discussed below.

RESTRAINING FORCES

Medicine

Medicine was mentioned as an important driving force. Paradoxically, it is also the major restraining force restricting the expansion of the nursing role. As indicated, during the twentieth century medicine has moved from an occupation peopled by a mixed bag of folk healers, country doctors, and well-trained practitioners to a well-educated, highly organized profession. It is probably the most highly professionalized occupation. When all of the public relations terms are laid aside, the key attribute of a profession is its autonomy,[29] or its power to control the terms, conditions, and content of its work.[30] To achieve this goal, medicine raised its educational requirements, restricted its membership, and sought not only to gain control over the practice of medicine but also to control the practice of all health occupations. The accreditation process, licensing, and the power of the hospital medical staffs were used as tools in this move for control.[31]

Although physicians in the past were willing to turn procedures over to nurses, including temperature taking, blood pressure readings, and patient observations, they tried to retain control over the formal decision-making process relative to patient care. When it became impossible for them to actually make all of the decisions about patient care, because they could not be present at all times, elaborate games were developed to maintain the pretense that physicians made all diagnostic and treatment decisions.

The Burden of the Feminine Norm

Physicians, probably could never have achieved this expansive definition of their prerogatives, however, if nurses had not allowed it; the reason they seemed to have allowed it is that most nurses were women. Nursing, probably more than any occupation except housewifery, reflects the stereotyped role of women. The norms and values of nursing are feminine and the relationships between nurses and physicians have reflected the extreme subordination of women with all of the male–female gamesmanship which tends to go along with that subordination. Moreover, the educational system has, at least in the past, tended to reinforce this feminine and subordinate picture of the role of the nurse, so that new generations of students have been taught to be ladylike, subservient, and manipulative.

Florence Nightingale set a precedent for this behavior pattern, although she was undoubtedly merely accepting the norms of her day. In Scutari, although she came with significant power delegated to her by the British Secretary of War, she refused to allow the nurses under her command to give any care to the suffering men until the surgeons "ordered" them to do so. This mechanism gained the support of the army doctors, who were very suspicious of her as well as the 38 nurses who came with her, but it also helped establish the surgeon as a superior power over the nurse.[32]

After the war Florence Nightingale started her monumental work of reforming the army to secure better pay and more humane treatment for the common soldier. She retired from public view and gradually secluded herself more and more, until she finally simply took to her bed, where she stayed for the last fifty years of her life. Sitting in her bed, she wrote letters, collected data, and wrote lengthy, well-documented position papers, but she never appeared in public to defend these positions. Instead she convinced her various male friends and admirers, including Sidney Herbert, who had been Secretary of War, that they should wage the public fight for reform. She claimed that she was a weak, feeble woman, and the work of public struggles had to be handled by great strong men. While this modus operandi was probably the key to her effectiveness, the precedent which she set for women and nurses has not been without negative consequences.[33]

There are still nurses who believe that they cannot and should not take any independent responsibility, or more accurately that they should not be held accountable for their own decisions. They are able to believe this in spite of the fact that often a patient's life may depend on their ability to assess the condition and act intelligently on that assessment. Of course, nurses do not actually avoid all decision making, they merely pretend to avoid it. The shortage of men in the profession and the quota system in medicine which operated for many years to limit the number of women admitted to medical schools made the sex segregation between medicine and nursing an extreme one, and stylized communication patterns have grown up between the two professions. These communication patterns are further distorted by the fact that nurses in hospitals and other institutional settings are also under the control of the administrators. Nurses have been forced to learn to negotiate, and gamesmanship has become a part of their lives.[34]

Most of the games nurses play with physicians are built upon the pretense that all decisions about patient care are made by physicians. When nurses make major decisions they handle the situation by invoking the name of the doctor to the patient, and pretending to the doctor that their idea was the doctor's idea. They do this by means of hints, flattery, and wiles rather than by making open statements. Such an approach is not unusual among groups of people who have little formal power; they learn to negotiate power by devious means. For example, Oriental wives and grandmothers are known for the power they are able to accrue through manipulation. But nurse–doctor relationships are remarkable when viewed against the more egalitarian norms of contemporary American society.

One of the best early descriptions of the doctor–nurse game was written by a psychiatrist, Leonard Stein. His article was originally prepared for a psychiatric journal, but it has been reprinted several times by nurses because it has the ring of truth. Stein was fascinated by the strange way in which nurses make recommendations to physicians and the reciprocal pretense on the part of physicians that nurses never make recommendations; yet successful physicians are careful to follow nurses' recommendations. Stein called the pattern a *transactional neurosis*.[35]

These tortured communication patterns and feminine withdrawal from an open admission of decision making have left their mark on present-day nurses. As the baccalaureate programs became more numerous in the 1960s, nurse educators tended to place their emphasis on giving emotional support to ill patients rather than diagnosing or treating the presenting complaints. The supporters of this approach felt that the patient care role should be divided into a "care" and "cure" component, with nurses giving psychosocial support and physicians carrying full responsibility for diagnosing and treating patients. This philosophy acted as a major deterrent to the development of educational programs to prepare nurse practitioners and critical care specialists at the collegiate level.[36]

The most helpful trend in overcoming these psychological barriers to role expansion has been the women's movement. At first this movement had difficulty gaining a foothold in nursing, and some feminists looked upon nurses as the worst possible examples of subordinate women and decided to avoid them. Now, however, nurses themselves have joined the movement. Assertiveness training has become a popular offering in continuing education programs throughout the country. As nurses become more assertive they realize that the care-cure dichotomy was based on a sexist argument, and some of them are willing to expand their point of view. They are assisted in this quest by the increased numbers of men entering nursing. They psychological restraining forces related to femininity are still present, but they are lessening.

In summary: the major driving forces increasing the functions of registered nurses include the improved educational system, the shortage of primary-care providers, the improving technology of health care, the physician's-assistant movement, and the aging population. The domination of medicine and the norms of femininity seem to be the major deterrents to role expansion.

For a time the law also served as a major restraining force limiting the expansion of the nursing role. Sociologists and political scientists have long been interested in the complex interrelationship between the law and social change.[37] In some cases it is possible to trace changes in the law to changes that have already occurred in the society;[38] in other cases the opposite causal sequence can be traced, with new laws creating significant changes in the society.[39] In nursing, both processes can be observed. Before 1971 the nurse practice acts, which forbade nurses the right to participate overtly in diagnosis and treatment, were a deterrent to role expansion. Employers worried about malpractice suits and the legitimacy of billing patients for nurses' services; nurses worried about the morality and safety of violating existing laws. The laws were a significant barrier to role change. As the laws were revised, this barrier was removed or lessened, but something else is happening now. As the momentum for changes in state nurse practice acts grows, an excitement is being generated and a bandwagon psychology is developing; more nurses are now willing to think about obtaining specialty training so they can move into one of the expanded roles. Thus the changing laws themselves are a factor supporting the revolution taking place in nursing.

REFERENCES

1. Kurt Lewin, *Group Decision and Social Change*, in READINGS IN SOCIAL PSYCHOLOGY, ed. E. Maccoby, M. Newcomb, and L. Hartley (1958).
2. Kenneth D. Benne and Max Birnbaum, *Principles of Changing*, THE PLANNING OF CHANGE 328–34 (2nd ed. 1969), ed. G. Bennis, D. Benne, and R. Chin.
3. Vern Bullough and Bonnie Bullough, THE CARE OF THE SICK: THE EMERGENCE OF MODERN NURSING 114–19 (1978).
4. American Nurses Association, FACTS ABOUT NURSING 12–13 (1974).
5. J. C. Vaughn and W. L. Johnson, *Educational Preparation for Nursing—1978*, 27 NURSING OUTLOOK 608–14 (September 1979).
6. New York State Nurses' Association, *Resolution on Entry Into Professional Practice* (Albany, 1974).
7. *ANA Convention; 1978*, 26 NURSING OUTLOOK 500–07 (August 1978).
8. M. Montag and L. G. Gotkin, COMMUNITY COLLEGE EDUCATION FOR NURSING 4–5 (1959).
9. B. Bullough, *The Associate Degree: Beginning or End*, 27 NURSING OUTLOOK 324–28 (May 1979).
10. American Nurses Association, FACTS ABOUT NURSING: A STATISTICAL SUMMARY 108 (1970–71).
11. *Educational Preparation . . . , supra*.
12. FACTS ABOUT NURSING, *supra*, 114.
13. *Educational Preparation . . . , supra*.
14. R. Fein, THE DOCTOR SHORTAGE: AN ECONOMIC DIAGNOSIS (1967).
15. Cambridge Research Institute, TRENDS AFFECTING THE U.S. HEALTH CARE SYSTEM 158 (DHEW Publication No. HRA 76-14503) (January 1976).
16. U.S. Dept. of Health, Education and Welfare, National Center for Health Statistics, HEALTH RESOURCES STATISTICS: HEALTH MANPOWER AND HEALTH FACILITIES 161 (1976).
17. E. Rakel, *Primary Care—Whose Responsibility*, 2 J. FAM. PRAC. 429–30 (1975).
18. E. Siegel & S. Bryson, *Redefinition of the Role of the Public Health Nurse in Child Health Supervision*, 53 AM. J. PUBLIC HEALTH 1015–24 (June 1972).
19. B. Noonan, *Eight Years in a Medical Nurse Clinic*, 72 AM. J. NURS. 1128–30 (June 1972).
20. H. Silver & L. Ford, *The Pediatric Nurse Practitioner at Colorado*, 67 AM. J. NURS. 1143–44 (July 1967).
21. H. Silver, L. Ford, & S. Stearly, *A Program to Increase Health Care for Children: The Pediatric Nurse Practitioner Program*, 39 PEDIATRICS 756–60 (May 1967).
22. E. A. Stead Jr., *Training and Use of Paramedical Personnel*, 277 NEW ENGL. J. MED. 800–01 (October 12, 1967).
23. A. Bergman, *Physician's Assistants Belong in the Nursing Profession*, 7 AM. J. NURS. 975–77 (May 1971).

24. *Executive Board Initiates Child Health Manpower Training Program in a Major Effort to Improve Pediatric Care,* 20 NEWSLETTER: AMERICAN ACADEMY OF PEDIATRICS 1, 4 (July 1, 1969).
25. *Guidelines on Short-Term Continuing Education Programs for Pediatric Nurse Associates,* 71 AM. J. NURS. 509–12 (March 1971).
26. Letter to Pediatric Nurse Associates from the American Academy of Pediatrics, January 16, 1974, signed by Robert G. Frazier, M.D., Executive Director (unpublished).
27. Committee on Nursing, *Medicine and Nursing in the 1970's: A Position Statement,* 213 J. AM. MED. ASSOC. 1,881–83 (September 14, 1970).
28. A. Berwind, *The Nurse in the Coronary Care Unit,* in THE LAW AND THE EXPANDING NURSING ROLE, 82–94 (1st ed., ed. B. Bullough, New York, 1975).
29. P. L. Stewart & M. G. Cantor, VARIETIES OF WORK EXPERIENCE: THE SOCIAL CONTROL OF OCCUPATIONAL GROUPS AND ROLES 1–6 (1974); A. K. Daniels, *How Free Should the Professions Be?* in THE PROFESSIONS, AND THEIR PROSPECTS 39–57 (ed. E. Freidson, 1971).
30. E. Freidson, *The Future of Professionalization,* HEALTH AND THE DIVISION OF LABOR 14–38 (1977).
31. E. Freidson, PROFESSIONAL DOMINANCE: THE SOCIAL STRUCTURE OF MEDICAL CARE (1970).
32. C. Woodham-Smith, FLORENCE NIGHTINGALE, 1820–1910 98–110 (1951).
33. Woodham-Smith, *supra.*
34. A. Strauss, L. Schatzman, D. Erlich, R. Bucher, and M. Sabshin, *The Hospital and Its Negotiated Order,* in THE HOSPITAL IN MODERN SOCIETY 147–69 (ed. E. Friedson, 1963); H. L. Smith, *Two Lines of Authority: The Hospital's Dilemma,* PATIENTS, PHYSICIANS AND ILLNESS 468–69 (ed. E. G. Jaco, 1958).
35. L. I. Stein, *The Doctor-Nurse Game,* 16 ARCHIVES OF GENERAL PSYCHIATRY 699–703 (1967).
36. American Nurses Association Education Committee, *First Position Paper on Education for Nursing,* 65 AM. J. NURS. 106–11 (December 1965); F. Kreuter, *What is Good Nursing Care?* 5 NURSING OUTLOOK 312–14 (May 1957); M. Rogers, REVEILLE IN NURSING (1964).
37. H. L. Ross, D. Campbell, & G. Glass, *Determination of the Social Effects of a Legal Reform,* 13 AM. BEHAV. SCIENTIST 494–509 (March/April 1970); W. G. Friedmann, LAW IN A CHANGING SOCIETY (1964); S. Nagel, THE LEGAL PROCESS FROM A BEHAVIORAL PERSPECTIVE (1969).
38. C. T. Dienes, *Judges, Legislators and Social Change,* 13 AM. BEHAV. SCIENTIST 511–21 (March/April 1970).
39. T. Lewis, THE IMPACT OF SUPREME COURT DECISIONS: EMPIRICAL STUDIES (1969).

5 The Third Phase in Nursing Licensure: The Current Nurse Practice Acts

BONNIE BULLOUGH

The primary focus of this chapter is the current changes in the nurse practice acts that are occurring to accommodate an expanding nursing role. An overview of some of the other features of contemporary codes is also included to give a more comprehensive picture of the laws regulating nursing.

There are nurse practice acts, or collections of laws regulating nursing, included in the codes of all fifty states, the District of Columbia, Puerto Rico, Guam, and the Virgin Islands. In spite of the fact that each of these states and territories enacted or amended its own statute, there are many commonalities among the laws and only a few significant differences. Moreover, as was indicated in the historical review of the development of the nurse practice acts in Chapter 3, it is possible to trace trends in licensure, so that once a given provision is included in the laws of a significant number of states it is likely to spread to most of the others.

In all but three of the jurisdictions, the task of administering laws related to nursing is delegated to a board of nursing or nurse examiners, which is responsible for drawing up the detailed regulations for accrediting schools of nursing, examining candidates, issuing licenses to qualified applicants, and disciplining people who violate the laws or regulations that relate to the practice of nursing. In New York this task is carried out by the Regents of the University of the State of New York and in Connecticut by the State Commissioner of Health. In Illinois the task is delegated to the Department of Registration and Education, but the state has recently appointed an advisory Board for Opinions on Professional Nursing and thus almost has a board of nursing.

Although there is some state-to-state variation in the percentage of provisions legislated and the percentage left to board regulations, the trend seems to be in the direction of leaving the details to regulations. For example, most of the state codes now simply indicate that the candidate for nursing licensure must have graduated from an accredited nursing school; the characteristics of the curriculum and the management of the school are left to regulations, rather than being spelled out in the law. In an earlier era, many of the laws called for specific theoretical or clinical content. Although the majority of the acts still require high-school graduation and a good character for registration, some of the new revisions allow the boards to specify even these basic criteria.

The interstate similarities in the laws and regulations, plus the use of state board pool examinations, makes the movement of registered nurses between states relatively easy. Registration in a second state is ordinarily possible without the necessity of repeating board examinations. Some nurses who move retain their original license, and some 15 percent of the registered nurses are included on the rolls of two or more states.[1] The situation for practical nurses who decide to move is more mixed: the standards for licensure still vary from state to state, and there are a few practical nurses who were originally licensed by waiver rather than by examination.[2] (Practical nurse licensure acts are more recent, and new acts tend to include provisions for coverage by waiver of the practitioners already in the field.) As older practical nurses retire, and the standards become more uniform, interstate movement will undoubtedly become easier.

The earlier problem of outsiders dominating nursing boards no longer exists (Table 1). The most common pattern is a board made up of registered and practical nurses, with the registered nurses in numerical superiority. Although there are often educational or geographic stipulations for board members, it seems apparent that the profession has a significant voice in its own regulation.[3] Moreover, the professional associations also have power: in many states, board members are selected by the governor from lists of candidates provided by the state nurses' association. In a few states, the language of the law emphasizes the influence of voluntary associations in an even more decisive manner. For example, the South Carolina State Board of Nursing is composed of seven members:

> The South Carolina Nurses Association shall be entitled to three representatives on the Board, who shall be members of the South Carolina Nurses Association. . . . The South Carolina Hospital Association shall be entitled to one representative on the Board. . . . The South Carolina Federation of Licensed Practical Nurses, Inc., shall be entitled to two representatives on the Board. . . . One member of the Board shall be a consumer of health care services.[4]

The major recent trend in board membership is the addition of consumer members. As Table 1 shows, there are now seventeen state boards with public members. Professional board members who have served with consumers find them a mixed group. The most effective are those who either bring some expertise or acquire enough expertise to serve as a sounding board for ideas. Effective consumer representatives remind professionals to think of the consumer

Table 1. Other Members of State Boards Besides Registered Nurses

Practical Nurses	Consumers
Arkansas	Arizona
Alabama	Colorado
Connecticut	California
Delaware	Florida
Florida	Idaho
Hawaii	Kentucky
Idaho	Kansas
Indiana	Maine
Illinois	Massachusetts
Kansas	Michigan
Kentucky	Minnesota
Maine	Nebraska
Massachusetts	Nevada
Maryland	New Jersey
Michigan	North Dakota
Mississippi	Vermont
Missouri	Washington
Montana	
Nebraska	Physicans
New Jersey	California
Nevada	Louisiana
New Hampshire	Massachusetts
New Mexico	Mississippi
New York	North Carolina
North Carolina	Tennessee
Ohio	Wisconsin
Oregon	
Rhode Island	Hospital Administrators
Puerto Rico	Massachusetts
Tennessee	North Carolina
Vermont	South Carolina
Virginia	Tennessee
Wyoming	Wisconsin
Psychiatric Technicians	Other
Arkansas	Massachusetts—
Kansas	Hospital Trustee
Michigan	New Jersey—
	Designee of the Executive
	Pennsylvania—
	Superintendent of Public Instruction
	Wisconsin—
	State Health Officer

Note: The only jurisdictions not included above are Georgia, Guam, Iowa, Oklahoma, Texas, Virgin Islands, and the District of Columbia; these boards are made up only of registered nurses. California, Colorado, Louisiana, Puerto Rico, Texas, Washington, and West Virginia have separate boards for licensed practical nurses.

point of view as well as serving as effective links to the outside world. Often, however, the consumer representatives neither know what is going on nor seem to care, and, instead of serving as an effective check on the professionals, lobby for their own special interests. Physicians still serve on seven boards, although the day of physician domination of nursing boards seems to be past.

Most of the boards regulate both registered and practical nurses. In a few jurisdictions there is a separate subcommittee for practical nursing, but the trend seems to be toward a single board with a broader nursing focus. There are, however, still seven jurisdictions in which there is a totally separate board for practical nurses or for practical nurses and psychiatric technicians. As indicated in Table 1, there are now 33 jurisdictions with practical nurse representation on the combined boards. This too represents an improvement over the situation five years ago, when the first edition of this book was written; at that time there were only 24 boards with practical nurse representation.[5] There are, however, still six jurisdictions in which practical nurses are not represented, either on the board or on a committee. The parallels between the medical domination of registered nurses and the RN domination of practical nurses are too apparent for comfort in this situation.

The goal of mandatory licensure, considered so important 30 years ago, has been achieved in all jurisdictions except Georgia and the District of Columbia. However, any feeling of accomplishment over mandatory licensure must necessarily be tempered with a certain amount of skepticism because of the many exemptions written into the codes. Gratuitous and emergency services are allowed in almost all states. In many jurisdictions, members of church groups operating within the tenents of their religion can give nursing care without licensure. In some states the list of people who are allowed outside the law is long. For example, Nebraska allows the three exemptions listed above plus nursing by domestic servants, friends, nursemaids, auxiliary nursing workers, out-of-state nurses who are accompanying patients, out-of-state nurses awaiting registration, new graduates, student nurses, federal employees, and nurses attending graduate school.[6] Also exempted in one or more states are people who administer home remedies, other health professionals, physicians' office employees, and attendants who work in prisons or other state institutions. Obviously the mandatory provisions written into the state acts have not been overwhelmingly restrictive toward non-nurses.

FACILITATING ROLE EXPANSION
FOR REGISTERED NURSES

As the profession and the state legislatures turn their attention to current needs for revision, most of the changes in practice acts are in the direction of lessening restrictions on nurses themselves, including most notably the prohibitions against diagnosis and treatment which were added to nurse practice acts after the publication of the 1955 model practice act by the American Nurses Association.[7] Indicative of the changing self-image of the profession are the model definitions of both professional and practical nursing published by the American Nurses' Association in 1976. No prohibitions against diagnosis are included in either of these statements:

> Practice of Nursing by a Registered Nurse
> The practice of nursing as performed by a registered nurse is a process in which substantial specialized knowledge derived from the biological, physical, and behavioral sciences is applied to the care, treatment, counsel, and health teaching of persons who are experiencing changes in the normal health processes; or who require assistance in the maintenance of health or the management of illness, injury, or infirmity or in the achievement of a dignified death; and such additional acts as are recognized by the nursing profession as proper to be performed by a registered nurse.
>
> Practice of Nursing by a Licensed Practical/Vocational Nurse
> Practical/Vocational nursing means the performance under the supervision of a registered nurse of those services required in observing and caring for the ill, injured, or infirm, in promoting preventive measures in community health, in acting to safeguard life and health, in administering treatment and medication prescribed by a physician or dentist, or in performing other acts not requiring the skill, judgment, and knowledge of a registered nurse.[8]

This new direction in nursing licensure can also be seen in the states. Table 2 summarizes the steps that have been taken to legalize an expanded nursing role in the four sections of the country. Only Rhode Island in the Northeast; Arkansas, Georgia, and West Virginia in the South; Ohio and Oklahoma in the Midwest; and Texas in the West have not taken some steps to legally recognize the expanded functions of nurses. Most of the states acted to revise their nurse practice acts, but Virginia[9] and North Carolina[10] have also revised their medical practice acts, while Tennessee and Delaware wrote provisions for practitioners into their regulations without changing the law.

None of the four other jurisdictions—the District of Columbia, the Virgin Islands, Guam, and Puerto Rico—has revised its practice acts in recent years. This means that there are a total of 12 jurisdictions that have not moved to sanction expanded nursing functions. Five of these (Georgia, West Virginia, Rhode Island, the District of Columbia, and the Virgin Islands) had not written a prohibition against diagnosis and treatment into their laws, so nurses in these areas can probably function without too much difficulty. However, in seven jurisdictions (Hawaii, Ohio, Arkansas, Oklahoma, Texas, Guam, and Puerto Rico) nurses are specifically prohibited from diagnosing and treating patients. These laws are clearly in need of revision.

Table 2. State Nurse Practice Act Support for Role Expansion

State	Diagnosis Allowed?	Treatment Allowed?	First R.N. Act	Expanded Role Recognized
\multicolumn{5}{c}{Northeastern States and the Four Other Jurisdictions}			
Connecticut	Yes—all R.N.	Yes—all R.N.	1905	1975
Delaware	No	No	1909	1978*
Maine	Yes	Yes—N.P.	1915	1974
Massachusetts	Yes—N.P.	Yes—N.P.	1910	1975
New Hampshire	Yes—N.P.	Yes—N.P.	1907	1974
New Jersey	Yes—all R.N.	Yes—all R.N.	1903	1974
New York	Yes—all R.N.	Yes—all R.N.	1903	1972
Pennsylvania	Yes—all R.N.	Yes—N.P. Protocols	1909	1973
Rhode Island	Not prohibited	No	1912	Not yet
Vermont	Yes—all R.N.	Yes—N.P.	1911	1974
District of Columbia	Not prohibited	No	1907	Not yet
Guam	No—if medical	No	1952	Not yet
Puerto Rico	No	No	1963	Not yet
Virgin Islands	No	No	1945	Not yet
\multicolumn{5}{c}{Midwestern States}			
Illinois	Yes—if not medical	Yes—if not medical	1907	1975 (Board for Opinions on Prof. Nursing)
Indiana	Yes—all R.N.	Yes—N.P.	1905	1974
Iowa	Yes—all R.N.	Yes—N.P.	1907	1976
Kansas	Yes—N.P.	Yes—N.P.	1913	1978
Michigan	Yes—N.P.	Yes—N.P.	1909	1978
Minnesota	Yes—all R.N.	No	1907	1974
Missouri	Yes—all R.N.	No	1909	1976
Nebraska	Yes	Yes—N.P.	1909	1974 (but problems with regs.)

North Dakota	Yes	Yes—N.P.	1915	1977
Ohio	No—if medical	No	1915	Not yet
Oklahoma†	No	No	1909	Not yet
South Dakota	Yes	Yes—N.P.	1917	1972 & 1976
Wisconsin	Not prohibited	No	1911	(in process)

Southern States

Alabama	Yes	Yes—N.P.	1915	1975
Arkansas	No—if medical	No	1913	Not yet
Florida	Yes—N.P.	Yes	1913	1975
Georgia	Not prohibited	No	1907	Not yet
Kentucky	Yes—all R.N.		1914	1978
Louisiana	Yes—N.P.	Yes—N.P.	1912	1976
Maryland	Yes—N.P.	Yes—N.P.	1904	1974
Mississippi	Yes—N.P.	Yes—N.P. Protocol	1914	1976
North Carolina	Yes—M.D. supervision	Yes—M.D. supervision	1903	1973
South Carolina	Yes—all R.N.	Yes—N.P. Protocol	1910	1975
Tennessee	Yes in regs. No in law	Yes in regs. Protocol	1911	1972
Virginia	Yes—N.P. Medical pract. act	Yes—N.P.	1903	1975—regs.
West Virginia	Not prohibited	No	1907	Not yet

Western States

Alaska	Yes—N.P.	Yes—N.P.	1941	1974
Arizona	Yes—all R.N.	Yes—N.P.	1921	1973
California	Yes—all R.N.	Yes—Protocol	1905	1974
Colorado	Yes—all R.N.	Yes—Nursing	1905	1974
Hawaii‡	No—if Medical	No—if Medical	1917	Not yet
Idaho	Yes—N.P.	Yes—N.P. Practice Policies	1911	1971 1977—rev.

(continued)

Table 2. (*continued*)

State	Diagnosis Allowed?	Treatment Allowed?	First R.N. Act	Expanded Role Recognized
Montana‡	Not prohibited	No	1913	1976
Nevada	Yes—all R.N.	Yes—N.P.	1923	1973
New Mexico	Yes—N.P.	Yes—N.P. Protocol	1923	1975
Oregon	Yes—N.P.	Yes—N.P.	1911	1973
Texas	No	No	1909	Not yet
Utah	Yes—all R.N.	Yes—all R.N.	1917	1975
Washington	Yes—all R.N.	Yes—A.R.N. S.R.N.	1909	1973
Wyoming	Yes—all R.N.	Yes—N.P.	1909	1975

*Although the Delaware law forbids diagnosis by nurses, the Board of Nursing has issued a 1978 statement recognizing Advanced Nurse Practitioners who hold certification from the American College of Nurse Midwives, the ANA, or the NAPNAP.
†Oklahoma board indicates law allows N.P. but statute sounds negative.
‡Board states that N.P. can practice.
Dates of the original nurse registration acts are from American Nursing Association, FACTS ABOUT NURSING, 69-71 (1977); other data is from the statutes.

MECHANISMS FOR CHANGE

The first state to change its nurse practice act in this new direction was Idaho. In 1971 the legislature inserted the following clause after the prohibition against diagnosis and treatment:

> except as may be authorized by rules and regulations jointly promulgated by the Idaho state board of medicine and the Idaho board of nursing which shall be implemented by the Idaho board of nursing.[11]

Following the passage of the amendment, the combined boards met and adopted such regulations. Nurses seeking to expand their activities to include acts of medical diagnosis or treatment are required to submit evidence to their agency that they have had the necessary special education. Then a committee or committees made up of nurses and physicians or dentists in the facility concerned would draw up standard policies and procedures under which the nurses with expanded functions could work. The 1977 revision of the Idaho practice act removed the prohibition against diagnosis and treatment and added a definition of "nurse practitioner" which reads as follows:

> Nurse practitioner means a licensed professional nurse having specialized skill, knowledge and experience authorized by rules and regulations jointly promulgated by the Idaho state board of medicine and the Idaho board of nursing and implemented by the Idaho board of nursing, to perform designated acts of medical diagnosis, prescription of medical therapeutic and corrective measures and delivery of medications.[12]

As Table 3 shows, the Idaho pattern is the most common mechanism for legitimating an expanded scope of practice for registered nurses; legislatures in 30 states have given the task of writing guidelines for expanded functions to the board of nursing alone or to some combination of boards. In some of these states the basic role of all registered nurses has also been broadened, while in others the expanded scope of function is reserved for nurse practitioners, midwives, or anesthetists, or some combination of these.

A disadvantage to this approach is the inevitable delay which occurs while regulations are drafted and agreed upon, particularly when the task is assigned to boards of both medicine and nursing, as is the case in twelve states; to the boards of nursing and health, as in Mississippi;[13] or to the special Illinois Board for Opinions, which includes physicians, hospital administrators, and nurses.[14] Minnesota has also complicated the regulation process by establishing an additional umbrella board to deal with all of the healing arts. In some states the delay between the law and the regulations has been as long as five years; two years seems the reasonable minimum norm for promulgating regulations. The Nebraska boards of nursing and medicine have experienced an additional

56 Nursing Practice Law

Table 3. Major Mechanisms for Role Expansion for Registered Nurses

	Board Regulations?	Expanded Definition of R.N.?	State Certification
Northeastern States			
Connecticut		Yes	
Delaware	Nursing		
Maine	Nursing		Midwives, anesthetists
Massachusetts	Nurs. and med.		Midwives
New Hampshire	Nursing	Yes	ARNP* (family, ob-gyn, child health, commun. health, psych/mental health, midwives)
New Jersey		Yes	
New York		Yes	Midwives, anesthetists
Pennsylvania	Nurs. and med.	Yes	CRNP† midwives (medical board)
Vermont	Nurs. and med.	Yes	
Southern States			
Alabama	Nursing		Midwives, anesthetists
Florida	Nurs. and med.	Yes	ARNP (fam., ped., adult, ob-gyn, diabetic, fam. planning, geriatric, college health, midwives, anesthetists)
Kentucky	Nursing	Yes	ARNP (Midwives, N.P.)
Louisiana	Nursing		Anesthetists (recog. national cert.)
Maryland	Nursing	Yes	
Mississippi	Nurs. and health		
North Carolina	Nurs. and med.		Midwives, ped. and family planning N.P.
South Carolina	Nursing		Recog. ANA certificate— midwives, anesthetists
Tennessee	Nursing		
Virginia	Med. and nurs.		N.P. (family ped.), anesthetists
West Virginia			Midwives, anesthetists
Midwestern States			
Illinois	Board of Public Opinion	Yes	
Indiana	Nurs. and med.		
Iowa		Yes	ARNP (several N.P. specialties named, midwives, anesthetists)
Kansas	Yes	Yes	ARNP
Michigan	Yes		Midwives, anesthetists, N.P.'s
Minnesota		Yes	
Missouri		Yes	
Nebraska	Nurs. and med.	Yes	
North Dakota	Nursing	Yes	
Oklahoma			Anesthetists
South Dakota	Nursing	Yes	N.P.'s anesthetists, midwives
Wisconsin			ARNP proposed

Table 3. *(continued)*

	Board Regulations?	Expanded Definition of R.N.?	State Certification
Western States			
Alaska	Nurs. and med.		ARNP, midwives
Arizona	Nursing	Yes	Practitioners in extended role (family, ped., midwives)‡
California	Nurs. and med.	Yes	Midwives§
Colorado		Yes	
Idaho	Nurs. and med.	Yes	N.P.'s
Montana			Midwives
Nevada	Nursing	Yes	
New Mexico	Nursing	Yes	N.P.'s
Oregon	Nursing	Yes	N.P.'s (family, ped., adult, ger., psych/mental health, women's health care, school, college, midwives)
Utah		Yes	Midwives
Washington	Nursing	Yes	ARNP, specialized registered nurse
Wyoming	Nurs. and med.	Yes	
Other			
Virgin Islands			Midwives

*Advanced registered nurse practitioner
†Certified registered nurse practioner
‡Arizona requires nurse practitioners to sit for a certification examination. The Board may waive this examination if the candidate has taken a national qualifying examination.
§California does not issue certificates for nurse practitioners, but the Board will evaluate candidates' credentials and send them a letter of approval. Family, adult, pediatric, and obstetrical-gynecological nurse practitioners are mentioned in the regulations.
Note: Arkansas, District of Columbia, Georgia, Guam, Hawaii, Ohio, Puerto Rico, Rhode Island, and Texas (not shown) have not yet passed any statutes facilitating role expansion for registered nurses.

problem. In accordance with a 1974 law, the two boards wrote up rules and regulations describing the additional acts appropriate to be performed by registered nurses, whereupon the Attorney General of the state ruled that the boards did not have this authority. He claimed that the legislature had improperly delegated the responsibility to write law, and therefore his office would not approve the regulations. The Nebraska nurses now must start again to seek new legislation.[15]

The second major approach to broadening the scope of practice is to expand the definition of a registered nurse to include diagnosis and management. The 1972 New York act and the 1974 California act use this mechanism. There are significant differences in the two laws, however. The New York law invokes the concept of a nursing diagnosis and a nursing regime. The statute defines a nursing diagnosis as follows:

Diagnosing in the context of nursing practice means that identification of and discrimination between physical and psychosocial signs and symptoms essential to the effective execution and management of a nursing regime. Such diagnostic privilege is distinct from a medical diagnosis.[16]

This language suggests that the act of diagnosis is somehow different when performed by a nurse rather than by a physician, but does not make clear how that difference appears in practice. Members of a nursing in-group who are familiar with the argument that the nursing diagnosis should be psychosocial rather than physical might well undertsand the language, but to the uninitiated the wording suggests that when nurses examine patients they place the signs and symptoms in two piles (one physical and one psychosocial); physicians presumably are allowed to be cognizant of the essential interplay between the psyche and the soma. This seems a peculiar way to distinguish a nursing from a medical diagnosis, particularly in light of the fact that the nursing educational system has for many years stressed the importance of the interplay between the biologic and psychosocial factors in illness, while medicine has been less interested in the holistic phenomenon. In spite of this apparent lack of clarity, thirteen states have used this definition of diagnosis, and several other states mention a nursing diagnosis or a nursing regime.

Probably the reality of the situation is that the cognitive processes used by nurses and physicians in diagnosing and planning a treatment regime are quite similar, although the two types of practitioners might well give priority to different patient problems—with nurses attending more to the social and psychological signs, symptoms, and treatment modalities. This generalization would hold only part of the time and would be influenced by the practitioner's specialty and the patient's needs. For example, coronary care nurses must necessarily be continuously aware of the physiological state of the patient; a psychiatrist must focus on the social and psychological problems presented by the patient.

Nurses generally seek more consultation and advice from physicians and other members of the health team than physicians seek, but even this does not neatly distinguish the nursing diagnosis and treatment plan from the medical one. There are also many humble physicians who seek consultation when needed. The point is that while there certainly are differences in the diagnostic and treatment processes carried out by nurses and by physicians, there are also significant similarities. The overlap makes clear definitions difficult, and any differentiation will probably become even more problematic as nurses gain in skill and confidence. Probably the only operational definition of a nursing diagnosis and care plan that would hold up over time and empirical study is a diagnosis and care plan done by a nurse, as distinguished from one done by a physician.

This was the approach used by some nurse practitioners for a time. They claimed that the work role of the practitioner fell under the general rubric of the terms "nursing diagnosis" and "nursing regime." However, more recently a backlash by at least one conservative board of medicine member has pointed up the problematic aspect of this conceptualization of the scope of nursing function. The case is a New Jersey one in which two nurse practitioners, Hirschman and Adler, are charged with practicing medicine without a license and their physician consultants at the Rutgers Community Health Plan are charged with aiding and abetting their practice. The specific charge against Hirschman is that she gave erythromycin to a child with an upper respiratory infection because the child was sensitive to penicillin. Adler's crime was finding in a woman's breast a lump that had been missed by the woman's family doctor. In addition, four New Jersey school nurses were charged with practicing medicine because they did physical examinations of children. The New Jersey Board of Nursing argues that the nurse practitioners are all functioning within the scope of practice outlined in the state's definition of professional nursing, which reads as follows:

> The practice of nursing as a registered professional nurse is defined as diagnosing and treating human responses to actual or potential physical and emotional health problems, through such services as casefinding, health teaching, health counseling, and provision of care supportive to or restorative of life and well-being, and executing medical regimen as prescribed by a licensed or otherwise legally authorized physician or dentist. Diagnosing in the context of nursing practice means that identification of and discrimination between physical and psychosocial signs and symptoms essential to effective execution and management of the nursing regimen. Such diagnostic privilege is distinct from a medical diagnosis. Treating means selection and performance of those therapeutic measures essential to the effective management and execution of the nursing regimen. Human responses means those signs, symptoms and processes which denote the individual's health need or reaction to an actual or potential health problem.[17]

However, when Edwin Albano, Chairman of the New Jersey Board of Medicine, read this definition, he reportedly said, "There are some states that recognize nurse practitioners, but not New Jersey. As far as I know there is no such entity." The case is now tied up in the courts because the disagreement of the boards leaves open a question of jurisdiction.[18]

Perhaps the New Jersey Board of Medicine would have found some other way to attack the nurse practitioner movement if the language of the nurse practice act had been less obscure. The 1978 statement on physician extenders made by the American Academy of Family Practice, as well as the earlier editorial in the *Journal of Family Practice*, suggests that there is a growing fear of competition from nurse practitioners and physician's assistants. These statements urge close monitoring of "physician extenders," with the possibility of terminating their use of some future date.[19] While a backlash movement seems to be developing, it would seem that language which invokes nursing jargon and is not clearly understood by everyone contributes to the problem. A law that allows nurses to diagnose patients' problems is more direct and more honest. On the other hand, a direct approach is not always possible, and part of the reason for the obscure New York language was also political. Although the original bill to amend the New York nurse practice act included some notion of nursing process that differs from a medical process, the original language did not stress the differences.[20] That bill was vetoed in 1971 because of medical opposition, and in his veto message the governor explained that the definition failed to differentiate between medicine and nursing. In 1972 the New York State Medical Association dropped its opposition, and the bill was again passed and was signed into law. The further differentiation of the medical versus the nursing approach through the addition of the concept of the nursing diagnosis seemed to have helped in this effort, although the vigorous campaign carried out by the nurses of the state in support of the bill cannot be overlooked as perhaps the more significant factor.[21]

By a very careful use of words, the California legislature managed to expand the definition of registered nursing without invoking the concept of a nursing diagnosis or treatment regime:

(a) Direct and indirect patient care services that insure the safety, comfort, personal hygiene, and protection of patients; and the performance of disease prevention and restorative measures.

(b) Direct and indirect patient care services, including, but not limited to, the administration of medications and therapeutic agents necessary to implement a treatment, disease prevention, or rehabilitative regimen prescribed by a physician, dentist, or podiatrist.

(c) The performance, according to standardized procedures, of basic health care, testing, and prevention procedures, including, but not limited to, skin tests, immunization techniques, and the withdrawal of human blood from veins and arteries.

(d) Observation of signs and symptoms of illness, reactions to treatment, general behavior, or general physical condition, and (1) determination of whether such signs, symptoms, reactions, behavior, or general appearance exhibit abnormal characteristics; and (2) implementation, based on observed abnormalities, of appropriate reporting, or referral, or standardized procedures, or changes in treatment regimen in accordance with standardized procedures, or the initiation of emergency procedures.[22]

Notice that the emotionally tinged word "diagnosis" is not invoked in this definition, so there is no need to explain it away. Rather, in section (d), a definition of diagnosis is substitued for the word. Of course, this supports the idea that there is a certain amount of gamesmanship involved in the construction of the new definitions, but that may well be one of the current political realities. It will be a better day when nurses not only can make their full potential contribution to patient care but also can openly admit that contribution. The careful tone of the new definitions suggest that the day is approaching but has not yet arrived.

The third major mechanism for role expansion seems to be a natural extension of the board responsibilities for regulation. The 1975 Washington State board started a trend when it drew up regulations defining advanced registered nurses and specialized registered nurses.[23] As Table 3 shows, there are now 19 states which grant a certificate to nurse practitioners with advanced preparation. A few boards have been able to do this on their own because they were originally granted general rather than specific regulatory authority by the legislature,[24] but in most of the 19 states the plan to certify originated in the legislature and has been carried out by the board of nursing or the boards of nursing and medicine.

To date the most popular umbrella name for the new specialist is Advanced Registered Nurse Practitioner, although there is considerable variation in the pattern. The older regulations for anesthetists and nurse-midwives are sometimes incorporated into the new certification plan. The longer standing of these two groups probably accounts for the fact that standards developed by their professional organizations are more likely to be accepted in the states than the more recently developed practitioner standards of the American Nurses' Association or the National Association of Pediatric Nurse Associates and Practitioners (NAPNAP). Most of the certification regulations are written in terms of educational standards.

In addition to these three major approaches—board rules, expanded definitions of nursing, and certification—there are two other mechanisms that appear in a few states. Protocols or standardized procedures are mentioned in the California practice act and in the Idaho regulations. In Tennessee, the Board of Nursing (without statutory obligation to do so) wrote regulations requiring registered nurses who manage medical care to use protocols jointly developed by the nurses and physicians in their agencies. Protocols are written for the administration of medications in Wyoming. This mechanism is explained in more detail in this book in Chapters 15 and 16. Although protocols have been criticized as a "cookbook approach," they probably have value in this transition period because they assure physicians and the public that nurse practitioners are caring for patients in a safe and orderly fashion.

Another approach to role expansion not covered in Table 3 is exemplified by the Maine practice act, which allows individual physicians to delegate the right to diagnose and treat. It indicates that professional nursing includes "diagnosis or prescription of therapeutic or corrective measures when such services are delegated by a physician to a registered nurse who has completed the necessary additional education programs."[25] Even before the current phase in nursing licensure there were state medical practice acts, including those of Arizona, Colorado, Florida, Kansas, and Oklahoma, which gave physicians broad powers to delegate medical acts to other workers.[26] As a consequence of the development of physician's assistants, most other states now provide exemptions to the medical practice acts for other workers when they act under physician supervision.[27] Some of these statutes allow physicians to decide to whom they are to delegate; others name specific categories, such as physician's assistants or nurses. The Arizona statute, which predates the current movement, indicates that "any person acting at the direction of . . . a doctor of medicine" is exempt from the prohibitions in the medical practice act.[28] The more recent Connecticut statute follows the trend toward more specificity and indicates that the following are exempt from the provisions of the medical practice act:

> Any person rendering service as a physician's trained assistant, a registered nurse, or a licensed practical nurse if such service is rendered under the supervision, control and responsibility of a licensed physician.[29]

It may be possible for nurses to sanction some expanded functions by using the delegatory provisions that have been added to medical practice acts, although there is some question as to their usefulness for this purpose. An expansion of the physician's right to delegate received support from officials of the Department of Health, Education and Welfare, who called for a moratorium on the development of laws to sanction new types of health workers but approved this approach.[30] It has been used as a major mechanism for giving legal coverage to physician's assistants, and this may well be a reasonable approach for physician's assistants, who have no basic license of their own except in Colorado.[31]

The nursing situation is different. Nurses already have a basic license. Their role expansion is taking place in varying degrees, so there is no single new nursing occupation. In the early days of the current revolution some people predicted that a new level of practitioner would develop, between medicine and nursing, with an identity separate from either of the other professions. Some authorities still hold this view and believe that not all nurses should be taught the techniques of diagnosis.[32] But the movement has not worked out so neatly. Rather, a large group of nurses seem to be in the process of expanding their role to a modest degree. In either in-patient or ambulatory settings, they are taking on a few new functions or admitting more honestly to the old functions that called for judgment. Some of the members of this group have acquired new knowledge through formal classes, but more have learned the new skills from the physicians with whom they work, or have enlarged their knowledge by reading the nursing journals, which have shifted their focus to include more information about diagnosis and treatment. The old nurse practice acts, which described nursing in a purely dependent and noncognitive way, are out of date for these people; but they are in no way members of any new occupational group. They are nurses who need and deserve better nurse practice acts.

On the other hand, there is a smaller group of nurses, perhaps about 20,000, who have taken on new titles in ambulatory or critical care. These nurses have moved further into what was formerly considered medicine's territory, and their need for either physician supervision or legal sanction is greater. Few of these practitioners need to have all their practice supervised by physicians because most of them still carry out significant nursing responsibilities. Physicians should not and cannot supervise everything that nurses do and still have any time for direct patient contact, which is what physicians are trained for. The new laws of Maryland and Minnesota clearly specify that not all nursing need be supervised by physicians. The Maryland statute indicates that:

> The practice of nursing includes both independent nursing functions and delegated medical functions, and may be performed autonomously or in collaboration with other health team members, or may be delegated by the registered nurse to other nursing personnel.[33]

In a similar view, the Washington statute indicates that "the registered nurse is directly accountable and responsible to the individual consumer for the quality of nursing care rendered."[34] These laws make an important point: all nurses are expanding their roles to a certain extent and becoming more legally accountable for their own practice, while a smaller group is moving into advanced specialties.

To summarize the recent legislation: provisions have been added to 40 nurse practice acts and one medical practice act to facilitate role expansion for registered nurses. This represents a significant trend to expand the scope of practice of registered nurses and is expected to continue as other jurisdictions revise their nurse practice acts. A variety of mechanisms are being used, including board regulations, expanded definitions of nursing certification of specialties, and standing orders. The best approach seems to be a combination of methods, including an expansion of the basic definition of the registered nurse and some type of regulatory mechanism to guide the practice and specify the educational needs of those nurses whose role expansion in the areas of diagnosis and treatment is signficant.

The revisions are best accomplished in those portions of the state codes that are considered nursing sections, rather than in the medical sections—unless nurses want regulation by medicine. Moreover, it is easier for nurses to ask for and achieve nurse practice act revision than medical practice act revision. Medical practice act revisions that increase the delegatory power of physicians do not seem to be a particularly desirable approach for sanctioning increased responsibility and accountability of nurses, who are already licensed to carry out delegated medical tasks.

The movement to expand the scope of function of nurses is probably related to other trends in the laws regulating nursing, including less domination of nursing boards by medicine and a beginning trend toward more consumer power in regulation. A major recent trend noted in this analysis is the movement to certify nurses as advanced specialists, including nurse practitioners, midwives, and anesthetists. It is a trend that can be expected to gain momentum, and if it does it will have far-reaching implications because it means that the states are giving positive sanction to an advanced level of nursing practice.

REFERENCES

1. American Nurses' Association, FACTS ABOUT NURSING 47, 72–73 (1974).
2. FACTS ABOUT NURSING, 156.
3. R. de Tornyay, *State Board Member*, 69 AM. J. NURS. 570–72 (March 1969).
4. SOUTH CAROLINA CODE § 40-33-210.
5. B. Bullough, ed. THE LAW AND THE EXPANDING NURSING ROLE 156 (1975).
6. NEBRASKA REVISED STATUTES § 71–1, 132.06.
7. *ANA Board Approves a Definition of Nursing Practice*, 55 AM. J. NURS. 1,474 (December 1955).
8. American Nurses' Association, MODEL PRACTICE ACT (1976).
9. VIRGINIA CODE § 54–275.
10. NORTH CAROLINA GENERAL STATUTES § 90–1814.
11. IDAHO CODE § 54–1413 (e) (1971 Revision).
12. IDAHO CODE § 54–1402 (d) (1977 Revision).
13. MISSISSIPPI CODE § 73–15–9.
14. ILLINOIS REVISED STATUTES § 35.35a.
15. Letter from Margaret Pavelka, R.N., Executive Director, Nebraska Board of Nursing, June 15, 1978; *NNA Asks Courts to Act on Rules for NP Practice*, 78 AM. J. NURS. 1,828–42 (November 1978).
16. NEW YORK STATE EDUCATION LAW Op Title 8, Article 139 § 6901.
17. NEW JERSEY REVISED STATUTES C. 45:11–23.
18. *News: Nurse Practitioners Fight Moves to Restrict Their Practice*, 78 AM. J. NURS. 1285, 1308, 1310 (August 1978); *Regional Review*, 3 NURSE PRACTITIONER 6 (May–June 1978); J. Adler, *Guest Editorial: You are Charged With* . . . 4 NURSE PRACTITIONER 6–7 (January–February 1979).
19. American Academy of Family Physicians, PHYSICIAN EXTENDERS, Policy Statement Adopted at the 1978 Annual Meeting; John P. Geyman, *Is There a Difference Between Nursing Practice and Medical Practice?* 5 J. FAM. PRAC. 935–36 (December 1977); Ingeborg G. Mauksch, *The Nurse Practitioner Movement—Where Does It Go From Here?* 68 AM. J. PUB. HEALTH 1074–75 (November 1978).
20. *Independence of Nursing Function Affirmed by New York Legislature* 7 AM. J. NURS. 1901–02 (June 1971); V. Driscoll, *Liberating Nursing Practice*, 20 NURSING OUTLOOK 24–28 (January 1972).
21. T. M. Schorr, *Where the Action Is*, 72 AM. J. NURS. 671 (April 1972).
22. CALIFORNIA BUSINESS AND PROFESSIONS CODE, Ch. 6, Art. 2, § 2725.
23. WASHINGTON STATE BOARD OF NURSING, RULES/REGULATIONS WAC 308–120–200 through 250.
24. Virginia C. Hall, STATUTORY REGULATIONS OF THE SCOPE OF NURSING PRACTICE, Joint Practice Commission (1975).
25. MAINE REVISED STATUTES Title 32, Ch. 31, § 2102.
26. M. S. Fish, *Nursing vis-à-vis Medicine. A Proposal for Legislation*, in American Nurses' Association, LICENSURE AND CREDENTIALING: PROCEEDINGS OF THE A.N.A. CONFERENCE FOR MEMBERS AND PROFESSIONAL EMPLOYEES OF STATE BOARDS OF NURSING and A.N.A. ADVISORY COUNCIL, 1972 14–22 (1974); E. H. Fogotson, R. Roemer, R. Newman, & J. L. Cook, *Licensure of Physicians*, in REPORT OF THE NATIONAL ADVISORY COMMISSION ON HEALTH MANPOWER, Vol. II, 294 (1967).
27. American Medical Association, EDUCATIONAL PROGRAMS FOR THE PHYSICIAN'S ASSISTANT 9 (September 1973). The list was updated by the addition of Tennessee.
28. ARIZONA REVISED STATUTES, 32–1421 (6).

29. CONNECTICUT GENERAL STATUTES, Ch. 370, Title 20–9.
30. L. Miike & H. Cohen, DEVELOPMENTS IN HEALTH MANPOWER LICENSURE AND RELATED HEALTH PERSONNEL CREDENTIALING 4–5 U.S. Department of Health, Education and Welfare Pub. No. (HRA) 74–3101 (June 1973).
31. W. J. Curran, *New Paramedical Personnel—to License or Not to License?* 282 NEW ENGL. J. MED. 1085–86 (May 7, 1970).
32. J. E. Lynaugh & B. Bates, *Physical Diagnosis: A Skill for All Nurses?* 74 AM. J. NURS. 58–89 (January 1974).
33. MARYLAND CODE, 54–275.
34. WASHINGTON REVISED CODE § 18.88.010.

Citations for all the Nurse Practice Acts (From American Nurses Association, FACTS ABOUT NURSING 1976–77, 69, 70, 71 [1977]; updated)

Alabama	Title 46, Code of Alabama of 1940, as amended.
Alaska	Ch. 68, Title 8, Alaska Statutes.
Arizona	Arizona Revised Statutes Annotated 1956, Ch. 15, §§ 32–1601 through 32–1667.
Arkansas	Arkansas Statutes 1947 Annotated, §§72–701 through 72–725.
California	Ch. 6, Business and Professions Code, enacted 1939, amended 1974.
Colorado	Ch. 12, Art. 38, Pt. 2 Colorado Revised Statutes, 1973, as amended.
Connecticut	Ch. 378 of General Statutes of State of Connecticut.
Delaware	Delaware Code, Ch. 153, Vol. 54.
District of Columbia	Code of Laws of D.C., 1974 edition, Title 2, Ch. 2.
Florida	Ch. 464, Florida Revised Statutes, 1975.
Georgia	Georgia Code Annotated, Title 84, Ch. 1001–1015, 1017–1021, 9915–9916.
Guam	Government Code of Guam, Ch. 3, Public Law 7–34.
Hawaii	Hawaii Revised Statutes, Ch. 457.
Idaho	Idaho Code, §§ 54–1401 through 54–1415.
Illinois	Ch. 91, Illinois Revised Statutes.
Indiana	Indiana Code 1971, Title 25, Art. 23, Ch. 1, §1–28. Amended by Acts 1971, Public Law 119, P.L. 376, and Acts 1974 P.L. 119 (Burns Indiana Statute Annotated 25–23–1–1 through 25–23–1–28 and Acts 1975, P.L. 272.
Iowa	Code of Iowa, Ch. 147 (general provisions—practice acts), Ch. 152 (practice of nursing).
Kansas	K.S.A., Ch. 65, Art. 11, Ch. 231, Laws of Kansas 1968.
Kentucky	Kentucky Revised Statutes, Ch. 314.
Louisiana	Louisiana Revised Statutes of 1950 as amended by Act 351, August 25, 1976.
Maine	Chapter 69–A (Enacted by Ch. 303, Public Laws of 1959), Ch. 31, Title 32, Revised Statutes 1964.
Maryland	1971 Replacement Vol. 1974 Supplement, as amended by Ch. 591 of the General Assembly of Maryland, 1975.
Massachusetts	General Laws, Ch. 13 and 112 as amended; Ch. 620 Acts of 1941; Ch. 693 Act of 1960.
Michigan	Act 149, Public Acts of 1967, as amended.

66 Nursing Practice Law

Minnesota	Minnesota Statutes, 1945, §§ 148.171–148.285, as amended.
Mississippi	Mississippi Code of 1942, §§ 8806–8831.
Missouri	Ch. 335, Missouri Revised Statutes, Supplement 1976.
Montana	Title 66, 1221–1246, 82A–1602.18, RCM–1947.
Nebraska	Compiled Statutes of Nebraska 71–1, 132.04–71–1, 132.42.
Nevada	Nevada Revised Statutes, 1963, Ch. 632.
New Hampshire	Revised Statutes Annotated, 1955, Ch. 326, Ch. 281, Laws of 1975.
New Jersey	P.L. 1947, c.262, as amended; Revised Statutes of New Jersey, Title 45, Ch. 11; Revised Statutes Cumulative Supplement, amended 1958 and 1966.
New Mexico	New Mexico Statutes 1953, Annotated, §§ 67–2–1 to 67–2–26.
New York	Education Law—Title VIII Education Law 1971, Art. 130 and 139.
North Carolina	North Carolina General Statutes, Ch. 90, Art. 9, 158–117.18.
North Dakota	Laws Governing Professional Nursing, N.D. Century Code 43–12–01 through 43–12–24.
Ohio	Ohio Revised Code, Ch. 4723.
Oklahoma	59 Oklahoma Statutes, 1971; 567.1–567.16.
Oregon	Oregon Laws, Ch. 678, §§ 678.010 through 678.410.
Pennsylvania	The Professional Nurse Law, 63 P.S. 211 *et seq.*
Rhode Island	Ch. 5–34 of the General Laws, 1956.
South Carolina	1962 Code of Laws of South Carolina, Vol. 5, Ch. 17, Art. 1 through 6.
South Dakota	Ch. 36–9, Session Laws of 1976.
Tennessee	Public Acts, Ch. 7, Title 63, Public Act Annotated 1967.
Texas	Vernon's Civil Statutes, Articles 4513–4528.
Utah	58–31–1 to 58–31–17 Utah Code Annotated, as amended to and including Session Laws 1963.
Vermont	Title 26, V.S.A. Ch. 27, §§ 1551–1552.
Virgin Islands	Virgin Islands Code Title 27.
Virginia	Code of Virginia, Title 54, Ch. 13.1 (as amended at the 1975 session of General Assembly).
Washington	Ch. 18.8, Revised Code of Washington.
West Virginia	Ch. 30, Art. 7, Code of West Virginia of 1931, as amended.
Wisconsin	Ch. 441, Wisconsin Statutes.
Wyoming	Wyoming Statutes 33–279.1 through 33–279.18.

6 Avoiding Legal Liability

JOAN P. RANDALL

"It may seem a strange principle to enunciate as the very first requirement in a Hospital that it should do the sick no harm."[1] While circumstances have changed vastly since Florence Nightingale wrote those words in 1859, they apply equally as well today. Patients and their welfare should still be the primary concern of health-care practitioners. As the legal definition of the scope of nursing practice has expanded, so has the responsibility, the absolute duty, the accountability, and the liability of nurses.

The purpose of this chapter is to help nurses become more aware of situations involving potential legal liability for themselves, for the physicians with whom they have a working relationship, and for their employing health institutions. All of the principles employed to lessen the chance of a legal encounter also promote sound nursing practice and the safety and well-being of patients.

Nurses can be sued and are being sued. The experience of being served with a summons and complaint and all of the subsequent events is unforgettable. It is a devastating emotional experience to live through months, even years, of interrogations, depositions, and finally the trial. It can also be a very costly experience in terms of lost wages, attorney's fees, and awards to the plaintiff which the nurse who loses a suit may be required to pay. This rather grim picture is a realistic one, but there are ways to improve it. The best way is to prevent the causes of such a suit. Another help is to have malpractice insurance. A professional liability insurance policy covers the insured for a stated period of time and for a stated amount of maximum coverage. The insured has a responsibility to report to the insurance carrier at the first indication that a suit might be pending. If there has been an obvious incident of harm to a patient where the nurse might be considered negligent, it should be reported. Some patients or their families might be unhappy, grumbling, and threatening suit because of a bill dispute, disappointment at not achieving an expected perfect result, poor rapport, misunderstanding, or actual professional negligence.

Insurance coverage will provide legal defense and will pay all sums of money for which the insured becomes legally liable, up to the limit of the policy. The amount of the settlement may be determined by the jury's evaluation of the damages suffered by the insured party. The jury is assisted by the testimony of expert witnesses who will help them to decide whether negligence was the cause of the harm. It would be legal malpractice not to prepare the nurse or other health professional properly for the deposition. The insurance company defense attorney will work closely with the client from the first report to the company. The accused should not discuss the case with anyone but the defense attorney, and should expect to spend a considerable amount of time with the attorney preparing for the deposition.

Since approximately eighty percent of malpractice cases are settled before the time of trial, the deposition is very important: it can win or lose the case. The deposition involves the attorney for the plaintiff questioning the accused in the presence of the defense attorney and a court reporter. This usually takes place at the office of the plaintiff's attorney, and although it may seem a casual event, it is not. Answers are given under oath and they may well determine the outcome of the case. If the case goes to trial, the accused is held accountable for all answers given at the deposition. Knowledgeable attorneys advise simple answers and suggest that clients do not elaborate, or volunteer information. Positive answers should be avoided when there is some doubt. It is a well-known fact that memory decays with time, and it would be very rare and probably suspicious to encounter someone who can clearly remember details or actual conversations which took place several years before. Records which are being used in questioning the accused are open to inspection, and this can be a big help in recalling circumstances. The plaintiff's attorney has the right to inspect and copy any material which is brought to the deposition to aid memory, so it is a good policy to show the defense attorney any such material for inspection and approval before the deposition.

Before the trial the accused will want to reread the deposition to refresh his or her memory and to aid in expressing himself or herself in a consistent manner.

When a case does go before a jury, many things can influence its outcome. The plaintiff (claimant) may be a very appealing person, arousing compassion in the jury. At times, even when negligence has obviously occurred, the plaintiff may have an abrasive personality and the defendant may win the jury over completely, resulting in a defense verdict. A trial is really a contest of impressions, so wise clients follow the advice of their attorneys on informal demeanor as well as on the formal strategy of the case.

Most suits are based upon negligence, assault and battery, invasion of privacy, or defamation of character. At times it is difficult to pinpoint the person actually responsible for the harm to the patient, but it is obvious that harm has resulted that would not have occurred in the absence of negligence. The responsibility is fixed under the legal doctrine of *res ipsa loquitur* (Latin meaning, "the thing speaks for itself"). An example of this would be the case of a patient who is taken to surgery for repair of an inguinal hernia and has his gall bladder removed. The nurse denies sending the wrong chart with the patient, the orderly denies preparing the wrong area for the surgery, both the anesthesiologist and the surgeon deny noticing the victim's lack of resemblance to the patient they saw before surgery—yet someone obviously made a mistake. Under such circumstances, everyone having contact with the patient is charged. Thus it is possible to be charged with negligence when you have actually not been negligent.

STANDARD OF CARE AS CRITERION FOR DETERMINING NEGLIGENCE

A thorough knowledge of the standard of care is the basis for preventing a malpractice suit and, naturally, the basis for providing the best care for patients. The term "reasonably prudent nurse" is often used in defining the standard of care, usually defined as care that is equal to the care provided by nurses with similar training and similar experience under similar circumstances. Negligence is defined as a failure to meet that standard. An expert witness, often a nursing supervisor or educator, may testify to help the jury understand exactly what the expected or required standard is.

Professional nurses must be aware of the provisions of the Nurse Practice Act in their state. They must not only avoid a breach of duty by failing to meet the standard of care, but are also expected to foresee any harm which might be caused to the patient if that standard is not met. There are many situations daily where the standard of care is not met, but fortunately most of these situations do not result in injury or harm.

An example of injury caused by a nurse not foreseeing potential harm is illustrated in the following hypothetical situation:

A nurse who had worked in the Emergency Room of a hospital for eight years was asked by the nursing supervisor to work in Labor and Delivery for a shift. Two of the three nurses ordinarily covering that area were out sick, and the patient load was rapidly increasing. The E.R. nurse agreed and, on entering the obstetrics area, asked the already overworked nurse there how often she should check fetal heart tones. The answer was, "With all that's going on, we'll be lucky to get them ever half hour." Deciding to be on the cautious side, the E.R. nurse set about making the patients comfortable and noting new orders, and managed to check fetal heart tones every twenty mintues. There were now five patients in active labor and a call to the supervisor for more help had not been returned. A few minutes after her fetal heart tone check, one patient, whose labor was being induced by Oxytocin drip, began having tetanic contractions. She complained of severe pain, so the helpful E.R. nurse administered an analgesic prescribed by the admitting physician. However, she did not recheck the fetal heart tones at that time, discontinue the I.V., or report to the regular obstetrics nurse. The fetal monitor which would ordinarily have been used on this patient was a new one and, even with the most careful application of the monitor lead, it did not register fetal heart tones. The manufacturer's representative had been called the day before and had not delivered another monitor and picked up the defective one as promised. The representative had been called three times.

Twenty minutes after the last check, the E.R. nurse checked the fetal heart tones again and found that the fetus was obviously in great distress. The admitting physician was called immediately but did not arrive for forty minutes. When he did arrive the patient delivered rapidly but the infant was pale, flaccid, had low Apgar score, and had to be intubated immediately. The child was maintained on life support systems for four days but had massive irreversible brain damage and died. There is no doubt that an injury occurred in this case. The result is clear but the causation is complex.

1. The E.R. nurse was working outside the area of her expertise and could not be held to as high a standard of care as the nurse regularly assigned to the unit. However, she was a nurse with many years of experience and should have been able to foresee the element of risk to the fetus involved when labor is being induced by Oxytocin. The nurse must consider the potential for trouble and base frequency of the checks on the potential for damage.

2. The experienced obstetrics nurse on duty was working beyond her capacity, but she still should have been able to foresee the possibility of harm to the patients from the understaffing problem. She was aware that the E.R. nurse needed supervision when she asked how often to check fetal heart tones. The element of risk began right there, but the O.B. nurse chose to give a casual answer and ignore the problem.

3. The nursing supervisor for the shift is liable also, for improperly staffing the units. She is responsible for being aware of qualifications and experience and for making appropriate staff changes. Even if the hospital has a chronic understaffing problem, it is still her responsibility to report the problem and to follow through on the solution to it. When a supervisor is reporting a problem, such as understaffing, which has the potential for patient harm, she would be well advised to submit her report in writing. She should maintain her own file of copies of reports and of efforts to follow through and to obtain a satisfactory and safe solution to the problem.

4. The hospital also has a duty to protect the patients from harm by providing adequate staffing and equipment. The hospital shares in the liability of the nurses because it is the employer of both the nurses and the supervisor. This is the doctrine of *respondeat superior*. This doctrine, "let the master answer," involves the hospital in the negligence of the nurse and extends the liability but does not dilute it. The supervisor can still be held personally responsible for her negligence as a supervisor. The individual nurses would also be held liable for not foreseeing the risk and taking action to prevent it. The nurse also has a duty to inform the physician of any condition endangering his patient. The E.R. nurse in this hypothetical example did notify the physician and she carefully documented

in the record the time of the notification, but her duty did not end there. When the doctor did not respond, her duty required her to notify her supervisor, to call any physician, and to report to the hospital administration.

5. The physician certainly has his share of problems in this case. He left the hospital while his patient was being induced by Oxytocin drip. He was aware of the risks and dangers to both mother and child in this situation and should have remained in the hospital. He was also aware of the malfunctioning fetal monitor.

6. This hypothetical case is also an example of product liability. The nurses had read and understood the manufacturer's instructions for the fetal monitor and were using it properly, so the liability rests on the manufacturer.

Now we have four individuals, the hospital, an equipment manufacturer, and all of their respective insurance companies and attorneys involved in a long, complicated legal battle. We also have a dead infant and two distraught parents. The quotation from Florence Nightingale at the beginning of this chapter still applies.

Nurses working in hospitals should be familiar with the hospital policies. These are not law, as they do not come from the government. However, if the written policy of the hospital is violated, it is in essence a violation of the standard of care. The policy is like a built-in expert to testify against the nurse by inference, so nurses should be very familiar with the written policies of their institutions. Some hospital policies are outdated and unsafe; the "reasonably prudent nurse" would call this to the attention of administration and help to formulate current and safe policies. If a nurse follows an unsafe policy and a patient is injured as a result, it would not be a very convincing defense to say that she would have lost her job if she had not followed the hospital rules, even though she realized there was a risk to the patient.

An example of an unsafe policy could involve the contact of patients with nonward personnel. If there is no policy requiring these personnel to check with the nurse before undertaking a procedure involving a patient, the degree of risk assumes great proportions. When an X-ray technician comes to the unit to do a portable check film, the nurses should be aware of it and should exercise some degree of supervision and control. It is their responsibility to safeguard the welfare of the patients. The X-ray technician might not be aware, for example, that a patient is being observed for a neck injury and, in the absence of this knowledge, positions the patient carelessly thus causing paralysis.

Patients also need to be protected from their own actions. Irresponsible and uncooperative patients increase the nurse's legal duty to protect them; once a nurse notices that a patient is uncooperative, additional precautions are called for. Patients are really all special risks; they are ill, they are medicated, and they are weak. They are very often placed in dangerous positions, for example, on X-ray tables and gurneys higher than their beds would be at home. It is mandatory that the rails be up and the straps fastened when the patient is on a gurney, the safety straps on X-ray tables are meant to be used, and bed rails are obviously for the protection of the patient. All patients in the hospital must be assumed to be a danger to themselves, and all possible precautions taken.

INTENTIONAL TORTS

Battery and false imprisonment are examples of intentional torts (a tort is a civil wrong, as opposed to a crime, which is against society). Consent is the general principal behind these two torts.

False imprisonment means the unlawful detention of an individual or the unlawful restraint of someone's personal liberty. This can be accomplished by the threat of force, chemical or physical restraint against the individual's will, or actual physical force. An implied force, by threats or gestures, can induce fear that physical force will be used.

There are exceptions in the liability of nurses, doctors, and hospitals for false imprisonment. Most state health and safety codes have sections covering the hospitalization of patients with some communicable diseases if such patients appear unwilling to be quarantined in their homes. Although there are laws allowing the temporary hospitalization of mental patients, in most states they cannot be held for more than a day or two against their will unless they present a clear danger to themselves or others.[2] If a patient is presenting a danger and needs to be restrained, care must be taken to only use as much force as is reasonable under the circumstances. More than this could make the hospital and employees liable for battery (battery means touching a person without his or her permission).

The example below will help clarify the difference between an intentional tort, such as battery, and negligence.

The evening nurse sedated an elderly patient for the night without helping him to the bathroom first. She also forgot to put up the side rails and did not notice that his bell cord was not plugged in. This placed the patient in a dangerous position and when he fell and was injured, it could easily be shown that the nurse did not use enough care to protect the patient. She did not mean to harm the patient, but she was negligent.

Circumstances such as these are of great help to the plaintiff's attorneys, who are able to prove that the nurse was negligent and, in turn, the hospital was negligent, under the doctrine of *respondeat superior*. The plaintiff thus has an opportunity to expand liability and possibly increase monetary damages. The settlement should be based upon lost earnings, projected loss of future earnings, medical costs both past and projected, and pain and suffering. If a nurse without professional liability insurance is being sued, and has meager financial resources, the plaintiff would not be able to collect much even if a large amount were awarded by the court, but when the hospital is brought into the suit, the possibility of collecting that large award becomes a reality. This is what a malpractice suit is all about. The plaintiff's attorney is trying to prove liability rather than guilt. The gain hoped for is monetary; fine and imprisonment do not apply. If an act such as battery has occurred and is the basis for a criminal complaint, there could be a separate trial.

CONSENTS

Another intentional tort involves the lack of consent. It is vital for nurses to realize that even after consent has been given, it can be withdrawn, verbally or by gesture. Consent is unique to the individual; the spouse has no right to give consent. When a patient has refused or withdrawn consent the nurse must immediately inform the supervisor and physician, and they have a duty to see that the procedure does not take place. A nurse who proceeds could be charged with both assault (an intentional act which makes the victim apprehensive of personal harm) and battery (the touching of an individual without his or her permission).

The doctrine of implied consent could apply when a patient is not lucid, whether from the effects of illness, drugs, or injuries. Consent by implication applies only to urgent care, however, not to elective procedures. An emergency sometimes removes the need for consent if the client is a minor or unconscious or delirious. It must, however, be shown that an effort was made to contact someone legally authorized to give consent (the contact could be by telephone). The situation must also be an emergency, in which not taking action would cause greater damage to the patient, as when immediate lifesaving action is needed. It is helpful to have consultants document the emergency nature of the situation.

A patient's consent to a procedure frees the individual carrying out the procedure from liability only for intruding on the patient's rights. The consent does not absolve anyone of negligence during the performance of the procedure.

A minor, someone seventeen years of age or less, has legal guardians who have full powers of consent. In cases involving minors, family members or guardians should be fully advised so they will be able to give their valid informed consent. The health-care provider should document the procedure fully, relating the risks, explaining possible complications, answering all questions, and noting that they were answered. The court will protect the rights of the child, if it believes that the decision of the parents to withhold consent threatens the child's life, by making the child a ward of the court. Most emergency rooms post the telephone numbers of several judges who can issue such orders.

"Emancipated minors" are those who have at any time been married, whether married at the present time or not, or those fifteen years of age or older who live away from home and manage their own financial affairs. They do not necessarily have to earn their own money—it can be obtained from their parents;

but they must manage their own finances. It is helpful for the nurse to document this; a sample nursing note might say: "The patient appears to be of stated age and seems to control all financial affairs." It is important also to note whether the minor appears to be mature enough to consent to his or her own treatment. This entry could read: "In my clinical judgment, this minor appears to be mature enough to understand the risks and implications of consent and treatment."

In many states, minors over twelve may give consent for treatment of contagious diseases. Drug problems, pregnancy and abortion, and the effects of rape can usually be treated with the consent only of the minor. A true informed consent should be obtained by the person who will carry out the procedure.

Ideally, surgeons should explain the risks and hazards of scheduled procedures in their offices before admitting patients to the hospital. Then the patient cannot later claim that the consent was signed under the influence of drugs. It is not acceptable for a nurse to approach a gurney heading for surgery and ask the patient, who has now been medicated and probably cannot read the form, to sign the consent form. Not only is the patient under the influence of a drug, but full disclosure might not have been made by the surgeon, who is actually the one legally responsible for obtaining the consent. This can be the basis for a malpractice suit. Informing the patient of the risks and hazards must be done carefully. If the hazards are minimized, the patient might be understandably upset about a complication. On the other hand, if every remote hazard is recited, the patient could be frightened to the point of refusing a procedure necessary for continued health. Nurses have been obtaining verbal consent, using disclosure, for a very long time, possibly without realizing it. A hypothetical situation such as the following happens with a patient who is about to be catheterized. The conversation might go something like this:

Nurse: "Good morning, Mrs. Grey."

Patient: "Good morning. What do you have there?"

Nurse: "This is a catheter tray. Your doctor has requested that we get a specimen of urine directly from your bladder, and the catheter is a tiny tube that we insert into the opening of your urethra."

Patient: "Is that going to hurt?"

Nurse: "It may sting a bit for just a moment. Now here's what you can do to help me prepare."

During this entire exchange the patient is being informed and questions are being answered; by accepting the answers and cooperating, the patient is giving her consent.

If the response is "Oh, no you don't. Get out of here with that tray . . ." consent has been expressly denied, and a nurse who insists could be liable for battery if the procedure is carried out and harm to the patient results. The nurse should not only document the refusal in the nursing notes and be sure that the doctor is informed, but also document the fact that the physician has been informed.

In summary, a lucid adult patient has the legally accepted right to consent to or refuse care.

GOOD SAMARITAN STATUTES

Good Samaritan statutes have now been enacted in all of the states, the first being passed in California in 1959. Their purpose is to encourage persons with knowledge and skill to render care at the scene of an emergency without fear of being sued. Formerly, many skilled professionals were afraid to stop and help for fear of being held liable for acts which they did or did not do. The wording of the statutes varies widely from state to state. Generally, the scene of an emergency is defined as outside the place and course of the individual's employment, and in most states such samaritans may not charge for their services. The nurse or physician is not required to stop at the scene of emergency and volunteer aid. There are no legal consequences for passing the scene. Nevertheless, most professional nurses would not hesitate to stop, because their skills may be superior to those of anyone else at the scene. The California statute, which established the pattern for many of the state laws, covers physicians and nurses licensed in that state, but not those licensed only in another state. It reads as follows:

> A person licensed under this chapter who in good faith renders emergency care at the scene of an emergency which occurs outside both the place and the course of her employment shall not be liable for any civil damages as the result of acts or omissions by such person rendering the emergency care. This section shall not grant immunity from civil damages when the person is grossly negligent.[3]

Licensed persons rendering aid in an emergency can be held to a higher standard of care than lay persons, but this is reasonable given their training. No matter what their specialized field of nursing might be, nurses who give emergency aid would be wise to become competent in cardiopulmonary resuscitation, the Heimlich manueuver, and first aid. Nurses who feel that their skills in these areas are not adequate can call the local branch of the American Red Cross or the Heart Association and learn the procedures. In some areas fire company paramedics also offer courses.

The samaritan who undertakes the care of a patient in an emergency situation must continue that care until the patient can be turned over to someone whose qualifications in the circumstances are equal to or above those of the samaritan, such as a physician or a paramedic. Samaritans cannot abandon patients. Their first responsibility is to the patient, and they must be careful about accepting lay help if in their professional judgment it would injure or endanger the patient. They can command someone else to go for help and supervise capable lay help, but should always make the safety and welfare of the patient their prime concern.[4]

REPORTING STATUTES

When there is a written statute applying to any area of nursing practice, the individual cannot do less than the statute requires, regardless of nursing practice in the rest of the community. Nurses in the public health field and emergency room nurses have more frequent contact with these situations than their counterparts in other areas of nursing. These statutes vary from state to state; full information is available from the state boards of nursing, medicine, and health. For immediate information, staffs of the local health department or an emergency room can be consulted.

A common reporting staute is the requirement that an injury from a dangerous weapon or a criminal act be reported immediately to the police. The patient may deny the cause of an injury, but if it is reasonably ascertainable that the cause was a dangerous weapon or a criminal act, it must be reported immediately. The purpose of this is to enable the police to investigate, and hopefully to prevent further injuries from the weapon or from the individual or individuals perpetrating the criminal act. Some states require that injuries noted when a patient is admitted to a hospital from a long-term care be reported. The person making the report is immune from liability for civil or criminal action for enforcing this law, and failure to comply with these requirements is punishable.[5] The purpose of such statutes is to enable the proper authorities to investigate and to prevent further occurrences.

Certain infectious diseases and animal bites are reportable in all states. Physicians are often required to report patients suffering from lapses of consciousness, so that the department of motor vehicles can determine the person's eligibility to operate a motor vehicle on the highways. Any case involving pesticide poisoning must also be reported to the local health office. Work-related occupational injury or illness are ordinarily reported to the state department of industrial relations. Most states require reporting of ophthalmia neonatorum and phenylketonuria in newborns. These are examples of the states' power to regulate preventive medicine and unfortunately arose out of the fact that some individuals neglected to assume that responsibility. Information about unlawful drug use, rape, attempted suicide, or criminal acts that the nurse learns while caring for the patient should be discussed with the attending physician or nurse practitioner immediately. There might be a legal duty to report these acts which would override what would ordinarily be considered privileged communication.

Statutes requiring the reporting of suspected child abuse have been enacted in all of the states. Impetus for these laws came from a 1963 Children's Bureau Report as well as the 1973 federal Child Abuse and Treatment Act. This law requires states to establish a reporting mechanism in order to be eligible for federal assistance in setting up child-abuse prevention programs.[6] The penalty for not reporting varies widely, ranging from no penalty to a fine or even a jail sentence. In most states nurses are required to report suspected abuse to the hospital administrator, the appropriate law enforcement agency, or the state welfare bureau. All of the statutes protect practitioners from liability in suits alleging defamation of the parents' character or invasion of privacy. This assumes that the report is made with a good-faith belief that the apparent facts in the situation are true.

In such reports, the name, age, and sex of the child should be included, and any available identification of the person or persons responsible for the care of the child and likely to be the perpetrator of the abuse. This might be parents, guardians, step-parents, relatives, or babysitters. A complete description of the child's injuries should be included. Any practitioner suspecting child abuse should check with other emergency rooms in the area to see if the child has been treated for previous injuries; this data should be included in the report. A school nurse will often question siblings. The nurse should also record the child's emotional state and should try to be alone with the child, as abused children may be afraid to show any emotion in the presence of the adults bringing them for care. It may be difficult to establish rapport with these children, because they are often withdrawn and fearful. A nurse who is called upon to testify about the child's condition should be nonjudgmental. It is wise to preface statements with "In my professional opinion. . . ." The reason for detailed, descriptive charting will be obvious. Quotations of what the child relates about the circumstances surrounding the injury can be included. Any X-rays needed as evidence should be carefully filed, as they may show old multiple fractures. Clinical observations are very important for the nurse who is called to testify at a hearing when the child is made a ward of the court while the parents receive the appropriate counseling to enable them to function as a family once more.

SCOPE OF FUNCTION

Licensing statutes are an important consideration in the practice of nursing today. Physicians who require or allow nurses in their employ to practice outside the boundaries of the nurse practice act or within the legal restrictions of the physician licensing act would be considered as aiding and abetting the unlicensed practice of medicine, and both the physician and the nurse would be running afoul of their own licensing statutes. Similarly, registered nurses and licensed practical nurses must be careful not to instruct or allow nursing assistants to perform the unlicensed practice of nursing. If a patient were injured during this sort of unauthorized nursing practice, an outraged jury might find everyone involved liable, including the hospital for not providing adequate staffing and for not exercising a reasonable degree of supervision and control.

In summary, these statutes require an absolute standard of care, and the individual who fails to observe them will be considered negligent. Many of these regulations are designed to prevent further damage. A hospital in-service program to keep health professionals aware of current laws affecting their practice would afford a great protection for the patients, the community, the nurses, and other health professionals.

CONFIDENTIALITY VERSUS A DUTY TO WARN

There are situations which require the nurse to warn someone which also take precedent over the right of confidentiality. If a patient's present condition constitutes a danger to others, the nurse has a duty to warn the police. However, it is possible to be sued for such action, because there has been an invasion of privacy. The best defense for such an action is the fact that there is a duty to warn which supercedes the right to confidentiality, a judicial standard of care involving the duty to protect the public. This standard would apply in the following hypothetical situation:

A patient came into a doctor's office with severe back pain; the doctor diagnosed the condition as a lumbar sprain and prescribed heat, rest, and muscle relaxants. The doctor asked the nurse to give the patient an injection of Demerol and to call someone to take the patient home. The nurse administered the injection, made the telephone call to the patient's wife, and explained to the patient the dangers of driving after being medicated (and noted it on the record). About five minutes later the nurse noticed that the patient was gone, and just then the patient's wife arrived. She told the nurse that her husband's car was not in the parking lot, although he had driven to the office. She supplied the license number and description of the car, and the nurse immediately called the police to alert them that the man was heavily medicated and presumed to be driving the car. Meanwhile, the patient began to experience such relief from his pain that he stopped and had several drinks. After leaving the bar, he had an automobile accident, and a passenger in the other car was seriously injured. Had the nurse not advised the patient not to drive after being given a drug that could cause sleepiness and not realized the duty to warn and called the police, the nurse would have been the target in the lawsuit. The patient would have been liable for contributory negligence because he stopped to drink and then drove again. But this nurse was aware of the duty involved in the situation and carried it out. A word of caution: when this situation is examined retrospectively, it is apparent that leaving the patient unattended for that brief period of time enabled him to slip out. If it was impossible to have someone observe him, his car keys could have been held, to be turned over to his wife when she arrived, and the unfortunate result could have been prevented.

A therapist told in confidence that the patient intends to harm someone else also has a duty to warn. A recent case concluded that the therapist is *required* to "disclose the contents of a confidential communication where the risk to be prevented thereby is the danger of a violent assault, and not where the risk of harm is self-inflicted harm or mere property damage."[7]

Some mentally ill patients, such as some with chronic brain syndrome, present a danger to themselves, others, or property but may refuse to consent to be hospitalized. In most states these patients may, with the proper authorization, be held for one to three days for psychiatric and medical treatment. The nurse who uses such emergency procedures must find out which agencies in the state are authorized to detain a patient, whether public or private hospital, clinic, psychiatrist, psychologist, or police officer. If a patient has to be held until a psychiatrist can arrive, the nurse may avoid a position of liability by calling the police. The nurse should also follow up to be sure the psychiatrist does see the patient; otherwise a charge of arbitrary imprisonment may be raised.

Some such patients are a danger to themselves and need to be detained for more than a brief period. This situation requires some type of conservatorship proceeding, enabling the patient to be admitted to the hospital. Additional powers must be granted to the conservator to hold and treat a patient who has not given consent. The hospital personnel must see the conservator's papers to be sure that the additional powers have been granted.

Doctors, nurses, and health facilities can also be sued for not holding a patient. If a patient is allowed to wander out of the hospital and becomes injured or injures someone, hospital personnel will have to justify their reasons for not using a seventy-two hour hold or getting a conservatorship. The statutes dealing with circumstances like those above are written to protect patients and those near them while trying to preserve patients' rights as much as possible.

INVASION OF PRIVACY

Defamation and invasion of privacy occur when information is given to a third person about someone and the dissemination of that information causes damage to a person's reputation. This charge cannot be made if it can be shown that the information given out is true and was given in good faith to a person who had a valid reason to receive it. Any member of the health-care team caring for a patient has a valid reason to receive or give to another member any information that would influence their care of the patient.

Invasion of privacy can also be charged if a patient has specifically requested that information be withheld from a specific member of the patient's family and that request is not followed. All members of the health-care team should be informed of the patient's request.

Some of the reporting statutes appear to cause an invasion of patients' privacy, which may be difficult for them to accept. The practitioners should carefully explain to patients that they would like to be able to protect patients' privacy, but the law requires a report of the situation; the patient should also be given the reasons for the law. In most instances, the state has the authority to limit the basic right to privacy when health and public welfare are endangered.

The American Hospital Association issued "A Patient's Bill of Rights" in 1973. This was not a legal document, but parts of it have been incorporated into the policies of many hospitals; it defines a standard of care and invokes a duty not to breach that standard of care.

A Patient's Bill of Rights

1. The patient has the right to considerate and respectful care.
2. The patient has the right to obtain from his physician complete current information concerning his diagnosis, treatment, and prognosis in terms the patient can be reasonably expected to understand. When it is not medically advisable to give such information to the patient, the information should be made available to an appropriate person in his behalf. He has the right to know by name the physician responsible for coordinating his care.
3. The patient has a right to receive from his physician information necessary to give informed consent prior to the start of any procedure and/or treatment. Except in emergencies, such information for informed consent should include but not necessarily be limited to the specific procedure and/or treatment, the medically significant risks involved, and the probable duration of incapacitation. Where medically significant alternatives for care or treatment exist, or when the patient requests information concerning medical alternatives, the patient has the right to known the name of the person responsible for the procedures and/or treatment.
4. The patient has the right to refuse treatment to the extent permitted by law, and to be informed of the medical consequence of his action.
5. The patient has the right to every consideration of his privacy concerning his own medical care program. Case discussions, consultation, examinations, and treatment are confidential and should be conducted discreetly. Those not directly involved in his care must have the permission of the patient to be present.
6. The patient has the right to expect that all communications and records pertaining to his care should be treated as confidential.
7. The patient has the right to expect that within its capacity a hospital must make reasonable response to the request of a patient for services.
8. The patient has the right to be advised if the hospital proposes to engage in or perform human experimentation affecting his care or treatment. The patient has a right to refuse to participate in such research projects.

No catalog of rights can guarantee for the patient the kind of treatment he has a right to expect. A hospital has many functions to perform, including the prevention and treatment of disease, the education of both health professionals and patients, and the conduct of clinical research. All these activities must be conducted with an overriding concern for the patient, and above all, the recognition of his dignity as a human being. Success in achieving this recognition assures success in the defense of the rights of the patient.[8]

PATIENT RECORDS

Medical records are all-important from the medical legal standpoint. They must never appear contrived or self-serving, or they will arouse suspicion and might be used as evidence against providers. The only reason for keeping the record is for the patient's benefit. It is best to write down only perceptions, not what the observer supposes to have happened. An obvious example of a wrong notation would be, "Mr. Jones fell out of bed," unless the writer actually saw him fall. The correct way would be, "Mr. Jones was found on the floor at the side of his bed." Direct quotations of remarks made by the patient can be included. Charting should be objective and not say anything derogatory about the patient that might appear later to be malicious. If an erroneous entry is made, a line should be drawn through it, but it should remain legible; note the date and time of the change and initial it, so that it will not appear to be a fraudulent alteration of the record. An illegible record can endanger a patient and shows disregard for the patient's welfare. The records should be reviewed frequently while the patient is in the hospital to see that all orders are carried out and changes in the patient's condition noted. Nurses should also check to see whether notes on successive shifts document changes in the patient's condition which were charted but not reported or acted upon. If a chart is not internally consistent, the discrepancies in it could support a lawsuit if noted by an attorney or medical expert reviewing a case.

Under some circumstances, a nurse has no legal duty to carry out a physician's orders. The nurse's first responsibility is to the patient. An illegible or ambiguous order endangers the patient and must be clarified before it can be carried out. The nurse has a duty to know what constitutes a reasonable order and to ask the doctor for an explanation if a dosage seems inappropriate. If the nurse carries out an order that was written in error and the patient is injured, the nurse is liable as well as the doctor. In an emergency, however, a nurse who superimposes a personal judgment on that of a doctor, by questioning an order, could be considered negligent if that conduct slows down the treatment and causes harm. A very delicate area is the administration of a controlled substance to a known drug user ("known" can mean presumed by past history). Under certain circumstances the physician writing the order and the nurse administering the drug can both be charged with violating their licensing statutes.[9]

Nurses in most states are not allowed to prescribe drugs unless there is a specific statute covering such a practice. In some states they are also not allowed to label a package of medication or to count out pills to put into a separate container for the patient to take home; only a pharmacist, physician, or dentist can legally do this.

A verbal order carries more inherent risk than a written order, but is still a legal order. If a patient is harmed by medication given following a verbal order, the evidence of a nurse who wrote the order down immediately has more than that of one who neglected the order or delayed writing it down.

Standing orders are legally valid if they are specific and not too broad. An unacceptable standing order would be "sleeping medication P.R.N." This places the nurse in a position of practicing medicine without a license, because the specific medication and the specific dose are not mentioned in the order. Lawsuits can be won or lost on "appearances," and overly broad standing orders could be interpreted as an example of mass-production medicine.

A secondhand order probably should not be accepted. The nurse's best protection is to get the order directly from the physician. It is very important to have only licensed staff members transcribing orders. There are many examples of malpractice suits originating from the harm done by a medication order which was incorrectly transcribed by a ward clerk or nursing assistant. This is considered negligent practice because these individuals do not have the education and experience in pharmacology necessary to avoid errors; it is unfair to them and to the patient to increase the risk of error in this manner.

Another important medication-related responsibility of today's nurse is awareness of drug interactions and cumulative drug effects. A patient, whether in an office or hospital setting, may be receiving medication prescribed by more than one physician. The nurse, who is probably observing the patient for a longer period of time than the physician, is in a better position to observe the synergistic or cumulative effects of medications. There could also be metabolic reasons for a patient's response to and absorption rate of a specific drug. Pharmacists are excellent resource people and should be consulted.

When it is necessary to write an "incident report," nurses should be aware that the only way to keep the report privileged and confidential is to make no copies and file the original in the office of the hospital's legal counsel. Any copy kept on file in the office of the administrator or the director of nurses will not be considered privileged and can be subpoenaed.[10] The right to privilege does not extend to information maintained in files outside the attorney's office. Insurance company records, physician's office records, and hospital records are not privileged. They may all be used as evidence.

When writing nursing notes, it can be very helpful legally to document instances of patient noncompliance. If this is done objectively, it could dilute the liability in a malpractice case by helping to show that the patient contributed to the problem or perhaps even caused it. When a patient is about to leave the hospital against medical advice it is important to do more than require a hasty signature on the A.M.A. (Against Medical Advice) form. Every effort should be made to have such patients read the form or listen while it is read to them. If they appear to understand, it is possible to chart in the record "A.M.A. form has been read to patient, who appears to understand and accept the risks and dangers of leaving the hospital against medical advice." If the patient will not stop long enough to listen, the record should read: "An attempt was made to inform the patient of the risks and dangers of leaving the hospital against medical advice, but patient signed the form and refused to read it or listen to the explanation."

In the following hypothetical case, the nurses appeared to have done a meticulous job of charting but were actually found grossly liable.

The patient, a young man, twisted his knee in a softball game. It was swollen and painful, so he went to a doctor, who diagnosed ligament tears and hospitalized him for surgery. The patient's leg was casted after surgery and the nursing notes reflected frequent checks of the circulatory status of that leg. They noted first the presence and then the absence of the pedal pulse; they noted the prolonged capillary filling time; they noted the change in temperature from warm to cool; they dutifully recorded the patient's rising temperature, the breakdown of tissue between his toes, the drainage and the foul odor emanating from the leg. They recorded administration of analgesics for the pain and antipyretics for the fever and conscientiously wrote observations about the patient's mood and appetite. The glaring omission was that no entry documented that the nursing supervisor and physician had been notified of the deteriorating circulatory status of the patient's leg. Since all of these events took place over a period of eight days, the patient required a midthigh amputation of his gangrenous leg and was lucky to survive.

The physicians were found liable, of course, and so was the hospital, through the doctrine of *respondeat superior*. The nurses had a much greater duty than to merely observe and record. They had a duty to safeguard their patient and to report and persist until action was taken. The harm was foreseeable, and the nurses were obviously negligent in their care of the patient.

The quotation from Florence Nightingale at the beginning of this chapter, "It may seem a strange principle to enunciate as the very first requirement in a Hospital that it should do the sick no harm," has been expanded and enlarged upon in the American Nurses' Association "Code for Nurses," as revised in 1976:

1. The nurse provides services with respect for human dignity and the uniqueness of the client unrestricted by considerations of social or economic status, personal attributes, or the nature of health problems.
2. The nurse safeguards the client's right to privacy by judiciously protecting information of a confidential nature.
3. The nurse acts to safeguard the client and the public when health care and safety are affected by the incompetent, unethical, or illegal practice of any person.
4. The nurse assumes responsibility and accountability for individual nursing judgments and actions.

5. The nurse maintains competence in nursing.
6. The nurse exercises informed judgment and uses individual competence and qualifications as criteria in seeking consultation, accepting responsibilities, and delegating nursing activities to others.
7. The nurse participates in activities that contribute to the ongoing development of the profession's body of knowledge.[11]

As professional nurses, we welcome our extended roles. We must, however, accept the responsibility and accountability accompanying our roles and "do the sick no harm."

REFERENCES

1. C. Woodham-Smith, FLORENCE NIGHTINGALE, 1820–1910 226 (1951). The quotation is from Nightingale, NOTES ON HOSPITALS (1859).
2. B. Ennis and L. Siegel, THE RIGHTS OF MENTAL PATIENTS: THE BASIC ACLU GUIDE TO A MENTAL PATIENT'S RIGHTS (1973).
3. Deering's BUSINESS AND PROFESSIONS CODE—ANNOTATED—OF THE STATE OF CALIFORNIA 106, § 2727.5 (1975).
4. R. Ratcliffe, THE GOOD SAMARITAN AND THE LAW (1966).
5. CALIFORNIA PENAL CODE, § 11161.8.
6. CHILD ABUSE AND TREATMENT ACT, Public Law 93–247; 88 Stat. 4 (1973); M. D. Hemelt and M. E. Mackert, DYNAMICS OF LAW IN NURSING AND HEALTH CARE 72–81 (1978).
7. Tarasoff v. Regents of California, 81 Cal. App. 3d 614 (1978); Tarasoff v. Regents of University of California 17 Cal. 3d 425, 441, fn. 13; 131 Cal. Rptr. 14, 555 P. 2d. 334 (1976).
8. American Hospital Association, A PATIENT'S BILL OF RIGHTS (1973).
9. Deering's BUSINESS AND PROFESSIONS CODE, Div. 2, §§ 2390 and 2399.5, and HEALTH AND SAFETY CODE, §§ 11154, 11170, and 11210.
10. Sierra Vista Hospital v. California Superior Court, 56 Cal. Rptr. 387 (1967).
11. American Nurses' Association, CODE FOR NURSES (1976).

SECTION TWO

Changing the Law and the Law as an Instrument of Change

7 The Political Process or The Power and the Glory

DONNA F. VER STEEG

There is supposedly an old Chinese saying that goes, "I curse you. May you live in a time of great change." Nursing is, in this sense, twice honored. Both as a profession among professions, and as a grouping consisting predominantly of women, we are living through a period of great change. These two identities have significant implications for the manner in which we participate in the political process that marks the changes. The implications of being female, of being a professional, and of having our practice controlled by laws are elaborated elsewhere in this volume. In this chapter we shall consider the power and the glory of the political process as it applies to all citizens and professions; but we will illustrate it with examples from ongoing research in health manpower legislation. Insofar as this can be construed as a "how-to" chapter, we shall include some comments on the particular problems of women and of nurses in politics, also drawn from ongoing research.

Although professions exist because of a mandate from society to perform certain functions, and many professions operate under legislative sanctions, there is a tendency among the rank and file members to forget this fact. There was a time when it was not considered "professional" to be involved in the political process. Professionals were somehow removed from the everyday world in which such decisions are made. This is an innocence which can no longer be excused. All kinds of decisions about areas of practice, distribution of resources, eligibility for care, etc., that were once the province of the professional alone, have been taken over by society, through its legislators. These legislators must be informed, and it is the responsibility of the professions to provide them with timely and accurate information.

We sometimes have the feeling that laws are unchangeable. They are not. The purpose of a system of laws is to express the collective interests and beliefs of society. These interests and beliefs change; eventually, the laws must change.

Portions of this chapter first appeared in Ver Steeg, *The Physician's Assistant: Interorganizational Influence on the Creation of a New Occupation* (Dissertation filed with University Microfilms, Ann Arbor, Michigan 78106, © 1973, Donna Lorraine Frank Ver Steeg).

When the laws on the books are too far out of step with the wishes of society, they frequently are not enforced. This is a dangerous situation because it breeds disrespect for the law. A credibility gap develops. A law ignored for "good reasons" is frequently followed by a law ignored for reasons of convenience; finally, good laws are ignored because one has grown used to the ignoring. We have such a situation in the health-care delivery system in the United States, and it is not good. A serious credibility gap continues to exist between our medical and nursing practice acts and medical and nursing practice in several states. In those states where nurses have succeeded in effecting changes in the practice acts to bring them into line with current practice, it is because they marshalled their forces and amassed enough power to influence legislators to change the law.

Because no law can ever answer all claims equally well, those groups which amass the most power tend to be most favored. In a pluralistic society this is only to be expected. It is therefore vital that concerned professionals learn how power is acquired and how it can be used. The exercise of political power has become a professional responsibility. Nurses need to address this responsibility. To do this they not only must understand the nature of power, they must learn to be comfortable with its existence and to feel good about their exercise of it.

AN ANALYSIS OF POWER

Power has been defined and analyzed in a number of ways, depending not only upon the academic discipline of the writer but also upon the problems to be analyzed. This chapter draws most heavily upon the work of Nuttall, Scheuch, and Gordon and of Eckstein.[1,2] The terms *power* and *influence* are sometimes used interchangeably and sometimes distinguished from each other; in this chapter they are used interchangeably.

Power can be real or only perceived as real. If we analyze power using these two dimensions, we can postulate four main categories. If an organized group has real power and is also perceived as having power, its power is *manifest*. If the organization has no power and is perceived as having no power, its power is *absent*. Between these two extremes are the two mixed categories, which must be of greatest concern to us. One is *reputational* power, which exists where an organization is perceived as having power when it actually does not. This is a very important category, particularly because we find that organizations with reputational power try to avoid change. They try to prevent decisions from being made that will reveal that they have less power than people perceive them to have. Closely related is the situation that exists when a manifestly powerful organization has only a limited amount of power to "spend." The organization is aware that when this power is gone it cannot easily be replaced. Such an organization will be reluctant to see decisions made that will use up the manifest power it has, reducing it to powerlessness for other, more pressing, decisions. Such organizations typically try to exert their influence by threatening to use power, hoping that their reputation for strength will prevent anyone from challenging them.

The final category includes those organizations that have real power but are not perceived as having power. Such organizations may themselves be unaware of how much power they have. Such organizations are said to have *potential* power. Obviously, it is to the advantage of adversary organizations to encourage society's ignorance of this power. History is full of stories of organizations and persons who were misled by an apparent lack of power or failed to appreciate the dangers of "arousing the sleeping giant." Sociologists are fond of studying the havoc that can arise in work situations when workers far down the hierarchy discover how much potential power they really have. Unfortunately, such discoveries usually lead to "illegal working arrangements," which operate to the detriment of the clients of such groups. Ideally, such discoveries should lead to a realignment of decision-making processes, which can be exercised openly and in a legal and accountable fashion. The client then has the opportunity to demand good services and has some recourse if quality is not received.

How does a group go about assessing its own or another organization's power? For political purposes, the most important assets are size, information base, professional expertise, physical resources (such as time and money), and the personal attributes of the members. In the discussion that follows, it is important to remember that an organization or group may be very deficient in one or more of these areas and still be very powerful because of its strength in other areas.

Size

The organization that has more members has more potential votes. If such an organization can demonstrate that its voters are interested and will show up on election day, the power of that organization is enhanced. In 1969 an attempt was made to change the California Nurse Practice Act without the informed participation of the mass of California nurses. For a variety of reasons, the bill was not acceptable, and a massive letter-writing campaign resulted against the bill. There are a lot of nurses in California. There is not a single legislator who can afford to ignore a visible nurse constituency that is agreed on how he or she should vote and is prepared to back up its beliefs at election time. The bill was defeated. When the California practice act was revised in 1974, the nurses who wanted it changed made sure the rank-and-file nurses were either supportive or neutral. The same is true in other states. The constituency must be united and visible for size to have an impact.

Information Base

An informed membership that understands the importance of verified information is a tremendous asset to an organization. Conversely, a membership that reacts to rumors with gut-level responses can sabotage itself without any help from an outside force. An organization that obtains and distributes information accurately and rapidly, so that its members can respond effectively, can be very powerful. This is a two-way responsibility. It is equally important for the membership to assist in obtaining accurate information and forwarding it to a central place. Not every opponent fights clean. In the political arena the use of innuendoes, half-truths, and, occasionally, total misrepresentation of the facts is not uncommon. These tactics can be harmful. It is important that members have access to the true situation. It is especially important that members recognize their own responsibility for verifying what they hear. It is important to remember that the prestige of the source does not automatically guarantee its veracity.

Another kind of information is political know-how and political know-who. There are rules for playing the political game. Understanding those rules is essential if an organized group wishes to have an impact on the political process. One of the more important ways of having access to this game is through the employment of lobbyists. Organizations that cannot employ lobbyists must depend upon volunteer efforts on the part of their membership to keep them informed of the day-to-day—sometimes minute-to-minute—changes that can go on in the legislative process. Ideally, an organization has both volunteers and lobbyists working in close harmony to get the message of the organization to the people who need to have it and to keep track of the activities of the other organizations whose interests may be different. A bill may undergo radical changes as it proceeds through hearings and discussions on the floors of the legislative bodies. There is no substitute for informed vigilance. A good lobbyist knows the system, knows the legislators and their staffs, and is known by them as a reliable source of information about the wishes of his or her employing constituency.

It is not required that all members of an organization agree with the organization's party line. It is important that dissident members who wish to be heard in the legislative halls make their dissatisfaction known to their organization and to whomever is monitoring legislation. It is possible for an organization to operate effectively in a situation of informed disagreement. However, dissent that the organization is unaware of in advance can be publicly embarrassing—it can confuse the legislators. Members must be aware that such activities weaken the organization for the day when those same members will be in agreement and want the organization to be strong.

Professional Expertise

In one sense professional expertise is another form of information base. It is, however, a special kind not equally available to all groups. We have tended, in nursing, to be so preoccupied with our search for academic respectability and an exclusive knowledge base that we forget how much special expertise we do have. In our search for the forest we have lost sight of the trees. A theory of nursing has two important functions in the political process. One is to help shape a meaningful redefinition of nursing for a new practice act; the other is to provide that sense of self-awareness or self-respect that individual nurses need to have when they offer their services to assist in the development of legislation in their particular area of expertise. General agreement on what nursing is all about and well-executed and well-documented research in the areas of practice in which nurses are involved are necessary. We possess a high level of expertise with an extensive knowledge base to support it. We need to have the self-confidence to share such knowledge and cite it when appropriate.

Nurses in the United States have a long history of working in organized health-care settings, and they have carried considerable responsibility for making those organizations function. As such organizations come under increasing government control, knowledgeable nurses need to be involved in helping design these controls. History has shown us that without the professional input of nurses and other members of the health-care team, the quality of care is ignored and cost of care becomes preeminent.

Physical Resources

Time, money, an organized means of communication (such as a journal or newsletter), personal influence, prestige, and visibility are all physical resources of an organization. Money may come from assessments, dues, and contributions from individuals or support from other groups with similar interests. On occasion, money is available in the form of grants to underwrite needed research or to support consultants. As nurses' incomes have improved they have become better able to contribute to their organizations. Political action costs money. Newsletters cost money, travel costs money, telephones and offices cost money, and staff salaries cost money.

As nurses become better known as qualified experts, and as they become known to legislators and the other members of government, they increase their chances of becoming members of influential groups. State legislatures are turning more and more to advisory groups to assist in developing solutions to difficult problems. Nurse members of such groups have an important opportunity to promote nursing goals for better health care. Increased participation by nurses in the decision-making bodies of their local governments, academic institutions, and the health-care institutions where they work develops another avenue to increased visibility and increased opportunity to affect the political process.

Prestige enhances the credibility of the group. Prestige can come from a legitimacy and special privilege that spring from recognized knowledge and technical competence. Prestige makes news coverage more likely. Where a prestigious group is in opposition to a less prestigious group, the less prestigious group may have to use extraordinary measures to be heard. There are times when informational access to the media is so unequally available that a news blackout may be essential to a fair settlement of the issues. Such was the case in the 1974 nurses' strike in San Francisco. Nurses insisted that their primary concerns were adequate staffing and the qualifications of personnel in specialized units. Further, they pledged full coverage for emergency units and critically ill patients during the strike. The news media concentrated on economic issues and on the statements of various individuals who claimed (erroneously) that emergency care was not being provided. Only after a federal mediator arrived on the scene and imposed a news blackout did the negotiation sessions proceed to a settlement satisfactory to the nursing profession.

There are other aspects of prestige that may work to the disadvantage of nurses. There is a tendency among groups with little power to depend on a collective equality that precludes the development of "stars." In such a group, those who excel may be seen as a threat to other members who lack the same qualifications. Nursing has for a variety of reasons been one of those groups. Efforts to upgrade the professional status of nursing as a whole have, in the past, led to unfortunately worded statements that have served to divide (and to risk being conquered by interests outside nursing). There is a broad spectrum of talents within the nursing profession to meet the broad spectrum of needs that nursing must fulfill if it is to be a responsible part of the health-care team. Prestigious members should be cultivated, not castigated. Less prestigious members need also to be honored for their own particular contributions to the profession.

Availability of and flexibility in the use of time are critical power assets. So long as nurses are employed in settings that do not allow for flexible working arrangements, they will be handicapped in the political process. Public hearings are not held at the convenience of hospitals and other agencies. We still have nursing supervisors who view using days off to attend political meetings as basically sinful, and probably subversive. Nurses need to be secure in their right to the free use of their own time.

Time has another dimension. In a society in which the decision-making powers are dispersed, time is required to reach decisions. The politically naive have a tendency to expect miracles. No group is powerful enough to impose its wishes without some sort of agreement with other groups. This requires time and a great deal of patience. If a favored program fails to get through one way, there is always another approach, another session, a new legislature, a new governor, or a new president. Stories about the passage of each of the new practice acts point up the importance of patience. At one time in the many behind-the-scenes discussions that led up to the passage of the California act, a group decision was made to be kind, courteous, patient—and fierce. Patience is sometimes mistaken for passivity. Patience can mean an implacable determination; this is the sense in which it is a political asset.

A power asset not always fully appreciated is geographic propinquity. Are you in the right place at the right time? There is a certain value to be gained from attending the right meetings and being seen attending them. Part of this comes from demonstrating that you care enough to show up. Showing up consistently earns you a reputation for faithfulness and concern. Also, you become familiar with the other people who attend meetings—able to recognize them on sight, familiar with who talks to whom, etc. Eventually, opportunities arise for you to introduce yourself to these people. One acquaintanceship leads to another, so that eventually you find yourself in a position to meet and talk with individuals who might not otherwise pay attention to you. There is a lot of vouching-for in the political arena: a screening process that should not be abused but of which you certainly should take advantage.

Personal Attributes

Members who speak for their groups are more apt to be effective if they display intelligence, style, and attractiveness. This does not mean physical beauty, although being handsome does not hurt. A certain physical and psychological presence that demonstrates that the individual knows who she or he is and is comfortable with that fact is necessary. Such individuals handle themeselves well in a variety of settings, and do not consistently require the assistance of other participants to "rescue" them. Unfortunately, this presence requires a knowledge base of skills that many women do not possess. For example, the public world of airplanes, hotel desks, and restaurants was not designed for women traveling alone or even in pairs. It was designed for men. This situation is changing rapidly for the better, but I expect that the remnants will be around for many years. Many women simply do not know how to buy plane tickets, how to register at a hotel, how to rent a car, or how gracefully to avoid having their meals paid for by others. The psychic costs to a woman traveling to a political meeting are high. She arrives with a psychic deficit. Married women particularly are at a disadvantage. It is difficult for anyone to maintain poise and attention to the purpose of a meeting when she is being quizzed for the umpteenth time about who is caring for her children and what her husband says about her being away from home. Such questions sometimes reach the point of absurdity. On one occasion I had to be in two distant but adjacent cities on a Saturday morning and a Sunday evening. In rapid succession I was chided for (1) being away from home so much, and (2) wasting money by spending the intervening evening and day with my family. Epstein has reported that women are denied participation in some decision-making processes because they may not appropriately appear at or do not choose to participate in otherwise all-male functions.[2] The rationale offered by Epstein's informants is that the men would feel uncomfortable telling jokes meant only for masculine ears. This taboo is lessening, partly because men are becoming more comfortable with the presence of peer-level women at such times, and partly, I suspect, because women are recognizing that this self-imposed restriction works to their disadvantage. It should be noted that the etiquette of such encounters has not yet become widely accepted; nor are all individuals yet comfortable or even knowledgeable about what such etiquette might include. There is a fine line between a social encounter and a business or political meeting between people of both sexes. Etiquette develops only through practice. There must be a mutual willingness to try. The simple solution would be for nurses to assume political tasks, as has been done in other female occupations—but this has other ramifications which make it inappropriate.

It is especially useful for individual members of organizations to make themselves known to their legislators. This may be done through letters on important issues about which the member has an informed opinion or in support of some action the legislator has already taken. It can also be done by visiting the staff and perhaps the legislator personally. An avenue that nurses are beginning to use is active participation in election campaigns, an approach that other professional groups have used for a long time. Nurses need to expand their activities in this area. Again, a coordinated effort is needed, so that the efforts of individual members are in concert rather than in opposition. As noted earlier in this chapter, the individual member can expect the organization to supply up-to-date and accurate information as well as to point out potential or obscure problems. Armed with such information, the individual is in a much better position to present an intelligent picture to those in positions of power.

Other assets can be included under personal attributes. Social skills, administrative skills, willingness to work closely together with other members of the organization, having the "right" value system, having gone to the "right" school—all these are assets of political power that are peculiar to the individual member. This is a matter of some concern to a professional group such as nurses, most of whose members do not come to the profession via the universities, where other professions (including politicians) receive their education. There is a disadvantage in educating professional-level people in isolation from the other members of their team. One might wish, in an egalitarian society, that such things were not important, but they are. People feel more comfortable working with others who speak the same "language" they do and are familiar with the same rules for behavior. Such skills can be learned, and need to be learned if the individual lacking them wishes to participate on an equal footing with others on the political scene. Many organizations provide an informal training program for their members, assuring that those who have the inclination will have the chance to develop political skills. Nurses have been lax in this area. The alternative is to restrict access to positions of power to those who already come to an organization with these attributes—an unpalatable and destructive alternative that should not receive the support of the membership of any organization.

THE POLITICAL PROCESS

Dahl has described political skill as "the ability to gain more influence than others, using the same resources."[3] With this in mind, let us now move to a discussion of how the legitimation of political decisions takes place in public performances and how the power assets already described can be used.

The process by which laws and organizational policies are constructed and implemented is designed to enhance the belief that "the will of the people" is being expressed. In point of fact, the people are rarely united in a single will. In a pluralistic society, legislators and leaders of large organizations are faced with the constant knowledge that whatever decision they make will render some portion of their constituency happy and another portion less happy, perhaps even furious. As with any social institution where strain exists, mechanisms evolve to reduce the strain. Gans, drawing on the work of Goffman, has characterized one such mechanism as being the development of two forms of government—the actual and the performing.[4] Using the language of the theater, a distinction is made between the backstage arena in which the supporting work, the basic decisions, the direction, the selection and casting of the performers, and the ultimate shaping go on, and the stage on which the play is presented to the audience. Those who are aware of the backstage activities and who are privy to the ultimate goals of the performance are "wise." Those who see only the play itself, even as participants, and have no backstage knowledge are termed "naive." Such an analogy might imply that the public performance is a sham and of no value except to dupe the public. This is not the case. Such performances fulfill an important function. Gans has suggested and research has confirmed that these performances are designed to establish a set of reasons or justifications for whatever the actual (backstage) government has decided is to be done. As will be noted later, the performances do not always succeed. Therein lies another opportunity for the use of power.

The initial and exploratory discussions between a governmental agency and an involved professional group regarding new laws or regulations are not usually public. They take the form rather of luncheon meetings, "hearings by invitation," office conferences, and corridor or telephone discussions. Eckstein cites a number of such instances, as do Gans, Dahl, Epstein, and Redman.[5] By the time a public performance—an open meeting or a formal hearing—is held, it can be assumed that the issues are fairly well delineated. The chair and leading participants have a clear view of what it is they wish to establish by such a performance. The "wise" participants who appear to report or testify are also well-versed in the process. A successful performance at such a meeting or hearing will lead to the results desired by those responsible for scheduling the meeting.

Because such a performance requires an audience, there is an element of risk involved: sometimes the performance goes bad or is spoiled. At the government level there are statutory ways of dealing with a spoiled performance.* In a professional organization, a spoiled performance must be handled

---

*California Administrative Procedures Act (1969), Section 11425, states: On the date and at the time and place designated in the notice the state agency shall afford any interested person or his duly authorized representative, or both, the opportunity to present statements, arguments, or contentions in writing with or without opportunity to present the same orally. The state shall consider all relevant matter presented to it before adopting, amending or repealing any regulation.

In any hearing under this section the state agency or its duly authorized representative shall have

carefully to insure preservation of the solidarity of the group. The mark of a skilled moderator is being able to sense when a performance is going bad and to decide the best way to deal with it. Several options exist: (1) the subject may be redefined as outside the purview of the group and be abandoned; (2) the performance may be terminated in as seemly a manner as possible and the matter referred back for further study; or (3) the "purpose" of the performance may be redefined (a) from the establishment of a position to "exploratory," giving it an interim quality that establishes the need for another, later, "final" performance or (b) from establishing a position to "tension release," in which those with deviant positions are given a further opportunity to present their own performance. It is probable that once a performance of this nature is begun, it must be continued until all of the deviant positions are heard or their proponents have given up from fatigue and gone home. At that point the performance can be concluded with some motion (e.g., to refer back to committee for further discussion) that preserves the appearance of solidarity of the group as a whole. Alternatively, a speech giving recognition to the differing concerns of the assembled members can be made, followed by a reminder of their higher responsibility to the common good. On occasion a recess can be ordered (assuming the spoilage occurs early in the day). Misunderstandings can be rectified and recalcitrant performers can be reasoned with privately.*

The importance of such public performances, properly presented, is in their utility as uncertainty absorption points.† A position stated, a fact testified to in such a performance becomes a citable event. It can later be used as established evidence to bolster some other performance.

The successful management of such performances requires a good deal of skill and organizational support. Not only the moderator (or chair) and the principal actors, but also selected members of the audience must possess essential political and organizational skills if the performance is to be a valid one. Where the performance is a symposium or other public program outside the usual framework of *Roberts Rules of Order,* the burden on knowledgeable participants is even greater, because the nature of the audience is less predictable.

A performance can be spoiled in a variety of ways. The most commonly observed is the introduction of evidence contrary to that accepted as valid. One must distinguish this from the scheduled discrediting that occurs during testimony, question-and-answer periods, etc. It is often possible to trace the origins

---

authority to administer oaths or affirmations *and may continue or postpone such hearing from time to time to such time and at such place as it shall determine.* [italics added]

*Merton discussed the genesis of such processes in his comments on the efforts made by groups to regularize the behavior of nonconforming members.[6]

†The concept of the "uncertainty absorption point" was developed by March and Simon to describe a specific location in a decision-making system.[7] This is the point at which a relatively diffuse group of data is reduced to an organized summation, which is thereafter used in place of the less clearly delineated and less concrete-sounding data from which it was developed.

of scheduled discrediting. A private investigation is made of a set of facts being advanced by an opponent. The results are reported back; not long after, loaded questions are asked at a performance. (This may not lead to discrediting if satisfactory answers to the loaded questions can be found.) Unscheduled discrediting is more likely to be done by naive performers—naive in the sense of not being an informed or planned part of the performance.

In the development of a political performance certain choices must be made about the facts to use to establish a formal basis for decision. These decisions cause what are seen by naive performers as errors of omission or commission. In their concern that the "whole" truth or the "real" truth be presented, naive or dissident performers may succeed in introducing to public view matters of which everyone is aware but which all have agreed privately to suppress. Whether this is "good" or "bad" depends on the intent of those scheduling the performance and the intent of those who cause the discrediting.

On one occasion that I observed, a meeting was held to draft a resolution. A dissident member of the group engaged in *sotto voce* comments during the performance, expressing dissatisfaction with the proposed decisions. A naive performer who really favored the proposed decisions actually succeeded in discrediting the entire performance by responding to the dissident comments (also *sotto voce*). This illicit dialogue raised issues that made it politically impossible for the other members to reach a decision that all could support, and a new performance had to be scheduled. At this second and successful meeting two differences were notable: (1) those who engaged in the *sotto voce* comments were not present, and (2) a fresh set of facts was presented to support the decision, which was then formally agreed to.

A second example concerns a public meeting during which a performer was challenged by a member of the audience about the validity of some information. The situation was eventually retrieved by a second performer who brought the escalating verbal exchange to an end with an appropriate statement. Closure was provided by a third performer, who promised that an investigation of the conflicting facts presented from the audience would be made.

A great deal can be done politically at a public performance without even being a public participant. One can "use" other people's plays to meet one's own goals. At one large gathering, a small group was heard complaining about what they felt to be the small amount accomplished: "It is just all a lot of talk." Conversation with members of this group revealed that they were unaware of the importance of informal contacts to be made in the corridors, the bar, the coffee shop, etc. Such encounters by performers with "the public" are sometimes cited by these performers as evidence in later public performances to support some official action.

An important aspect of symposiums and workshop meetings is that although the agenda may be fixed, it is essential to the credibility of the performance that there be at least an appearance of full participation by the entire group. This can be anxiety producing even for the skilled moderator. One of these was heard to remark of a participant, "He's got a hidden agenda, but I can't figure out what it is." Skilled participants with hidden agenda of their own can "take over" from a less skilled moderator and reshape the entire focus of the session. This is particularly easy if the participant has greater occupational or other prestige (such as expertise) and therefore higher status than the moderator. Anyone who has attended a professional convention can recall occasions when a renowned and senior person—whether member of the audience or one of a group of panelists—has taken over and dominated the remainder of the session. It should be noted that on some occasions this domination is an agreed-upon arrangement that precludes the emergence of a different outside person as dominating member.

Moderators of workshops and symposiums may maintain control by trying to avoid recognizing members of the audience whom they suspect of wanting to make a negative contribution. When the majority of the audience is in sympathy with the aims of the moderator, this can be done fairly nicely and with finesse. Where the audience is not in complete sympathy, it may side with the suspected deviants, forcing their recognition by subtle, and not so subtle, means. This is a case where being attractive, attired in proper establishment dress, and well-spoken can be a distinct advantage to the person seeking recognition. Being a sympathetic figure is a useful ploy where it is fairly certain that the audience will be swung to the side of the individual seeking recognition. It can also be a dangerous ploy if one's efforts backfire. In more sophisticated groups, such an intruder may be listened to in silence, after which the meeting continues as though the speech had never been made. Regardless of the intent of the intruder, the message is more likely to be heard if it is cast in terms that at least appear to fall within the rules of the game. "You've explained the problem very well," said one such intruder, "but my constituency has some particular problems." How, he went on, was he to explain the actions of the group to the people back home? He was then able to present "new facts" in a manner that was within the rules for that particular gathering.

The "rules" for making inputs vary with the kind of performance. If testimony is to be offered at a legislative hearing, it is considered courteous to notify the author of the bill being spoken to in advance of the hearing. Again, it is presumed that in such a situation the individual wishing to testify will have notified his or her professional organization in advance. Not to do so will weaken the apparent strength of the organization. A legislative hearing sometimes assumes the character of a morality play, with villains and good guys and innocent maidens to be protected by our heroes, the legislators. Legislators do not take kindly to being made to appear foolish. Although they may speak to each other in public in a critical fashion, these criticisms fall within the rules. Embarrass one legislator and you may well raise the defenses of the others.

THE GLORY

Few feelings compare with those that come with the successful completion of a political campaign—whether it be the enactment or defeat of a bill or the election or defeat of a candidate. Few feelings can compare with the despair when the victory goes to the opponent. I have had the privilege in recent years of watching California nurses grow into a more organized and politically effective group. The qualitative changes in their participatory efforts, the growing awareness of their own political muscle, the realization that politics is not only essential, but also fun, have been a wonder to see. We are living in a time of great change. It may be a curse, but it is surely also a blessing.

REFERENCES

1. R. Nuttall, E. Scheuch, & C. Gordon, *On the Structure of Influence*, in COMMUNITY STRUCTURE AND DECISION-MAKING: COMPARATIVE ANALYSES (T. Clark, ed., 1968); H. Eckstein, PRESSURE GROUP POLITICS; THE CASE OF THE BRITISH MEDICAL ASSOCIATION (1960).
2. C. F. Epstein, WOMAN'S PLACE (1971).
3. R. A. Dahl, WHO GOVERNS (1961).
4. H. J. Gans, THE LEVITTOWNERS (1967); E. Goffman, THE PRESENTATION OF SELF IN EVERYDAY LIFE (1959).
5. Gans, *supra;* Dahl, *supra;* Epstein, *supra;* E. Redman, THE DANCE OF LEGISLATION (1973).
6. R. Merton, SOCIAL THEORY AND SOCIAL STRUCTURE (rev. & enl. ed., 1957).
7. J. G. March & H. A. Simon, ORGANIZATIONS (1958).

8 The Washington State Success Story

JOAN P. WHINIHAN

Amendments modernizing Washington State's nurse practice act were signed into law on March 19, 1973. However, the first chapters of this success story were written some two or three years earlier. In early 1970 the Washington State Nurses' Association, through its Commission on Nursing Practice, appointed an ad hoc committee to study the state's law regulating the practice of registered nursing. After several months of study and review, the committee recommended that a bill be drafted that would bring the state law into conformity with current nursing practice. As so often happens, practice had preceded the law; every day nurses were being asked and, in fact, expected to perform acts that were clearly outside the scope of nursing practice as then defined in the state statute.

At the same time that the ad hoc committee was making its recommendation to the WSNA Board of Directors that changes were needed in the law, the Association prepared and submitted a proposal to HEW for a grant to conduct an intensive and collaborative study of the state's nursing practice act. The overall objective of the study was to be the updating and modernizing of the act in order (1) to better define nursing; (2) to reflect the expanded role of the nurse; (3) to clarify the relationship of the professional nurse with others in the health-care field; (4) to explore questions of continuing education for licensure; and (5) to explore the question of the composition of the board of licensure. The grant proposal was approved for one year—from June 1971 to June 1972.

During that year, meetings were held with representatives of the Licensed Practical Nurse Association; the state medical, hospital, and health facilities associations; and various government agencies to obtain advice, support, and cooperation in planning for the proposed changes. Information also was gathered from neighboring states regarding the status of their nurse practice acts and their plans for the future of nursing. Copies of recently revised practice acts were requested from the few states that had already successfully pursued the updating of their state laws.

In addition, in this twelve-month period, a series of workshops were held throughout the state to gather input from nurses and to get their reaction to the

The Washington State Success Story   101

broad concepts of change. Armed with this information, the ad hoc committee then set about the task of coming up with the actual language of the proposed amendments, in consultation with the association's legal advisor.

As the grant period neared its conclusion, it became apparent that it would not be possible in the time allotted to complete either the stated objective of the study or the final report, which was to consist of the proposed legislative package with a draft of a revised nurse practice act. Therefore, the association requested an extension of the contract from HEW; this was granted, for an additional six months. Under the extension, the study was scheduled to be completed at the end of 1972, just prior to the opening of the regular session of the Washington State Legislature in January 1973.

During the last six months of 1972 a draft of an amended nurse practice act was presented to nurses, consumers, other health workers, the public, and state legislators at twelve regional seminars conducted throughout the state. The proposal included a provision for mandatory continuing education as a condition for relicensure.

The meetings were well attended, with several hundred people turning out for each of the twelve sessions. Since the state legislative campaigns would be under way at the same time the seminars were being held, it was decided to invite current legislators and legislative candidates to attend the seminars. Also, a selected legislator was invited to participate in each of the sessions, speaking on the legislative process.

A good percentage of legislators and candidates responded positively to the invitations and not only attended but also took an active part in the open discussions. This was advantageous from many standpoints. The large audiences at the seminars demonstrated to the lawmakers that there were large numbers of nurses in the state; many legislators were introduced to the thrust of the association's legislative proposal before the legislature was in session, thus substantially reducing the time the association's director of government relations would need to explain the background and rationale for the bill; the seminars offered an excellent opportunity to gain media exposure about the need for changes in the nurse practice act.

One very tangible result of the regional meetings was the deletion of the mandatory continuing education provision from the draft of the bill. This decision was based on the nurses' strong opposition, expressed vocally as well as in writing on the seminar evaluation forms to making continuing education (CE) mandatory. Some legislators at the meetings stated that their support for the bill was contingent on the CE provision being dropped, because they had heard objections to it from their nurse constituents.

Although the nurses' stand in opposition to mandatory CE in the proposed bill was loud and clear, it also was clear that nurses overwhelmingly endorsed the *concept* of mandatory CE. They were unwilling, as some put it, "to buy a pig in a poke." Before they would support the inclusion of this provision in the law, nurses demanded to know that there would be ample CE opportunities available where they worked and where they lived.

The culmination of the seminars was an all-day meeting in mid-November of 1972, which focused on nurses' views of the changing role of the nurse and consumer's views of new roles for nurses. In addition to nurses and consumers, physicians, hospital representatives, and government officials attended this meeting.

Thus, well before the nurse practice act proposal was introduced into both houses of the state legislature, a great deal of communication about the need for changes in the law had been accomplished with four important publics— registered nurses, state legislators, others in the health-care field, and health consumers.

Because the chairman of the Senate committee on Social and Health Services was a strong supporter of an amended nurse practice act, the bill was moved first through the Senate. At the Senate committee hearing, the Hospital Association stated its overall objection to the changes being proposed and then requested some minor amendments, which the nurses were willing to accept. The Medical Association, University of Washington School of Medicine, and State Board of Medical Examiners all presented impassioned statements in opposition to the bill, stressing their particular aversion to that part of the new definition of nursing that gives final authority to the Board of Nursing to determine through its rules and regulations the additional acts that are jointly recognized by the medical and nursing professions as proper to be performed by nurses. As part of its testimony, the Medical Association insisted on an amendment that would give the Board of Medical Examiners veto power over the Board of Nursing's decisions.

The Senate committee rejected the amendment, voicing grave exception to the idea of one statutory board presuming to take authority over another. The physicians also expressed concern that nurses would venture into areas far beyond their abilities. To allay these anxieties the Senate committee itself wrote and adopted a clarifying amendment:

> This chapter shall not be construed as . . . (15) permitting the performance of major surgery, except such minor surgery as the board may have specifically authorized by rule or regulation duly adopted in accordance with the provisions of chapter 34.04 RCW; (16) permitting the prescribing of controlled substances as defined in schedules I through IV of the Uniform Controlled Substances Act, chapter 69.50 RCW.

The testimony presented by the president of the Washington State Nurses' Association and the chairman of the State Board of Nursing at the hearing before the House of Representatives Committee on Social and Health Services, which follows, summarizes succinctly the rationale for the changes in the law and the amendment accepted by the Senate Committee.

> Mr. Chairman, Members of the Committee, I am president of the Washington State Nurses' Association, the professional association for registered nurses. I wish to speak in support of S.B. 2213—amendments to the law regulating the practice of professional nursing in Washington.
>
> In June 1971, WSNA was awarded a grant from the Department of Health, Education and Welfare to conduct a study of the state's Nurse Practice Act. The results of that exhaustive 18 month investigation are the amendments which you have before you in Senate Bill 2213.
>
> Our study indicated that the current Nurse Practice Act had some serious flaws. It not only includes limitations for the expanded role of the nurse, but also contains language explicitly forbidding nurses from doing many of the acts which they now are expected and, in fact, are *required* to do in the regular course of their practice. Because of the serious legal implications, the language in the current law that prohibits nurses from doing "acts of diagnosis or prescription of therapeutic or corrective measures" is deleted and a new definition of nursing has been inserted.

The new definition reads:

> The practice of nursing means the performance of acts requiring substantial specialized knowledge, judgment and skill based upon the principles of the biological, physiological, behavioral and sociological sciences in either: (1) the observation, assessment, diagnosis, care or counsel, and health teaching of the ill, injured or infirm, or in the maintenance of health or prevention of illness of others. (2) The performance of such additional acts requiring education and training and which are recognized jointly by the medical and nursing professions as proper to be performed by nurses licensed under this chapter and which shall be authorized by the board of nursing through its rules and regulations. (3) The administration, supervision, delegation and evaluation of nursing practice; provided, however, that nothing herein shall affect the authority of any hospital, hospital district, medical clinic or office, concerning its administration and supervision. (4) The teaching of nursing. (5) The executing of medical regimen as prescribed by a licensed physician, osteopathic physician, dentist, or chiropodist.

In her testimony, the WSNA president continued:

> This new definition of nursing more accurately describes the broad scientific knowledge base necessary to give safe nursing care to the public and also reflects the current education and preparation of registered nurses. You will note the definition of nursing includes the words "assessment" and "diagnosis." All professional health workers diagnose—physicians, dentists, nurses, psychologists, social workers, and others. The word "diagnosis" is not limited to medical practice.
>
> The practice of any profession requires assessment of the patient's problem, arriving at conclusions based on this assessment, and action to remedy or alleviate

the patient's problem. Such a process can properly be termed "diagnosis" and "prescription of therapeutic or corrective measures."

The expanding responsibilities of the nurse, therefore, represent an evolution in such traditional nursing practice in that they involve primarily more elements of diagnosis and treatment and more sophisticated intervention within the framework of continuing close collaboration with members of the medical profession.

Item 2 of the new definition of nursing provides a mechanism for collaboration between the professions of medicine and nursing and establishes an orderly procedure for identifying the requirements of education and training for nurses to qualify to perform specialized and advanced levels of nursing practice.

Item 3 of the new definition broadens the responsibility of supervision and delegation to include administration and evaluation of nursing practice. In recognition of the concern expressed by the Hospital Association that item 3 would cloud the issue of who was responsible for the administration of the hospital, the Senate Committee on Social and Health Services added the following amendment to clarify item 3: "Provided, however, that nothing herein shall affect the authority of any hospital, hospital district, medical clinic or office, concerning its administration and supervision."

Item 4 of the new definition provides for the inclusion of the teaching of nursing and item 5 deals with the dependent role of nursing in which nurses carry out the medical regimen as prescribed by a licensed physician, osteopathic physician, dentist, or chiropodist.

Sections 4 through 20 of the bill deal with changes in the State Board of Nursing and a redefinition of the Board's responsibilities. The amendments provide for strengthening practitioner input on the Board as well as the addition of a public member. The State Board of Nursing has prepared a statement for presentation at this hearing and its testimony will speak to the specifics of the changes in this area.

In Section 27 the language is deleted from the act that prohibits the conferring of any authority to practice medicine or to undertake the treatment or care of disease, pain, injury, deformity, or physical condition in violation of chapter 18.71; or the conferring of authority to practice osteopathy or osteopathy and surgery in violation of chapter 18.57.

As medicine and nursing have evolved and continue to evolve, nurses have moved and will continue to move into areas of practice previously considered medical practice. The nurse who has been adequately prepared and who knows the cause and effect of her actions is able to contribute effectively to the ongoing development of nursing roles within the ethical and legal framework for practice. Removal of this legal barrier to expanding responsibilities can enhance the opportunity for nursing to make health care more available and accessible to all citizens.

Many tasks that physicians are asking and expecting nurses to do today are considered medical acts. Removal of this restrictive language is needed to protect the nurse from being in violation of the law. I also would call your attention to the fact that the Senate Committee amended Section 27 to set specific prohibitions and limitations as to those additional acts which may be authorized by the Board of Nursing through its rules and regulations to be performed by nurses who have been determined to have the required education and training. In addition, this Senate

The Washington State Success Story 105

Committee amendment specifically prohibits nurses from prescribing controlled substances as defined in schedules I through IV of the Uniform Controlled Substances Act.

In the preamble to the act . . . the statement has been added that "The registered nurse is directly accountable and responsible to the consumer for the quality of nursing care rendered." This statement was amended on the floor of the Senate. For clarification the word "individual" was inserted before "consumer." In fact and in law we know the nurse is responsible and accountable for his or her own acts, as is any professional. This is spelled out in the preamble to reaffirm to the nurse and the public she serves the intent of the Nurse Practice Act which is to assure safe nursing care to the people of our state.

Throughout the law, the word "professional" has been deleted before "registered nurse." This is a housekeeping item to change the title "professional registered nurse" which is redundant to "registered nurse."

The remaining two Senate Committee amendments to SB 2213 will be found in Sections 3 and 27. Language was added to Section 3 to answer the Hospital Association's concern that the practice act for professional nurses not limit the practice of other health workers such as physicians' assistants who are not licensed but who are authorized by state law. A further amendment adds the category "nursing home" to the section stating ". . . (4) nor shall it be construed as prohibiting auxiliary services provided by persons carrying out duties necessary for the support of nursing service including those duties which involve minor nursing services for persons performed in hospitals, nursing homes or elsewhere under the direction of licensed physicians or the supervision of licensed, registered nurse. . . ."

It is essential that the Nurse Practice Act be brought into alignment with the practice of nursing and the delivery of health care as it is taking place today. The successful passage of these amendments is important not only to the nurse, but also to the consumer of health care, if in fact, nurses are going to be expected to function to their highest abilities in the health care system.

Following this statement by the WSNA president, the chairman of the State Board of Nursing gave this testimony:

The Washington State Board of Nursing has worked closely with the Washington State Nurses' Association in its study of the practice act and wishes to testify in support of the amendments proposed in Senate Bill 2213.

Sections 4 and 5 of the bill provide for changes in the size and composition of the Board of Nursing. To insure practitioner input on the Board, two members are required to be nurses at the level of direct patient care. Also, because nursing believes it is time the consumer had a voice at an effective, decision-making level, a public member is added to the Board. In making these changes, the Board is enlarged from five to seven members.

In Section 7, the responsibilities of the Board are redefined. In this section, the Board is authorized to be responsible for standard-setting in nursing practice and education and for helping the public to identify those practitioners who are adequately prepared to assume expanded practice responsibilities.

In this same section, the Board is charged with the responsibility of establishing criteria as to the need, type, size, and geographical location of nursing programs. This is done to insure quality of educational programs and capability of practitioners as well as the most efficient use of tax dollars.

In Section 20, the requirement is added that those nurses changing from inactive to active license status after three years on the nonpracticing list must provide proof of reasonable currency of knowledge and skills as a basis of safe practice.

Section 21 deals with the grounds for revocation and suspension of license. The grounds have been clarified and strengthened. This will safeguard the public by providing adequate mechanisms for the Board of Nursing to hold practitioners accountable for performance and quality of nursing practice.

The Nurse Planning Council, Section 18.88.040, is deleted. This is in keeping with the modern philosophy that advisory committees are appointed to accomplish a specific task rather than being perpetuated through statutory provisions. Also, the National Commission on Nursing Education has recommended the appointment of a Statewide Master Planning Committeee to assist with planning in nursing education. The nursing profession in this state is moving in this direction.

By busload and carload, nurses converged on the state capital for the Senate and House Committee hearings. In addition to testimony of the WSNA president and Board of Nursing chairman in support of the changes in the nurse practice act, testimony also was given by a staff nurse in a nursing home, a director of nursing service, a coronary care unit nurse, a nurse midwife, a nurse anesthetist, a nurse educator, a public health nurse, and a clinic nurse in a rural setting. Consumers and physicians were also among those giving full support to the nurses' position.

The coronary care nurse said, in part:

> With the increasing number of trauma and coronary care units being installed in hospitals, nurses are expected to judge, evaluate, and determine what is needed to be done. Five minutes could mean the patient's life. I and other staff nurses who function in these specialized units find ourselves practicing in gray areas which are not authorized under the current nurse practice act. This is the real world of nursing and patient care and our practice act must reflect this real world. There are those who would like us to believe that what we are doing is covered under those actions permitted in emergency situations. Since we are given specialized training to prepare us to function at this level and we are regularly employed to staff these units, we would have difficulty proving we are dealing with emergencies which were not anticipated.

The staff nurse who practiced in a large nursing home testified:

> Nursing homes are essentially nursing care facilities. There is no full time house staff. Because of this, daily medical leadership by a physician in unavailable. . . .
> In the absence of medical direction, professional responsibility for patient care is

carried by skilled nursing service. . . . The nurse is expected to identify that a nursing home patient who has suddenly become confused . . . probably has a urinary tract infection. The nurse is expected to order a urinalysis for culture and sensitivity and notify the physician. The nurse also is expected to make continual assessment of toxic and therapeutic effects of drugs. Discontinuation or withholding of drugs are the responsibility of the nurse in the nursing home.

The real world of nursing in a small isolated rural town was described by a clinic nurse:

In the clinic, I do much of the initial screening, referring those needing more complex care to the physicians. Then, on assigned weekends and when the physicians are out of town, I am expected to handle patients' problems and emergency situations that arise. What I am allowed and capable of doing on Monday to Friday becomes expanded on the weekend and during physicians' vacations.

The historical evolution of the functions of physicians and nurses was cited by one nurse speaking in support of change. She said:

Nurses and physicians, working together over the years, have faced an onslaught of new knowledge and technology, combined with ever-increasing demands for health care. By mutual agreement, over 50 procedures have been delegated to the nurse that were once carried out only by the physician. These range from taking temperatures to defibrillating patients. If we are to be successful in establishing an effective system for delivering health care services, we must continue working together to define functions as needs change and knowledge emerges. Further, we must describe these functions in such a way as to reflect professional practice for consumer protection.

The president of a visiting nurse service and the chairman of the nurse clinic board in a remote, rural community gave well-documented, yet emotionally charged, appeals for passage of the amendments to the nurse practice act. A public health officer and a child psychiatrist in private practice helped complete the nurses' case. The psychiatrist made a telling point when he observed that it was perfectly legal for him to resuscitate heart patients, though he was not at all skilled in this area—but, that the specially trained and highly skilled CCU nurse who did this was performing an illegal act.

At the House committee hearing, the medical association once again attempted to have the bill amended to give veto power to the Board of Medical Examiners. And, once again, it failed in its attempt.

The excitement and ingredients of an old-fashioned cliff-hanger prevailed when the nurse practice act bill came to the floor of the House for final passage on the last day of the regular session. If action was delayed, the bill would be sent back to the house of origin and it would have to go through the entire process again during the special session following adjournment of the regular session.

Failure to gain passage of the bill during the regular session would have signalled defeat for that year's session, because the legislature had decided that only bills having budgetary impact would be considered during the special session.

All appeared to be going smoothly until it was noted that several of the representatives had left their desks and were conferring with the Speaker of the House. One of the representatives began scanning the visitors' galleries, caught the eye of the WSNA director of government relations, and motioned her to come to the doors leading to the House floor. This took place as bills were being voted and the nurse practice act was coming up fast on the day's calendar.

A representative who was also a pharmacist had decided to attempt to place a floor amendment on the bill because of his concern over the language dealing with the prescribing of controlled substances. If the bill was amended on the floor of the House this would force it into a conference committee, and passage would then require a concurring vote of the Senate—this when the bill was perhaps five minutes away from the House vote. By speaking to the controls in the Board of Nursing, which would have to promulgate rules and regulations for the implementation of this section of the law, and with considerable assistance from nurses' strong supporters in the House, the WSNA director of government relations was successful in persuading the pharmacist-legislator to withdraw his floor amendment.

The representatives who had been huddled with the WSNA director in the hall then returned to their seats in the House. The bill was called, and the votes flashed on the electronic call board—all green, a "go" for the nurse practice act. The bill drew a 100 percent "yes" vote in both the Senate and the House, and was one of the very few bills to successfully pass the legislature during the regular session.

The Governor signed the bill on March 19, 1973, after item-vetoing the subsections that spelled out the criteria for the nurse members of the State Board of Nursing. It was explained that requirements for members of state boards were being deleted whenever possible because this type of detailing could be unduly restricitve.

In his covering letter to the Senate, the Governor wrote, "This act comprehensively reformulates the law relating to the regulation of nursing practice. This legislation has the effect of bringing the law up-to-date with many currently accepted nursing practices and building into the administrative processes sufficient flexibility to meet future needs of the profession."

Nurses in Washington waged a winning campaign for change. However, the true measure of the success of the Washington story will not be known for some years to come, for the challenge lies in implementation, and that challenge is a continuing one.

9 Institutional Licensure— Panic or Panacea?

LUCIE YOUNG KELLY

Despite a variety of patchwork reforms, health-care systems (or nonsystems, as some would have it) remain the target of serious criticism. Major focus has been on the undeniable fragmentation of services, accelerating costs, and poor utilization and maldistribution of health manpower. Credentialing of health manpower, one of the factors that probably contributes to these problems, has been given special attention by legislative and governmental-consumer groups for some years. Needless to say, this pointed scrutiny has aroused new, or at least renewed, interest on the part of the health occupations and professions.

Licensing of individuals is probably one of the most authoritative mechanisms of credentialing, since it is a function of the police power of the state. Its primary purpose is to protect the public; therefore the state, through its licensure laws, sets standards and qualifications for the licensed practitioner and holds the power to punish those who violate the law. At the same time, licensure, as it stands currently, has definite advantages for the licensee—at the least, status and protection of title (R.N., L.P.N., M.D.); inevitably, certain economic gains also accrue.

Other methods of credentialing for individuals or institutions have also evolved. Whether official, quasi-official, or voluntary, most purport to provide assurance of quality or safety to the public as well as undeniable benefits for the credentialed. And therein lies the dilemma. As one expert in the credentialing field noted:

> It is true that any professional society or group, no matter how socially oriented, will tend to develop barriers to protect itself. . . . Among the contemporary protective mechanisms for the health professions are accreditations, certification, licensure, and registration. All four of these mechanisms medicine has employed with excellent results, if not always for the benefit of society, at least for the benefit of most members of the profession. And now many of the numerous other health professions wish to adopt, if they have not already done so, the same steps which medicine had fashioned to meet the needs of society *and its own protection*.[1] (emphasis added)

This phenomenon has not escaped the notice of consumers or the government. Since the health professions as a whole did not seem to show rapid progress in remedying the more questionable aspects of credentialing, particularly licensure, a series of blue-ribbon panels, high-level committees, and prestigious task forces were formed at state and national levels. For instance, since 1968 Health, Education and Welfare Department committees have produced at least six major publications on the credentialing of health manpower personnel.[2] Furthermore, in 1970-71 the Carnegie Commission on Higher Education looked at both higher education and some aspects of health professional education,[3] and in 1972 the Commonwealth Fund supported an extensive study of accreditation.[4] All of these groups presented firm recommendations for strengthening, changing, or eliminating various forms of credentialing, but it was the 1971 HEW report that first gave official recognition to the concept of institutional licensure.

The HEW report made clear not only that health manpower credentialing was no longer immune from public criticism and that it must reflect the public interest, but also that the federal government had every intention of seeing that action was taken, by using its authority in very specific ways. Preceding the recommendations was an invitation—and a warning:

> This department has a definite role in the process of credentialing progress—a role for catalytic action and support. While the Federal Government cannot solve these problems by itself, it is also apparent that meaningful solutions may not be forthcoming, on a timely basis, without a greater Federal interest. The needs in this field offer great opportunity for significant public-private cooperation.[5]

Of the recommendations—support of a moratorium on licensure of new health personnel and expansion of current acts to extend broader delegational authority; use of national examinations and development of meaningful equivalency and proficiency examinations; strengthening of licensing boards to help maintain quality health services, including requiring assurance of the practitioner's continued competence—the most immediately controversial was probably the last: "The concept of extending institutional licensure—to include the regulation of health personnel beyond the traditional facility licensure—has important potential as a supplement or alternative to existing forms of individual licensure. Demonstration projects should be initiated as soon as possible."[6]

CONCEPTS OF INSTITUTIONAL LICENSURE

Institutional licensure as a process by which a state government regulates health institutions has existed for over 30 years. Usually, requirements for establishing and operating a health facility have been concerned primarily with such matters as administration, accounting requirements, equipment specifications, structural integrity, sanitation, and fire safety. In some cases there are also minimal standards of square footage per bed and minimal nursing staff requirements. The issue in the new institutional licensure dispute is whether personnel credentialing or licensing should be a part of the institution's responsibility, under the general aegis of the state licensing authority.

There are a number of interpretations of just what institutional licensing means and how it should be implemented. Lawrence Miike, an HEW physician-lawyer, considers it "instructive to view institutional licensure not as a developed concept, but more appropriately as a convenient descriptive term applied to the concept of a unified health delivery system."[7] He adds that the "Hershey model" has become to many people synonymous with institutional licensure and has led to some confusion. Nathan Hershey, professor of health law at the University of Pittsburgh, has indeed criticized individual licensure for years. Instead of licensing of individuals, he advocates regulation of institutionally based health workers by that institution, within bounds established by the appropriate state regulatory bodies:

> Because the provision of services is becoming more and more institution-based, individual licensing of practitioners might be legitimately replaced by investing health services institutions and agencies with the responsibility for regulating the provision of services, within bounds established by the state institutional licensing bodies.
> The state licensing agency could establish, with the advice of experts in the health care field, job descriptions for various hospital positions, and establish qualifications in terms of education and experience for individuals who would hold these posts. Administrators certainly recognize the fact that although a professional nurse is licensed, her license does not automatically indicate which positions within the hospital she is qualified to fill. Individuals, because of their personal attainments, are selected to fill specific posts. Educational qualifications, based on both formal and inservice programs, along with prior job experience, determine if and how personnel should be employed.[8]

Hershey further suggested the development of a job description classification similar to that used in civil service. Personnel categories could be stated in terms of levels and grades, along with descriptive job titles. Under such a system, the individual's education and work experience would be taken into consideration by the employing institution for the individual's placement in a grade; basic qualifications for the position, expressed in terms of education and experience, would be set by the state's hospital licensing agency.

Thus, a professional nurse returning to work after ten or fifteen years, Hershey indicates, might be placed in a nurse's aide or practical nurse position, and move on to a higher grade after she "regained her skills and became familiar with professional and technological advances through inservice programs."[9]

Hershey is rather evasive about the place of the physician in this new credentialing picture, implying that physicians might be excluded because the current practice of medical staff review is really a pioneer effort along the same lines and it might as well continue to serve the same function. However, he does list as sites all institutions and agencies providing health services—nursing homes, physicians' offices, clinics, and the all-inclusive "et cetera."

In the three years after Hershey's article (and before the HEW report), institutional licensure as an alternative or, in some cases, an adjunct to individual licensure, generated serious discussion by assorted groups, especially the American Hospital Association and its affiliates, but an interest in this subject is not immediately visible in the nursing literature, despite its serious ramifications for the nursing profession.

A survey of papers, articles, and position statements issued in that period, some of which are cited in the 1971 credentialing study,[10] indicates some variations on the theme. McAdams, for instance, suggests that most of Hershey's proposed structure be kept intact, but that either the Joint Commission on Accreditation of Hospitals or some new private body, instead of the state, be responsible for setting basic qualifications of health personnel and, presumably, policing for compliance.[11] Lloyd offered still another interpretation of the term "institutional licensure." He proposed that all present licensing statutes be replaced and that medical, dental, nursing, medical technology, medical therapy, and institutional licensure be substituted. Each license would recognize only general skills, and an individual could change or upgrade into another category. Medicine would cover (besides physicians) optometrists, podiatrists, pharmacists, and nurses performing medical functions. In this proposal, institutional licensure would be for those personnel directly involved in the operation of institutions: hospital and nursing home administrators, medical record librarians, hospital dieticians, and medical social workers. He suggested, however, that all should have national certification for specialities for group identity.[12] Such certification, it should be pointed out, is usually considered the prerogative of the professional association. Lloyd's concept was not dissimilar to a New Jersey Hospital Association proposal which raised the possibility of one license in each of six areas: medicine, dentistry, nursing, medical technology, medical therapy, and institutional licensure.

Roemer, a health law expert, suggested 20 options for improvement of the licensure situation and considered institutional licensure worth experimentation, but suggested the licensure of health teams in an organized employment setting, where the head of the team would be licensed as an individual and authorized to supervise certain kinds of unlicensed personnel working on the team, provided specific criteria of good patient care were met. Although Roemer admitted to some administrative and legal constraints to this plan, she saw it as protecting the public because it "distinguishes between health practitioners to whom the public has direct access and personnel working in an organized setting."[13]

The final recommendation of the AHA Special Committee on Licensure stated only that institutional licensure should be expanded to include use of personnel,[14] but a later AHA statement—one relating to health-care corporations, a part of AHA's Ameriplan—was more specific. This policy statement saw health-care corporations as having specific responsibility for quality and effective delivery of care by all providers, including physicians.[15] More interested in principle than in style of implementation, the Illinois Hospital Association, in its "White Paper," recommended that "Licensed hospitals should be privileged to utilize the services of competent health care personnel without reference to whether they are individually licensed or whether they are reimbursed by the hospital for these services."[16] Whether or not individuals are qualified to do a job, the association maintained, is more important than whether or not they are licensed. It advocated that current licensure acts be amended to exclude practitioners working in a licensed hospital.

Of the professional associations, only the American Medical Association took an early stand. In a 1970 review of licensure problems and possible alternatives, the AMA interpreted institutional licensure as exempting independent practitioners such as physicians, but affecting "dependent" practitioners such as nurses, physician's assistants, physical therapists, and medical technologists. The report noted that the "concept of employer accountability for personnel working under that employer's supervision or direction seems to be workable for the physician as well as for the health care institution." A number of problems were foreseen, however, and support for institutional licensure was not among the final recommendations in the report.[17]

PROBLEMS OF INDIVIDUAL LICENSURE

Criticism of individual licensure is implicit or explicit in all of the proposals for institutional licensure. Particularly in the first years of interest in the topic, the evils of individual licensure (some quite justified) were cited, but there was little recognition of actions taken to remedy the faults. Evolving changes (which were indeed often slow in evolving) were brushed off as too little and too late. Edward Fogotson, a physician-lawyer who directed a study of licensure for the National Advisory Commission on Health Manpower, enumerated some of the key criticisms of individual licensing.

1. Most licensure laws for the health professions do not mandate continuing education requirements to prevent educational obsolescence. Therefore, the minimal standards of safety, theoretically guaranteed by granting the initial license, may no longer be met by some (perhaps many) practitioners.
2. Educational innovations in the health professions may be stifled by the rigidity of statutorily specified courses and curricular requirements. Changing these requirements to make them responsive to the rapid informational and technological explosion is a difficult and time-consuming process, and the result is the possibility that existing minimal standards may lag behind the practice realities.

3. Definitions of the area of practice are generally not specific, so that allocation of tasks is often determined by legal decisions or interpretations by lay people. On the other hand, some limitations of practice—ones that are not congruent with changing health care needs—are delineated.
4. Most licensing boards are composed of members of that particular profession (or, in some cases, the professional superior of that group), without representation of competent lay members or of allied health professions. This is seen as allowing these professionals to control the kind and number of individuals who may enter their field, with the possibility of shutting out other health workers climbing the occupational ladder and also limiting the number of practitioners for economic reasons. Moreover, the members of a one-profession board may lack overall knowledge of total expertise in the health care field, so that the scope of functions which could be delegated to other workers is not clearly determined. This creates the possibility that others capable of performing a particular activity may be prevented from doing so by another profession's licensing law.[18]

In addition to these generally reiterated criticisms, the HEW report also pointed to the lack of geographic mobility for some health professionals, who may be licensed in one state but barred from another unless they obtain a new license.[19] Only nursing, with its State Board Test Pool Examinations, which are used in every state, allows for licensure by endorsement (i.e., assuming that other criteria for licensure are met, a nurse need not take another examination when relocating to another state). Even then, nursing does not completely escape the mobility criticism, since in the last few years various state boards of nursing have adopted rather idiosyncratic internal criteria. And, of course, not all health occupations are licensed; of the 32 that are, only ten are licensed in every state.* Nevertheless, it seems that almost all of the established or fledgling health occupations—over 250 at last count—look toward licensing as a primary means of credentialing. The licensure problems of one health occupation, obviously, are not necessarily the same as those of all the others. Yet, because the majority of health workers function in institutional settings, the various weaknesses of the licensing laws of all health occupations, the inconsistencies and varying standards of those seeking licensure, and the sheer numbers involved appear to be the bases for whatever enthusiasm exists for institutional licensure.

DOES INSTITUTIONAL LICENSURE SOLVE THE PROBLEMS?

Nurses are often reassured that institutional licensure would not include or affect them or their practice. But it is difficult to see how institutional licensure would not affect them, when, at the least, others would decide the duties of nursing

---

*The ten health occupations licensed in all states are physicians, osteopaths, professional and practical nurses, physical therapists, optometrists, podiatrists, dentists, dental hygienists, and pharmacists.[20]

personnel whom nurses would supervise. It is also unrealistic for nurses to expect to be exempted when many of the tasks once considered in the realm of professional nursing have been assigned to those with less preparation when this is expedient. On the other hand, tasks that have been part of another group's responsibility suddenly become part of nursing's responsibility when that serves the purposes of the institution. The classic tale of a practical nurse in charge of a nursing unit after 3 P.M., under the "supervision" of an R.N. on another floor or in another building, is not fantasy.

Whether that L.P.N. has had special preparation for those assigned responsibilities—has the knowledge, or just the external skills—to carry them out is often questionable. (Still, it is this external manifestation of activity, not quality, which is observed by nonnurses doing job analyses.) Today there are nurses who protest that kind of staffing. But what kind of protest to such a situation could be made under institutional licensure? There is no guarantee even that an R.N. would have to supervise, from any distance. Will this improve patient safety?

Anyone who thinks that hospitals would not be inclined to take the risks involved in institutional licensure should consider the evening or night supervisor who currently dispenses needed medications from the locked pharmacy, thus practicing pharmacy illegally. Institutional licensure might make this act legal, but will it make it any safer?

One advantage cited for institutional licensure is that job descriptions and classifications, combined with inservice training or other experiences and education, would allow health practitioners to move from one classification to another. But is this new? Such a plan has already been adopted by some of the more progressive hospitals. More to the point is the determination of whether all agencies would be willing to initiate the expensive and extensive educational, evaluative, and supervisory programs necessary to fulfill the basic tenets of institutional licensure. Hospital administrators, especially, have been complaining bitterly at the expense of orientation and inservice education programs, cutting back on them as much as possible (sometimes even more than is acceptable to the Joint Commission on Accreditation of Hospitals). This raises the specter of a return to the corrupt apprenticeship system of early hospital nursing in the United States. Probably a hospital's own personnel would be used as teacher-preceptors. Who then would do their jobs? How would they be compensated for the extra role? How long would a "student" be expected to function in one position with its lower salary while "practicing" a new, higher role? And with what kind of supervision? What kind of testing program would there be for each level? Testing by whom? With what kind of standards? Such sliding positions might well cut manpower costs, but might they not also indenture workers instead of freeing them to new mobility? Problems of criteria are obvious. If 50 states cannot now agree on criteria for individual licensure, why would they be any more likely to agree on institutional licensure?

Considering the more than 7,000 profit and nonprofit hospitals, with bed capacity ranging from tens to thousands, in rural areas and urban, with administrators and other key personnel prepared in widely varied ways, and the even larger number of extended care facilities, clinics, and home care agencies equally dissimilar, a state of confusion, diversity, and parochialism is an overwhelming probability. Instead of facilitating interstate mobility, institutional licensure would more likely limit even *inter-institutional* mobility. A worker who qualified for a position in institution A would have absolutely no guarantee that this qualification would be acceptable at institution B. Moreover, the disadvantages to those health professions that have fought to attain, maintain, and raise standards might be disastrous to patient welfare. Nurses, particularly, who are just beginning to fulfill their potential for providing total health care and are proud to be accountable to the patient and not to an administrative hierarchy or a physician for their professional acts, may find themselves relegated increasingly to technical tasks, substituting for a more expensive physician and being substituted for by the less prepared (not nurse practitioners, but physicians' assistants; not primary nursing, but nursing by direction). Will this save patients money, or deprive them of optimum health?

Even if many of these practices exist today—de facto institutional licensure—as one proponent asserted, it hardly seems progressive to legalize what is already considered an unsatisfactory situation. And let there be no mistake, under the proposed system an institution would have the power to determine the specific tasks and functions of each job and to indicate the skill and proficiency levels required, regardless of the employee's licensure, certification, or education.[21] Institutional control would be almost complete, since guidelines to be developed by the state institutional licensing agency are intended to be general.

But, then, would the state guidelines not give the consumer, if not the employee, protection? Presumably the state licensing agency would be empowered to review the institution's utilization and supervision of health personnel to determine whether employees were performing functions for which they were qualified, but how realistic or feasible could such an evaluation possibly be? No one believes that any army of experts knowledgeable in all the subcategories of health care could be recruited, employed, and dispersed to check the hundreds of thousands employed in the multiple subcategories of workers in the thousands of care-giving facilities in any state. Rather, review would consist of inspection by paperwork. The ineffectiveness of such surveillance is reflected in recent nursing-home scandals and the admitted deficiencies of various municipal, state, and proprietary hospitals. In all of these situations, the institution reviewed was given an official blessing, while actual conditions varied from merely unsafe to life-threatening. Generally approval was given on the basis of an institution's written self-report, with or without a visit by harassed, overworked surveyors. (When surveyors did recommend closings of institutions, they were frequently overruled or ignored if it was politically expedient.) Would institutional licensure miraculously avoid these pitfalls?

Finally, what about those health professionals providing care outside the walls of a health institution? Is the possibility of independent practice to be eliminated? Or will multiple systems of certification, individual, and institutional licensure add to the confusion we already have?

ACTIONS AND REACTIONS

Given the inconsistencies of institutional licensure, its economic advantages to certain employers, and its perceived threat to established professions, a polarity of reactions was to be expected. Continuing to voice general approval were the hospitals and hospital administrators, but organized nursing, finally awakened, arose to rally an opposing constituency. The first major action was a strong resolution approved by the ANA House of Delegates in 1972, reaffirming commitment to individual licensing and individual accountability as an essential of safe, high-quality care and promising opposition to any efforts intended to shift this accountability from individual to institution. Institutional licensure, the ANA pointed out, would vest in the employing agency the major responsibility for defining the scope of nursing practice, long held to be the profession's prerogative and responsibility. (This reasoning applies equally to other professions.) In addition, the ANA noted that the wide variation among institutions prevents rather than enables geographic mobility of health practitioners.

A short while later, the executive committee of the National League for Nursing Board of Directors reaffirmed its 1971 position in favor of separate nurse licensure. Its 1972 statement asserted that it was "unalterably opposed to the concept of extending institutional licensure to include the regulation of nursing personnel." Similar resolutions or statements opposing institutional licensure were made by the National Association for Practical Nurse Education and Service and the National Federation of Licensed Practical Nurses, the board of the Association of Operating Room Nurses, the Nurses Association of the American College of Obstetricians and Gynecologists, and state nurses' associations.[22] In early 1973, the National Commission for the Study of Nursing and Nursing Education also reiterated its position that the public was best protected by individual nurse licensure;[23] and at its June 1973 convention, the AMA passed a resolution opposing the extension of institutional licensure in lieu of individual licensure to physicians and nurses. Representatives from nursing organizations and from the National League for Nursing spoke in support of the AMA resolution. Other health professions were also alerted to the danger of institutional licensure (often by nurses) and began to adopt negative positions.

While these reactions were being aired, the federal government took action on implementing two of their recommendations. First HEW's Bureau of Health

Manpower Education granted a contract to the Institute of Public Administration in Washington, D.C., to explore the feasibility of a national system of certification, conceived as an umbrella system at the national (not federal) level, which could provide coordination and direction of certification practices for selected health occupations through voluntary participation. Such a system, it was said, would enable the establishment of common policies and practices and determination of the desirability of extending certification to new occupational groups and specialties.

Second, two demonstration projects on institutional licensure were funded. Ironically, at the same time that the governor of Illinois signed into law a bill retaining individual licensure, the Illinois Hospital Association's proposal to explore institutional licensure was funded for a year by HEW and began in June 1972. Although this project purported to study only unlicensed personnel, the fact that nurses are responsible for the nursing regimen, as well as for seeing that the medical regimen is carried out, mandated participation by the Illinois Nurses' Association. It was made clear that this participation did not in any way negate the association's commitment to individual licensure, but it was expected that the INA would have the opportunity to contribute significant nursing input to the project. Various disagreements and misunderstandings apparently occurred, and when neither the INA nor the Illinois Medical Society were given the opportunity to review the continuation proposal for HEW, both organizations withdrew from the project.

The project was nevertheless funded for another year, with plans to put a credentialing model to work in midfall. These plans did not materialize. When the project terminated in 1974, the report concluded that although certain aspects of institutional licensure were theoretically feasible, the concept was not practical in terms of the needed resources and potential cost of an effective program. The computerized data showed that the majority of the seventeen hospitals studied could agree on the majority of the job descriptions of the unlicensed personnel employed; nevertheless, implementation of a whole system, with legal responsibility, could be an overwhelming task. It was also pointed out that the tremendous resistance of various professions toward the proposal which was encountered in the study would be equally formidable in a total implementation of the institutional licensure concept.[24] Since no aspect of implementation was attempted in this project, there was some assumption that this logical next step might be carried out in Pennsylvania, where the Hospital Educational and Research Foundation of Pennsylvania, an arm of the Hospital Association, had also been funded for an institutional licensure grant. The foundation proposed a three-year demonstration project, involving six to 12 health-care institutions, "to examine an alternative method of regulating health personnel." The project was to include, among other things, a plan for selection and utilization of hospital personnel regardless of existing licensure regulations. However, halfway through the second year of that project (at the end of 1974), no hospitals had yet been selected to participate in such an experiment. Some preliminary studies with X-ray and laboratory personnel had been done in one hospital, with no fanfare, but the results were not published. The project director did draft legislation (never introduced) which would authorize suspension of existing licensure laws for experimental purposes, an action suggested in the original project proposal. When HERF was flooded by protests from nurses and others, it issued a statement that this proposed legislation was intended only to protect the participants in the experiment from violating the licensure laws of other health professionals and was actually very similar to a California law already in existence.

The law referred to was probably AB1503, considered by some to be California's version of institutional licensure. The original intent of AB1503 was to allow nurse practitioners to continue to function after the California Medical Board had issued a cease and desist order. In essence, the law states that, for purposes of experimentation in health-delivery systems, "a select number of publicly evaluated health manpower pilot projects should be exempt from the healing arts practice acts." (Thus, nurse practitioners could not be accused of violating the medical practice act as they practiced in their expanded roles.) Safeguards for the public were written into the law, and the state Department of Health was given the responsibility of designating experimental programs. Actually, implementation of the law was a bit unwieldy, since nurse practitioners were forced to maintain trainee status under the supposed supervision of an educational program, even though they had completed the program and were employed in a variety of settings. Moreover, after passage of a new nursing practice act that legalized expanded practice, the law continued to operate, presumably to cover the expanded role of the medical auxiliaries and dental auxiliaries, as well as maternal-child care, pharmacy, and mental health personnel, which were among the designated programs that could be approved for experimentation. Some of the participants in the experiment had been minimally trained workers serving certain poor and otherwise unserved areas in California with something of a "barefoot doctor" status. As the law nears its demise, many of these experimental workers remain uncredentialed. Since they represent political influence groups, it is not unlikely that the law will remain on the books, with an unknown effect on the health-care system.

In other states, there have also been some overt attempts to legislate institutional licensure, which were kept in committee or killed, primarily through the efforts of organized nursing. Attempts to consolidate or eliminate the licensure boards of the various health occupations—seen by some nurses as an indirect approach to institutional licensure, since they tend to attenuate nursing's control over its practice—have had varied success. One of the first efforts was in Massachusetts in 1973. The governor's proposal would have abolished the Board of Registration in Nursing, along with other health professions' licensing boards, and assigned their regulatory functions to a new Health Systems Regulation

Administration. Nurses would have had almost no input. Additional legislation was proposed to provide that anyone employed in a licensed or approved health-care facility could provide nursing services, as long as such services were provided under the supervision of a registered nurse or licensed practical nurse. Of major concern to nurses was the quality of nursing care under such loose and perhaps unenforceable conditions, as well as the question of how both Massachusetts nurses and those from other states wishing to practice in Massachusetts would have been licensed. Strong protests by the nurses of Massachusetts and other states, however, including a series of resolutions passed at the NLN convention, aroused the interest of the public and legislators. As a result, the governor submitted a revised plan. Nevertheless, changes were eventually made and the power of the Board of Registration in Nursing to develop rules and regulations was taken away (but not placed elsewhere). Finally in 1976 the power to promulgate and enforce regulations was restored to the Nursing Board—thanks to the cooperative political and legislative efforts of the Massachusetts Nurses' Association with other groups.[25]

The trend toward weakening the power of the professional association in licensure seems to be growing. In 1977 one of the results of significant changes in Wisconsin's licensing laws was consolidation of the funds, personnel, and financial management of all boards, theoretically intended to ease the administrative burdens of the boards. However, the next proposed legislative step was to establish a board composed entirely of lay persons, "responsible for promulgating the rules and regulations governing the practice of all licensed professions."[26] All boards that were not eliminated would act only in an advisory capacity. Connecticut's nursing board is already in such an advisory position, and it faces total elimination in 1981. Both plans are similar to that which has been in effect in New York with the Board of Regents since the beginning of licensure there.

In Illinois in 1978, nurses clashed with the director of the Department of Registration and Education, whom they accused of making decisions in the areas of "licensure, approval of nursing schools, maintenance of standards of nursing education and practice, and the autonomy of the profession."[27]

It is clear that legislation in other states is also being directed toward plans that take legal control of the health profession out of the hands of the health professionals. Is this a step toward institutional licensure or a strong reaction to what has frequently been termed the unresponsiveness of *all* professionals to the public's complaints? And will the end results be the same?

WHAT NEXT?

It is true that some of these actions were predictable. In the spring of 1974, a follow-up report on the 1971 HEW report on licensure was published (dated June 1973). It presented a general overview of state activities in the various aspects of licensure and personnel credentialing, including institutional licensure and anticipated continued activity in the state arenas. In the foreword, Dr. Charles Edwards, then Assistant Secretary for Health, recommended an extension of the moratorium on licensing of new health personnel through the end of calendar year 1975, citing the need for more time "to assess properly some of the new directions that have been taken by State legislatures, licensing boards, professional organizations, and the educational community with respect to the credentialing of health manpower."[28] He also reiterated that the examination of health personnel credentialing would continue to be a significant departmental activity.

The section on institutional licensure was extremely brief, probably because there were as yet no meaningful reports from the two funded projects in Illinois and Pennsylvania. Moreover, the strong objections to the concept by various professional groups were recognized: the denial of individual licensure to emerging professions; the threat to presently licensed groups; the danger involved in nonprofessionals' wielding ultimate authority in clinical situations; and the possibility that institutional licensure would be geared primarily to administrative convenience.[29]

However, the idea that institutional licensure was just a concept, a developing experimental model, was again put forth, and the need to test the concept was emphasized. Of particular significance was the statement that health-care delivery today is already a form of institutional licensure, with actual scopes of duties restricted by prescribed competency levels through such modalities as certification, hospital staff regulation, and even voluntary specialization within allied health fields. Demonstration projects in institutional licensure were seen as one means of documenting the extent of the de facto situation. Perhaps as a reassurance to objecting health professions, the report added:

> Documentation of such practices does not necessarily mean that formalizing the structure will improve the system. Before that is done, such changes would have to be justified by showing that it is of greater value than accommodating the present licensing system to such practice; moreover, it would have to be demonstrated that it would function more effectively than the de facto situation.[30]

Apparently, these hopeful words influenced no one, and the continuing organized objection to institutional licensure and the rather negative report of the Illinois study combined to dim governmental enthusiasm—for the time being. At any rate, the 1977 credentialing report stated only that, on the basis of "studies of the feasibility of a national certification system and institutional licensure as alternatives to the traditional model of occupational licensure in health . . . the Public Health Service (PHS) has concluded that the certification alternative should be further developed, whereas the institutional licensure approach—because of the intense controversy that it generated—should not receive further consideration at this time."[31]

Many of the recommendations made in that report were similar to those in the 1971 report—relating to national standards the criteria for and improvement of licensure; competency measurement and the need for continued competence; and a major push for a national voluntary system for allied health certification (supposedly not to include nurses). A Certification Council did organize, with no official ANA participation—by its own choice. The purpose was to certify the certifiers—an overall group that would include the organizations that certified allied health professionals, but also set certain uniform standards and guidelines. There were, of course, varied degrees of objection from various groups about the recommendations, but few failed to detect a new note of governmental persistence—the suggestion that if health practitioners chose not to make some of the needed changes, there were other ways in which changes could be made—e.g., setting standards through Medicare-Medicaid or national health insurance legislation or requiring conformity for reimbursement. Neither the recommendations nor the suggestions for enforcement were much different from alternatives to institutional licensure set forth by various experts in health law, and some action is being taken by almost all the health professions.

In nursing, certain very positive actions were and are being taken. The ANA and NLN took action on the issues of open curriculum, mandatory continuing education for relicensure, and certification. Most states have revised their nurse practice acts—broadening the scope of practice, adding consumers to their boards, and requiring evidence of current competence through various means, including continuing education. Nurses in the field have continued to strive toward techniques of peer evaluation, implementing standards of practice, and voluntary continuing education. State boards have given increased attention to removing or rehabilitating incompetent nurses. Educators are working seriously on equivalency and proficiency examinations and other methods of providing flexibility and upward mobility for nursing candidates. Finally, a major study of credentialing, sponsored by the ANA, made some daring proposals in 1979, suggesting, among other things, the establishment of a national nursing credentialing center, possibly a federation of organizations with "legitimate interests" in nursing and credentialing, "as the means of achieving a unified, coordinated, comprehensive credentialing system for nursing. The purpose of the center would be to study, develop, coordinate, provide services for, and conduct credentialing in nursing."[32]

Other professions have also given increased attention to these matters— some admittedly for the first time. Indeed, the criticisms of current credentialing processes involve all. None of the concerns belongs exclusively to any one health discipline, and it is possible that they cannot be resolved by any one health discipline. The moratorium on licensing new health personnel is over, according to the calendar, but the problems that instigated the moratorium are not over: they continue. Even if individual licensure is improved, what of the unlicensed worker? Will certification provide the answer or simply duplicate the problems of licensure and leave no legal recourse? Has the geometric increase of health-care providers improved patient care? Is there another answer? Resolution of the problems posed could well help to resolve some of the other problems of health-care delivery. And if one group must take the lead in initiating cooperative action, why should it not be nursing?

REFERENCES

1. National Committee on Accrediting, STUDY OF ACCREDITATION OF SELECTED HEALTH EDUCATION PROGRAMS. PART 1: STAFF WORKING PAPERS: ACCREDITATION OF HEALTH EDUCATIONAL PROGRAMS (1972).
2. U.S. Department of Health, Education and Welfare, REPORT OF THE NATIONAL ADVISORY COMMISSION ON HEALTH MANPOWER. Vol. 1 (1967); Vol. 2 (1968); Green, K., OCCUPATIONAL LICENSING AND THE SUPPLY OF NONPROFESSIONAL MANPOWER (U.S. Department of Labor, 1969); U.S. Department of Health, Education and Welfare, REPORT ON LICENSURE AND RELATED HEALTH PERSONNEL CREDENTIALING (1971), DEVELOPMENTS IN HEALTH MANPOWER LICENSURE (1973), and CREDENTIALING HEALTH MANPOWER (1977).
3. Carnegie Commission on Higher Education, HIGHER EDUCATION AND THE NATION'S HEALTH: POLICIES FOR MEDICAL AND DENTAL EDUCATION. SPECIAL REPORT AND RECOMMENDATIONS (1970), and LESS TIME, MORE OPTIONS: EDUCATION BEYOND THE HIGH SCHOOL, SPECIAL REPORT AND RECOMMENDATIONS (1971).
4. National Committee on Accrediting, STUDY OF ACCREDITATION OF SELECTED HEALTH EDUCATION PROGRAMS. COMMISSION REPORT (1972) (SASHEP).
5. REPORT ON LICENSURE. . . , *supra*, 71.
6. *Ibid.*, p. 77.
7. L. Miike, INSTITUTIONAL LICENSURE: AN EXPERIMENTAL MODEL, NOT A SOLUTION (Paper presented at New Jersey League for Nursing Symposium on Institutional Licensure: What It Means to You, February 27, 1973).
8. N. Hershey, *Alternative to Mandatory Licensure of Health Professionals,* 50 HOSP. PROG. 73 (March, 1969).
9. *Ibid.*, p. 74.
10. REPORT ON LICENSURE . . . , *supra,* 65–70.
11. D. McAdams, *Institution-based Licensure System May Help Solve the Licensure Dilemma,* 50 HOSP. PROG. 52 (July 1969).
12. J. J. Lloyd, *Arguments for State Regulation of Health Professions.* 51 HOSP. PROG. 71 (March 1970).
13. R. Roemer, *Legal Regulation of Health Manpower in the 1970's: Needs, Objectives, Options, Constraints, and Their Trade-Offs,* 86 H.S.M.H.A. HEALTH REP. 1,062 (December 1971).
14. American Hospital Association, *Statement on Licensure of Health Care Personnel,* 45 HOSPITALS (March 16, 1971).
15. American Hospital Association, Special Committee on Provision of Health Service, Policy Statement (1971).
16. Illinois Hospital Association, HOSPITALS, MANPOWER, LICENSURE AND THE 1970's 5 (November, 1971).
17. American Medical Association, Council on Health Manpower, LICENSURE OF HEALTH OCCUPATIONS 4 (December, 1970).

18. E. Fogotson, LICENSURE, ACCREDITATION AND CERTIFICATION AS ASSURANCE OF HIGH QUALITY HEALTH CARE (paper presented at National Health Forum meeting, Los Angeles, March, 1968).
19. REPORT ON LICENSURE . . . , *supra*, 43.
20. *Ibid.*, 136.
21. N. Hershey & W. Wheeler, HEALTH PERSONNEL REGULATION IN THE PUBLIC INTEREST, QUESTIONS AND ANSWERS ON INSTITUTIONAL LICENSURE 13–14 (California Hospital Association, 1973).
22. American Nurses' Association, *Resolution on Institutional Licensure*, 72 AM. J. NURS. 1 106 (June 1972).
23. *Institutional Licensure Opposed by NCSNNE*, 72 AM. J. NURS. 701 (April 1973).
24. R. Tucker and B. Wetterau. CREDENTIALING HEALTH PERSONNEL BY LICENSED HOSPITALS: THE REPORT OF A STUDY OF INSTITUTIONAL LICENSURE (1975).
25. *New Massachusetts Law Restores Autonomy to Board of Nursing*, 76 AM. J. NURS. 831 (May 1976).
26. CREDENTIALING OF HEALTH MANPOWER—CONFERENCE REPORT 12 (National Health Council, 1978).
27. *Illinois Nurses Say State Nursing Act Is Being Violated*, 78 AM. J. NURS. 185 (February 1978).
28. THE STUDY OF CREDENTIALING IN NURSING: A NEW APPROACH. VOL. 1, THE REPORT OF THE COMMITTEE (1979).
29. DEVELOPMENTS IN HEALTH MANPOWER LICENSURE, *supra*, 47.
30. *Ibid.*, 48–49.
31. CREDENTIALING HEALTH MANPOWER, *supra*, 6.
32. THE STUDY OF CREDENTIALING IN NURSING, *supra*, 91.

10 Denver: A Case Study

CRAIG BARNES

In Denver, in 1977, the published beginning salary for entry-level staff nurses was less than that for sign painters—$316 a month less. A Graduate Nurse I was also paid less than a Plumber I, Tree Trimmer I, Tire Serviceman I, Oiler I, Gardener Florist I, or Parking Meter Repairman I. Entry-level nurses were routinely required to have a baccalaureate degree and several years of experience, partly because Denver's hospital is a training hospital for interns. But these nurses were assigned a published salary rate lower than that of the Arborists, Cement Finishers, Automotive Mechanics I, Spray Booth Operators, Mower Shop Foremen, and Automotive Mechanic Helpers. All of these higher-paid jobs, in 1977, were filled by men. Ninety-seven percent of the nursing jobs were filled by women.

At the top of the nursing ladder, in the same year, the Director of Nursing Service was also paid less than men in comparable positions. The Director in Denver in 1977 (a woman) supervised approximately 575 employees and administered an annual budget of $3.5 million. The position required 17 years of education, a master's degree, and five years of experience and was denoted by the city as an "administrative" post (rather than, for example, "professional" or "technical" or "sales"). In 1977 there were 19 city job classifications filled entirely by men that required the same or less combined education and experience and the same or less supervisory responsibility, but were nevertheless paid more than the Director of Nursing Service. The highest of these classifications received $553 a month more than the Director of Nursing Service. The median in-grade salary of the incumbents of all 19 of those male-dominated job classifications was 8.7 percent more than that of the top-level nurse. The only other city job requiring the same pre-employment education and supervisory levels which was also denoted "administrative" was the Director of Environmental Health. The male director in that year was paid $497 a month more than the female Director of Nursing. He was not required to have more experience than the Director of Nursing, nor did he exercise more supervisory responsibility. He was not required to be licensed. The nurse was, of course, required to be licensed by the State of Colorado.

Nurses work hard; they are, typically, on their feet through most of an eight-hour shift. They are exposed to contagious disease and regularly subjected

125

to personal health risks. They must be prepared to react swiftly, expertly, and with professional aplomb in emergencies; they are expected to be at work no matter what the weather or road conditions. They are to be family counselors, teachers, and even spiritual guides. They are, in short, responsible for the preservation of human life.

Still, in Denver, parking meter repairmen are paid more. For every level of nursing from LPN to Director, including clinical specialists, head nurses, and all those in between, there are a multitude of male-dominated classifications which require similar qualifications in terms of education, level of supervisory responsibility, and experience, but which nevertheless are paid more than the corresponding nursing level. This was true in 1977. It was also true in 1974. It was true when the nursing classifications were compared to classifications which were exclusively filled by men; it was true when they were compared to classifications filled 75 percent or more by men. There were 35 exclusively male-occupied classifications requiring fewer combined years of education, experience, and supervisory responsibility that were paid more than the Graduate Nurse III, Denver's grade for the head nurse on a ward. Head nurses were paid a starting salary $137 a month less than the mean starting salary of these 35 male-occupied classifications, including, for example, Traffic Signal Technician I and Plumber II.

When, on the basis of these facts, seven Denver nurses sued the city for sex discrimination, they also commissioned a formal job-worth analysis. On the basis of an unpublished professional evaluation by Dr. Richard L. Beatty of the University of Colorado, each of the approximately 800 job classifications was analyzed in terms of factors contributing to job value, or job worth. At the lower range of job worth, including low-level nursing jobs and comparable male-dominated jobs, the nurses suffered a 55 percent monthly salary disadvantage, according to Beatty. In the middle range, including head nurses and other jobs requiring similar skills, physical effort, and mental responsibility, nurses were paid 44 percent less than comparable male-dominated jobs. At the top level, the Director, Assistant Director, and other nurses with highest responsibility were paid 80 percent less than comparably valued male classifications.

According to Beatty, sex discrimination in public employment in Denver was not limited to nursing. Of approximately 800 job classes in Denver in 1974, 325 were filled entirely by men. By 1977, the number had increased to 375. Predictably, the mean salaries of the classifications filled 100 percent by men exceeded the mean salaries of those filled 100 percent by women in both 1974 and 1977. What was surprising was that while the classifications filled by women suffered a mean salary disadvantage of 26 percent in 1974, by 1977 that disadvantage had increased to 46 percent. Further, Beatty reported, there was a general tendency for salary to track with male domination of the classification. When Beatty analyzed all the jobs in the city by sex and by salary, he discovered that the starting salaries of jobs held 80 to 90 percent by women were lower than those of jobs held only 70 to 80 percent by women. That is, the more men within the brackets, the higher the mean starting salaries within those brackets. Jobs occupied 50 percent by men were, on the whole, paid less than jobs occupied 60 percent by men, which were in turn paid less than jobs occupied 70 percent by men, and so on. While there were some exceptions, as a general rule one could know whether a given job was likely to be paid more than another by knowing the sex ratios of the incumbents of those jobs. The more men, the higher the pay.

This was the general environment that Beatty probed to analyze the situation for nurses specifically. The job-worth analysis was an effort to screen out the influence of other societal factors which might influence the higher salaries for male-dominated jobs. Thus, if all the jobs were compared on the basis of the same worth criteria, such as mental responsibility, working conditions, and other objective factors, one ought to be able to measure salary equity between the sexes by determining whether jobs of approximately equivalent worth are paid on a par. What Beatty found, however, was that at any level, regardless of the fact that the worth of the nursing jobs was equivalent to that of the male-dominated jobs, they were paid less. At the top of the scale the salary deficiency suffered by the nurses was 80 percent.

Anyone familiar with nursing or nursing history will not find such figures surprising. According to Bonnie Bullough, Dean of the School of Nursing, State University of New York at Buffalo and Ph.D. sociologist, nurses have been in a substantially sex-segregated profession for 600 years. The City of Denver salary program is designed to replicate community salaries for nurses, and as the community is affected by that 600-year history, so is the city. "The prevailing wage" is the city's stated goal, but this means, of course, paying what history dictates.

The lawsuit brought against the City of Denver is known as the *Lemons* case, after Mary Lemons, who, at the time the case was brought, was Director of Nursing Service at Denver General Hospital and one of the seven plaintiffs alleging sex discrimination. The suit was in preparation from 1974 through 1977 and was tried in federal district court in April 1978. With the aid of Bullough, the nurses alleged that since the Middle Ages their profession had been largely sex-segregated, that its original practitioners were paupers, nuns, alcoholics, and even prostitutes, all of whom were of a low social status and who could command either no pay at all or minimal pay. There was a parallel from the earliest times between nursing as a female profession and low pay, and the Denver nurses charged that sex and low pay were related as cause and effect. For centuries an employer had only to know the sex of the incumbent of the position to know that nurses would work for less.

The Denver nurses further charged, and Bullough testified, that when Florence Nightingale revived the respectability of the profession in the late 1800s, she did so in the image of femininity. "Every woman is a nurse," said Nightingale, and she taught her trainees obedience, chastity, and nurturing and caring roles. She did not teach them analysis or curative roles. Nursing, as Nightingale conceived it, was to be an extension of the traditional feminine virtues. Even the name "nursing" carries a double female meaning. As nursing entered modern times, therefore, it did so sex-segregated, low-paid, and stamped with a "female" label which would keep it sex-segregated in the minds of employers. The Florence Nightingale Training Schools were for women only, medical schools were known to exclude women, the Army and Navy nurse corps excluded men, and, finally, nurses built their sex stereotypes into their own protective legislation.

In Colorado, the Nurse Practice Act picked up and carried forward Florence Nightingale's feminine terminology for nursing. This law characterizes the function of a nurse as "supportive and restorative,"[1] the very *feminine* adjectives that Nightingale used. The Medical Practice Acts, by contrast, which describe the role of the doctor, who traditionally has been male, prescribes "curative and analytical" functions, which are traditionally male functions.

Here then, embodied within existing Colorado law, is sex stereotyping. It is similar to the black-white segregation laws of the Old South and has the effect of directing women toward one profession and men toward another, as well as identifying male and female roles in medicine. Despite the fact that nurses at one time and for other purposes saw these laws as an advance, such laws also reflect the modern-day continuation of sex roles and the prevalence of such roles in community awareness.

It is to this community, in which there is a cause-and-effect relationship between female sex and low pay, that the City of Denver turns to determine its pay for nurses, 97 percent of whom are female. Since low pay and femaleness are consistently economic handmaidens, it follows that the City now pays nurses less than parking meter repairmen.

History also works to the disadvantage of women in that discrimination tends to flatten or contract pay scales. The range of possible advance in salary within women's jobs tends to be less than within men's jobs. In the *Lemons* case, testimony to this general condition came from Barbara Bergmann, a widely published professor of economics at the University of Maryland. The nurses' case included testimony that Denver offered only a nine-step salary range for beginning level nurses, while nearly every one of the hundreds of male-dominated jobs enjoyed an 11-step salary range.

The city uses a complicated calculation of mean salaries to develop its salary range for any job. The formula produces 11 steps on paper for all jobs, including nurses. Then, testified the Assistant Director of Nursing Service, Lois Cady, the city typically imposes an actual nine-step limit on nurses and several other classes, all but one of them predominately female. Cady testified that the more compacted range for nurses had to be, and was, specifically approved each year by Denver's governing personnel authority, the Career Service Board. The practice became known as the Board Approved Hiring Rate, or BHR.

Removing two possible steps of salary increase from the salary of the "key" class, Graduate Nurse I, was in itself, according to the nurses, discrimination between themselves and the male classifications with longer salary ranges. Furthermore, since every other nursing job in the city was tied to the salary range established for Graduate Nurse I, the discrimination against that class produced a salary effect in every other nursing class. Every nursing salary in city employment was thus adversely discriminated against by this one practice of adopting the Board Approved Hiring Rate.

City witnesses at the trial protested that the purpose of the practice was to the advantage of nurses in allowing them to be hired, initially, at a rate *above* the rate which could be derived from the regular mathematical formula. It was a special dispensation to nurses to eliminate the bottom two salary steps through which other, male-dominated, job classes had to progress. The city did not, however, address the fact that in eliminating the bottom two steps it failed to add two more at the top.

In effect, Denver was not conscious of the fact that the BHR had created a narrower, more compacted salary range for nurses, an affirmative reconstruction of the flatter salary scales inherited from the discrimination-affected market. Interestingly, the objective mathematical formulas which the city uses to develop its pay scales, if actually applied, do not alone result in compaction. It is an affirmative act of the board to adopt the BHR which cuts down opportunity for women.

Paying nurses on the basis of historical sex stereotypes is particularly insidious, because such stereotypes exist in the culture and in the mind and are largely unconscious. Most male employers would deny any prejudice against women as employees, believing that since such prejudice never has been formed in an affirmative, articulated thought pattern, it does not exist. The unconscious thought pattern is not recognized.

The Denver nurses in the *Lemons* case sought to demonstrate the existence of the unconscious thought pattern by analyzing in great detail the ways in which city personnel managers actually administered their system, regardless of protestations of sex neutrality. The analysis required identification of the incumbents of every job in the city and, over four years, consumed thousands of hours of nurses' volunteer time. At the end of that period the nurses claimed that they had laid back the flesh from the bones of the city's system and had found extensive use of sex stereotypes, in spite of the official protestations to the contrary.

This exhaustive study was required because the days of easy victories in sex discrimination are over. The cases of blatant differences in pay for men and women doing the same work, bearing the same title, are fewer and farther between. Statutes that say what men can do or what women can do and articulate the stereotypical expectations in, for example, weight lifting or estate administration or child care, are dwindling. The new arena is the proof of stereotyping circumstantially, rather than on the basis of overt, stated objectives. The Denver nurses sought to break through this new conceptual barrier by the use of organizational statistics.

Since the city is bound by its charter to pay to its own employees the community's "prevailing wage," it must survey certain community jobs which it uses as benchmarks for all remaining city jobs. Thirty jobs are surveyed annually, among them accountant, dietician, and entry-level nurse. Each of the surveyed jobs is called a "key" class. Other jobs are then related to the key classes, and pay for the additional jobs is based on this relationship. By analyzing which jobs the city classifiers related to which other jobs, the Denver nurses sought to provide the circumstantial evidence of sex discrimination.

The jobs that were clustered together in relation to Graduate Nurse I, for example, tended to be held primarily by female incumbents. The jobs that were related to the Dietician (also traditionally female) also tended to be held primarily by female incumbents. The jobs related to the Administrative Clerk key class were also predominantly female. By contrast, the jobs related to the Civil Engineer were held primarily by men, as were those related to the Heavy Equipment Operator and the Accountant I.

The system may be illustrated as follows. First the classifiers select the key class and assign it a salary based on the community survey:

Graduate Nurse I

Then to the key class is related another class:

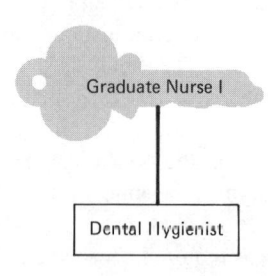

Graduate Nurse I
|
Dental Hygienist

The dental hygienist is then assigned a salary—for example, "up two pay grades," meaning that this classification is paid the salary of the Graduate Nurse I plus two pay grades. Often an additional class may be related to a related class:

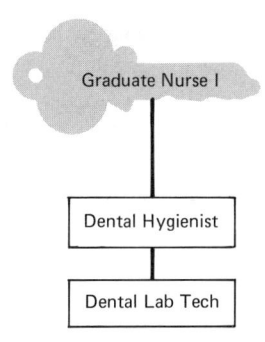

```
        Graduate Nurse I
              |
      ┌───────────────┐
      │ Dental Hygienist │
      └───────────────┘
              |
      ┌───────────────┐
      │ Dental Lab Tech │
      └───────────────┘
```

In this way a hierarchy of jobs is built and all of the jobs in the city are eventually related, sometimes through as many as eight or nine intervening classes, to the key classes. A typical cluster of jobs achieved through this process looks like this:

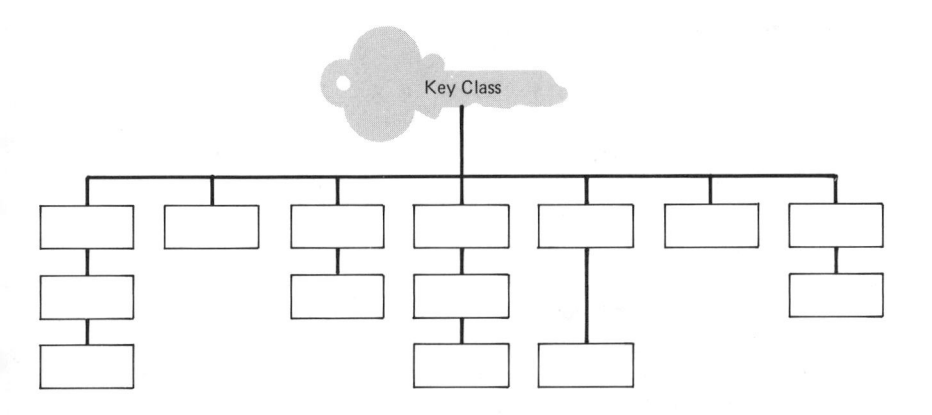

[Diagram: Key Class at top branching to multiple boxes representing job classes]

In 1977 the city had organized 30 of these key class clusters or groups. When the nurses analyzed the incumbency of those jobs which the city's classifiers had lumped together, they discovered that twenty-six of the clusters were highly sex-concentrated. Each of those twenty-six groups was made up 75 percent or more of members of the same sex.

The nurses therefore suspected that sex was the organizing criteria, or the factor which caused one job to be related to another for pay purposes. This became a major allegation in the *Lemons* case. The city, for its part, vigorously denied any use of stereotypes and claimed that various jobs were related because of job "similarities." Sometimes these were similar management responsibilities. Sometimes the jobs were clustered because they were "low-level" salaried jobs. Sometimes they were grouped because they were in the same physical facility, for example, a hospital. Sometimes they were grouped because they dealt with the same subject, for example, nursing or food services. The city claimed that such flexible criteria were necessary, and the city's chief classifier testified that the selection of competing criteria was on the basis of what criteria was "best," "most reasonable," or made the classifier "comfortable."

In this circumstance the employer was armed with multiple justifications, any one of which could be used at any given time to resist requests for integration of male- and female-dominated jobs in pay clusters. There were no written criteria, and no records of decisions adequate to trace the criteria that had been used in any one decision.

Twenty-six of the thirty clusters consisted of 75 percent or more members of the same sex, and no objective criteria existed by which it could be determined that sex stereotyping of the job had not been a factor. Testimony was given that the city classifiers' decision to include a job in a cluster with the key class Graduate Nurse I, or any other key class, was made as a result of informal meetings and discussions. In effect, the classifiers sat in informal session and asked, "Where shall we put the Family Health Counselor?" Information they regularly had before them at such sessions showed the sex of the incumbents of the job being discussed. They also knew the general sex tradition of the jobs already grouped. Thus the Family Health Counselor, a new job created in 1977, was clustered with Graduate Nurse I. The city said it was because both the nurse and the counselor worked in the "same physical facility," i.e., a hospital. But the nurses suspected it was because both jobs were held mostly by women, and the evidence upon which they based that conclusion was the subjective nature of the process and the overall sex-segregated result for the system as a whole.

A factor adding to the weight of the nurses' conclusion was that a very large percentage of the groups or clusters were of jobs requiring the same number of years of education. Jobs which, for example, required no post-high-school education were typically grouped together; jobs requiring a bachelor's degree were linked; jobs requiring more than a bachelor's degree tended to end up in the same groups. One complete group was described as a "college-level" series. The nurses concluded, therefore, that education was a de facto organizational criterion. The classifiers who met in informal conference to decide where to put a new job appeared to follow this criterion to a substantial degree.

A review of the educational prerequisites for all the job classes clustered together in 1977 revealed that commonly three quarters or more of the classes linked together were required to have the same years of education or college degree. In fact, 84 percent of the clusters displayed this tendency toward educational homogeneity; of the 30, only five did not reflect it.

There were, however, deviations from the norm—that is, five groups in which education did not appear to be the organizing standard. Some other standard, some other criterion, appeared to be more important to the classifiers in these cases. Four of these five deviant clusters were occupied predominantly by women. The nurses therefore claimed an additional circumstantial fact of sex discrimination: sex appeared to be a factor in the organization—perhaps unconscious, but nevertheless controlling—which overrode the usual guide of educational level.

According to the nurses, when the city's classifiers met to determine into which pay group to put the new job classification of Family Health Counselor in 1977, these informal discussions should have revealed that the Graduate Nurse I cluster contained master's-degree nurses, psychologists, and top-level administrators. Had the classifiers followed the educational norm used in all but one male-dominated cluster, they would have said, in effect, that since Family Health Counselors are not required to have any post-high-school education, that job should not go into the group with bachelor's- and master's-degree classifications. Instead, however, given the fact (and, the nurses alleged, *because* of the fact) that health counselors are known to be primarily women, and nurses are known to be primarily women, the decision was made to include counselors in the group with nurses. This cluster thus ended up with a wide range of educational levels, a deviation from the practice followed in all but one of the male-dominated clusters.

The nurses alleged this to be sex stereotyping. In the absence of clearly enunciated criteria for the establishment of these groups, they said, sex became the dominant criterion, erasing other criteria used in the cases of groups dominated by males. Clusters consisting of women were formed because the incumbents were women, but groups consisting of men were formed because of education, job similarity, or some other factor.

The net effect of all this was that women's pay scales were based on their relationship in the cluster to some other "women's job," rather than to a job of similar responsibility or effort or working conditions. Mary Lemons, Director of Nursing Service, found her job in the cluster related to beginning-level staff nurse, Graduate Nurse I, and the Family Health Counselor. The beginning nurse was not required to have even a bachelor's degree. The Counselor was not required to have any post-high-school education. Lemons, by contrast, was required to have a master's degree and five years experience and to supervise 575 people and a budget of $3.5 million. Nevertheless, the city set Lemons' salary using Graduate Nurse I as the starting point, and low community pay scales for Graduate Nurse I dictated a low base for the calculation of Lemons' salary. By relating women to women, the city assured that Lemons' salary remained low.

The city claimed that it related Lemons to the Graduate Nurse I classification because the two jobs were functionally similar—i.e., both were nurses—and that therefore the choice had nothing to do with sex. But the nurses pointed out that the top-level administrative nurse had no more similarity, functionally, to the bedside nurse than did the hospital administrator, typically a man, who is not included in the same pay group. There is no functional similarity between the desk job of the Director of Nursing Service and the nursing shift of the staff nurse.

The alternative which the city did not follow in Lemons' case was to pay her a salary equivalent to that paid other administrators of a similar level of responsibility. The example above of the Director of Environmental Health illustrates the point. Lemons was more an administrator than a nurse; that is, she occupied a desk; administered a large budget; supervised other supervisory personnel; directed recruitment; supervised policy drafting, shift management, and inservice training; and seldom if ever went near a hospital bed. Her job was labeled by the city itself as "administrative" rather than "professional," which is the label given the bedside nurse. Still, the city chose to pay Lemons according to nurses' scales rather than its General Administrative Series scale, where it included such other directors (male) as the Director of Environmental Health. Since the pay of the latter was based on an amalgam of pay given to professionals and administrators in the Denver area, and since Lemons' salary was tied to the pay of the beginning-level staff nurse, it is not surprising that Lemons suffered a $497-per-month disadvantage.

All the other nurses in the Denver system claimed similar disadvantage in pay because of what they claimed to be a subjective, stereotype-ridden system.

The city did not in the *Lemons* trial attempt to rebut the use of stereotypes and subjectivity, nor the resultant salary disadvantages, nor the use of the BHR. The circumstantial evidence of the nurses was rebutted, instead, by a kind of circumstantial evidence of the city's own. The city said, in effect, that as an employer it was acting in good faith and out of a necessity to meet competition. The dictates of competition required, said the city, that the top-level administrative nurse be clustered with the beginning staff nurse because both were nurses. To put the top-level administrative nurse into the General Administrative Series would break up the natural identification of all nurses with the same pay scale which occurs in the marketplace. By way of rejoinder, the nurses pointed out that the Accountant Series was divided into two parts: top-level Accountants III and IV were split from low-level Accountants I and II and placed in the General Administrative Series. If this can be done for accountants (male), why can it not be done for nurses (female)? It could, replied the city, if there were a need, but the best system is to follow the market and link all nurses' salaries together.

The heart of the matter therefore came down to this: is absence of conscious bad faith and the "necessity" to meet competition an adequate defense to the challenge that a city's pay system is sex-based, depends upon sex stereotypes, uses different criteria for the organization of women than for men, incorporates by reference the residual effect of 600 years of sex discrimination, compacts and restricts promotional opportunities to nine pay grades while all but one of the hundreds of male-dominated jobs enjoy 11 steps, and has a resulting disadvantageous salary impact as high as nearly $500 a month?

The trial judge in this case said yes. Admitting the invidious history and the disadvantage presently existing, Fred M. Winner, Chief Judge, United States

District Court for the District of Colorado, presiding, held that to measure the impact upon nurses' salaries by comparing nurses to nonnurses would lead to a disruption of the entire American economy. The law, said Judge Winner, allows comparison of male nurses to female nurses and redress of disparate pay scales between the two if such exists, but the law does not require a comparison of the Director of Nursing Service to the Director of Environmental Health.

The Chief Judge thus limited Denver's nurses to the relief which would have been available to them under what is known as the Equal Pay Act of 1964.[2] Violation of that act had not been alleged by the nurses, but the judge incorporated the provision of that act into the Civil Rights Act of 1965,[3] violation of which had been alleged, and said that if the earlier act had not been violated, then neither had the latter. In effect, the judge said, the limits of sex discrimination law as we now know it, or which can now be enforced, are the limits achieved by the breakthrough of the Equal Pay Act of 1964.

To date, therefore, one must view the Equal Pay Act of 1964, which proscribes paying male nurses more than female nurses, as the high-water mark of the law of sex discrimination as it affects nursing. The *Lemons* case is, at this writing, on appeal. But the status of the law, absent success on appeal or revision in the statutes, is that the use of sex stereotypes (if proven by statistical rather than direct evidence), the use of different organizing standards for women than for men (if proven by circumstantial rather than direct evidence), the use of subjective standards of organization which contain no system to screen out possible sex predilections, and the resultant massive, across-the-board impact are insufficient to prove a violation of the Civil Rights Act of 1965 (Title VII). The employer which responds that it is acting in good faith or that it is meeting competition has stated an adequate defense.

At least that is so in Judge Fred M. Winner's court in Denver, Colorado. It is possible that the Denver nurses ran into more resistance than others might. At one point the judge inserted into the trial the fact that the Declaration of Independence states that all *"men"* are created equal. It is an age-old problem, a history with which we are dealing, he said, rather than a present problem.

Whether the problem lies in the unconscious stereotyping of judges or the unconscious stereotyping of employers, the Denver experience indicates that the mandate of the law as it exists is not clear enough nor articulate enough to force equality of pay between nurses and male professionals, even when a 600-year history of discrimination is made part of the record. It may be that the Court of Appeals or the U.S. Supreme Court will reverse Judge Winner. If that does not happen, then it will be time to seek stronger legislation.

Perhaps the most troubling ambiguity in the law for which new legislation is needed is that of the equation currently being drawn by other judges, in addition to Winner, between the Equal Pay Act of 1964 and the Civil Rights Act of 1965. The former was intended to eliminate differentials in pay between men and women "working in the same establishment" doing essentially the same kind of work. A year later the much broader Civil Rights Act was passed, proscribing discrimination not only in pay but also in "terms and conditions of employment," "status," and job "opportunities." The latter act, by its broad application in race cases, could be interpreted to proscribe also acts such as unconscious sex stereotyping and discrimination based on a rigid adherence to market (which means, in effect, adherence to historically depressed, discrimination-based wage scales). These acts affect pay even though they are not expressly pay problems. Several courts, however, have said that if women seek a pay increase they are bound by the earlier, narrower, Equal Pay Act to show discrepancies between men and women "in the same establishment." The effect is to eliminate the showing of the sorts of acts which blacks and Chicanos may use to prove discrimination under the Civil Rights Act of 1965 from the arsenal of weapons available to persons alleging sex discrimination, whether they be men or women.

There is no legislative history to justify such a narrowing of the Civil Rights Act of 1965 as it applies to sex. But there is a provision in the 1965 act which says that the later act shall not be interpreted to render invalid any act "authorized" by the 1964 act. This language is now known as the "Bennett Amendment," after the Utah Senator who was its author. The Bennett Amendment has been interpreted by Judge Winner and others to allow stereotyping, uneven application of criteria, and incorporation of discriminatory history into the salary scales of women because they are not "prohibited" by the Equal Pay Act of 1964. The advocates for the nurses in Denver argued that the allowance in the later law is only for those acts "authorized" by the earlier statute, and is not a loophole for anything "not prohibited" thereby, which is a much broader idea. The distinction is significant. But this argument did not succeed in Denver. It has also failed elsewhere, notably including the important *Christensen*[4] case in Iowa, which creates the need for a statutory clarification.

When that hurdle is overcome and sex stereotyping which leads to pay differences between men and women is eventually declared by statute or a court as cognizable under the Civil Rights Act of 1965, there is abundant other case law which should give hope to victims of sex discrimination.

The United States Supreme Court in *Griggs* v. *Duke Power Co.*[5] declared, for example, that the 1965 act proscribes a practice "neutral on its face" and neutral in its intent, if the practice has disparate impact on a protected class (e.g., women), unless the practice can be justified by "business necessity." Thus a testing program which screened out black applicants from employment was struck down in *Griggs* even though neutral on its face, because it had the effect of picking up the disadvantageous results of a discriminatory history, perpetuating that history. Similarly, nurses may argue that they suffer from a discriminatory history and take advantage of the *Griggs* precedent.

Thus, if nursing was conceived of as a feminine profession, and if for centuries there has been a causal relation between sex and low pay, then the history bears some of the same marks of disadvantage as that suffered by blacks.

It is ironic that while the City of Denver views its reliance on the market as evidence of its neutrality and complete absence of sex-based decision making, nurses see the same reliance as the root of the problem. Absent the Bennett Amendment, the nurses might expect to make progress under the precedent of *Griggs*.

There is also case law that an employer whose practices produce a disparate impact upon a class protected by the Civil Rights Act of 1965 may be in violation of that act if the employer's system is operated subjectively, and does not have built-in objective criteria by which to screen out bias. See, for example, *Muller v. United States Steel Corp.*[6] An employer, therefore, like Denver, which decides to group for pay purposes women's jobs with women's jobs and men's jobs with men's jobs and which explains such organization on the criteria of what is "best" or "reasonable" or "comfortable" might be expected in the face of such precedent to have some difficulty (assuming, that is, that the Bennett Amendment has been removed).

At this writing no case has yet broken the conceptual hurdle which currently prevents nurses' salaries from being compared to, for example, those of other administrators who are not nurses. Even under the Civil Rights Act, that has not occurred, because none of the other protected classes has precisely the same problems as do most women who are qualified across job boundaries. This method of analysis has occurred in one or two other cases in a tangential way (see, for example, *Christensen v. Iowa* and *Sledge v. J.P. Stevens Co.*[7]), but has never been dealt with directly. In the end, this kind of comparison is the conceptual barrier of the most promise but also the most difficulty. If a case like the *Lemons* case does not make this breakthrough, then it seems likely that the breakthrough will have to come through legislation. Unless, as a result of such legislation, some other criteria than history and market are taken into account, it is possible that for a long time to come nurses will be paid less than the parking meter repairmen.

REFERENCES

1. COLORADO REVISED STATUTES, 1973, §12-38-202 (9) (b).
2. 29 U.S.C. §206(d).
3. 42 U.S.C. §2000-e, *et seq*.
4. *Christensen v. State of Iowa*, 563 F.2d 353 (8th Cir. 1977).
5. *Griggs v. Duke Power Company*, 401 U.S. 424 (1971).
6. *Muller v. United States Steel Corporation*, 509 F.2d 923 (10th Cir. 1975).
7. *Sledge v. J.P. Stevens Company*, 10 E.P.D. ¶10,585 (E.D. No. Carolina, Dec.22, 1975).

Section Three

Nurse Practitioners, Clinical Specialists, and Physician's Assistants

11 Nursing Functions in Other Countries: Insights for the United States

RUTH ROEMER

The problem of what a nurse does, should do, or is allowed to do is neither new nor unique to the United States. Scope-of-practice questions are not novel, because nursing functions have been expanding ever since nursing began. This process of change is reflected in enlarged nursing functions in health-care institutions, in the enrichment of curricula of nursing schools, in modernized nursing practice acts, in rulings of licensing boards, in joint statements of the nursing and medical professions as to functions appropriately performed by nurses, and in advisory opinions of attorneys general in some states.[1]

Several general forces explain this dynamism in nursing functions. First, scientific and technologic advances, commonly referred to as the biomedical revolution, have impelled new tasks and functions. Would anyone have thought a generation ago that nurses would be performing complex tasks, making critical decisions, and monitoring highly sophisticated equipment in intensive and coronary care units? Second, advances in nursing education have contributed to enlarged functions, especially since many nurse practice acts define professional nursing as acts based on knowledge and application of scientific principles acquired in an approved school of professional nursing. The introduction of new subjects into the curriculum, more profound examination of certain fields, the teaching of new techniques, and more interdisciplinary studies have all given the nurse a richer background for performance of nursing tasks, for supervision of auxiliary personnel, and for decision making and nursing assessments. Third, increasing recognition of health care as a human right drives toward expanded nursing functions; wide acceptance of the idea that health care is a human, if not yet a legal, right is expressed in measures to improve access to health care and to promote its quality. Perhaps the clearest acknowledgment that health care should be a right is contained in measures to spread the financial burden of health services through social insurance, as under Medicare for the aged and the totally disabled and as proposed under various forms of national health insurance. The

The research on which this chapter is based was supported by Public Health Service grant NO1–MI–34090(P) (Milton I. Roemer, M.D., Principal Investigator).

141

concept of health care as a human right raises questions about how the limited resources of a country, including its health personnel, are to be allocated to provide the needed services. Who will provide the care? Who will and can do which tasks?

The same forces that have impelled the evolution in nursing functions in the United States are also operative in other countries. Scientific advances, improved education, and increasing recognition of health care as a human right are compelling re-examination of the roles of health personnel and the ways that health services are organized and financed in other countries. It is natural that this scrutiny should turn to the key health profession of nursing—the health profession that has the largest numbers and the longest tradition of service. Nevertheless, the issue may arise in different ways, and change may occur at different rates, depending on the particular conditions in each country.

In resolving questions concerning nursing functions and the law, it may be helpful to examine the experience of five other countries—all relatively affluent countries and all countries in which access to health care has been facilitated by a national system for the social financing of health services. Studies of the health manpower policies of Australia, Belgium, Canada, Norway, and Poland were undertaken to obtain insights for the United States as it moves to enact some form of national health insurance. A key issue concerned the ability of these countries to assure the necessary health personnel once the cash barrier to care had been removed. In all the countries studied it was found that, despite differences in approach, strategies had been devised for providing vastly increased health services to the people and, moreover, that expanded nursing functions were an important element in assuring such care.

Obviously, the five countries studied varied in the degrees to which they resembled the United States. Australia and Canada, as large, federated, mainly English-speaking common-law countries, are most similar. Like the United States, Australia and Canada consist of federated states or provinces, with major authority for health matters vested in the states or provinces but considerable influence still exerted by the federal government. All three countries are characterized by pluralistic health systems, with multiple public and private agencies and varied patterns of organizing medical care.

Of course, just as there are similarities, there are also differences. Some of these differences are historical, social, and cultural, with greater influence of the United Kingdom on both Australia and Canada than on the United States. Some of the differences relate to the health-care system, and the most important of these is probably the system of financing health care. In both Australia and Canada, government financing of health care is further developed than in the United States.

Both the Australian and Canadian systems for financing health care differ from ours. In 1974, Australia enacted a new program called "Medibank" for financing both physician's and hospital care through insurance, administered largely through private insurance companies, with co-payments by patients.

Prescribed drugs have been a public benefit (except for a one-dollar charge per prescription per patient) in Australia since the Pharmaceutical Benefits Scheme was adopted in the 1940s.[2] The Canadian health insurance system started with enactment of a national program of hospital insurance by the Canadian Parliament in 1957, with each province entering the program in different years thereafter. A similar federal-provincial program for physician's care was enacted in 1966, and each province has enacted various other benefits in addition. With all ten provinces of Canada in the system, a national health insurance system for both physician's care and hospitalization operates across Canada.[3]

Belgium, despite its small geographic size, has many similarities to the United States, including a high degree of industrialization, cultural diversity, local sovereignty, and particularly great strength in the private sector. Belgium's system of health insurance is highly pluralistic, consisting of six national health insurance organizations (under the general supervision of a National Institute for Sickness and Invalidity Insurance) composed of about 150 regional groupings of about 2000 small mutual aid societies at the local level.[4] These mutual aid societies receive claims and indemnify their members for medical care expenses. Not only does this system resemble the pluralistic American system composed of Blue Cross, Blue Shield, commercial insurance companies, and governmental programs, but medical practice is also characterized by fee-for-service, solo practice, and "free choice of doctor." The Belgian medical profession prides itself on being governed by two legal doctrines—that of "therapeutic liberty" guaranteed by the 1967 royal decree on the healing arts and that of medical confidentiality—both of which assure great autonomy to the doctor in medical practice.

Norway resembles the United States in its strong democratic tradition, its "frontier" character, its tradition of local government, and, at the same time, its increasing trend toward centralized authority. Norwegian health services differ from those in the United States in that hospital services are provided by salaried specialists in governmental hospitals, and general practitioners do not practice in hospitals but rather in the community.[5] Still, many of the lessons from Norway concerning staffing rural areas and regionalizing health services are relevant to our own problems, and Norway's long experience—since 1909—with health insurance makes insights from its health services particularly important.

The country with the greatest differences from the United States is the Polish People's Republic, where health care is a legal right, and health services are organized in a unified and integrated national system which provides care, trains personnel, operates both ambulatory and inpatient facilities, and controls distribution of drugs and medical equipment.[6] Despite these great differences, socialist Poland with its national health service provides the full range of lessons possible on health manpower policies.

Within all these health-service systems, as in our own, nursing functions are in transition. Before turning to current developments in nursing practice, however, it may be helpful to sketch briefly the kinds of nursing personnel in each country and the educational and regulatory systems affecting nurses. From this review, contrasting approaches emerge—with perspectives, perhaps, for the United States.

NURSING FUNCTIONS IN AUSTRALIA

Australia has two levels of nurse: the registered nurse, with three years' training and a basic certification in general or psychiatric nursing; and the nursing aide or enrolled nurse, with one year's training and practical experience. Nursing assistants are untrained personnel.[7] Basic nursing education for registered nurses in Australia is generally provided in hospital schools of nursing. The Nurses' Registration Board in each state is responsible for setting the required curriculum and for the final examinations leading to registration, except that very recently the most populous state, New South Wales, has separated the regulation of education and of registration into two agencies. Postbasic education in hospitals or colleges provides specialist qualifications for registered nurses in midwifery, geriatrics, intensive care, obstetrics, infant care, and other specialties. Australia has the interesting system of regulating specialist qualifications through its Nurses' Registration Boards in the six states. A nurse who has completed basic training and midwifery is "double-certificated"; a nurse who has completed basic training, obstetrics, and infant care is "triple-certificated."

Although nursing education in Australia has long been conducted predominantly as an apprenticeship system, it is beginning to change. Basic nursing programs are now being offered in academic institutions, called colleges of advanced education. For some time, colleges of nursing have offered postgraduate training—both full-time courses in nursing administration and other specialties and shorter courses as a form of continuing education—and these colleges now offer basic training in an academic setting as well. The trend is in the direction of separating nursing education from nursing service. One of the major problems facing the nursing profession and the health services of Australia has been the serious loss of nurses from the profession because of family needs, job dissatisfaction, inadequate salaries, difficult hours, lack of child-care facilities, and other reasons.[8] It is hoped that improved education and improved working conditions will keep larger numbers of professional nurses in active practice.

Because the vast majority of Australian nurses are employed in hospital rather than ambulatory settings, the most dramatic change in nursing functions has been in the development of intensive care units, where nurses have been called on for new functions because of new technology. Authorization for new functions has come about in two ways. One way is that the State Hospital Commission, which regulates hospital services and reimbursement, issues general instructions on the appropriate scope of practice for nurses. Under these instructions, hospitals can make specific determinations. Another way is that, in some states, the Nurses' Registration Board specifies what a nurse may properly do.[9]

The legal scope of nursing practice has not been a prominent issue in the hospital setting in Australia. Some moderate expansion of general nursing functions has occurred, and nurses now take blood samples, cross-match blood, and start intravenous therapy. But when asked about authorization for new functions, representatives of Nurses' Registration Boards and governmental officials in health services reply that once nurses are properly educated and registered, their functions tend to be the responsibility of the institution that employs them. This attitude toward the problem of scope of practice—more matter-of-fact than that in the United States—may be related to the relatively low incidence of malpractice actions in Australia.

In the context of community health services, however, nursing functions in Australia are a more lively issue. Australia has not in the past had a generalized public health nurse in the American sense. Rather, specialized nurses have provided well-baby care in baby health centers, care in child health centers for children with physical or emotional problems, school health services, and home nursing services.[10] As mentioned, nurses receive postbasic training in various specialties, including psychiatric and geriatric nursing.[11] Recently, a new type of nurse has emerged in conjunction with the national initiative to develop community health centers. The community health nurse is a registered nurse, with additional training for ambulatory care in the community, who will replace the various specialized nurses now functioning in different settings. The community health nurse provides clinic services and domiciliary care and works with infants, children, adults, and the aged in connection with physical and psychosocial problems. In some places, community health nurses function in a capacity analagous to that of generalized public health nurses in the United States. In others, they are assuming responsibility for home nursing services, with a strong mental health component. In South Australia, where primary doctors have been in short supply, they may serve as community practice nurses to extend the reach of the limited supply of doctors.

In 1973 the Karmel Committee, reporting to the Australian Universities Commission on Medical Education, recommended development of registered nurses to work in an expanded role in conjunction with doctors in community health centers and as practice nurses in large group practices.[12] In this capacity, nurses would assist in screening the degree of urgency of calls, carry out certain procedures, interview patients, and take histories. The Karmel Committee favored offering a graduate program to prepare nurses for these functions, rather than creating a separate program for "assistant doctors."

Current training programs for community health nursing vary in length and depth. In Melbourne, the College of Nursing is offering a one-year postgraduate program leading to a diploma in community nursing. In other places, shorter courses with considerable on-the-job instruction are offered. The curricula also vary, some being developed along traditional public health lines and others incorporating a new component on diagnostic techniques, history taking, and patient assessment.

Ample precedent exists in Australia for expanded functions of nurses. So-called "Bush" nurses have long been the main source of medical care for aborigines and others in vast stretches of central Australia. In fact, the outstanding record of the "Bush" nurses is cited as clear demonstration of the capacity of registered nurses to undertake an expanded role. But despite this experience, there has been no movement to extend the functions of nurses generally into diagnosis and treatment. The new community practice nurses relieve doctors of the need for performing many procedures in primary care, but diagnosis and treatment remain medical functions. The emphasis in Australia has generally been on developing a postgraduate training program in family medicine and increasing the number of doctors specially trained in family medicine.

NURSING FUNCTIONS IN CANADA

Canada has two main classes of nurse: the registered nurse and the registered nursing assistant.[13] There are also untrained personnel: orderlies, nurse's aides, practical nurses, and psychiatric aides. A variety of educational programs exists for the registered nurse in Canada, as in the United States: diploma programs (in both hospitals and community colleges), baccalaureate programs, and postbasic programs. Canada, again like the United States, has developed clinical nurse specialists in various fields. The registered nursing assistant is generally trained in ten-month programs. The regulatory system consists of registration by the College of Nurses or a similar body in each province, and the prerequisites for registration include graduation from an approved nursing school, passing of a national examination designated by the college, and payment of the registration fee. In Quebec, proficiency in French is also required unless special exemption is granted.

Unlike Australia, in Canada considerable explicit attention has been directed to the issue of nursing functions. In 1964, the Royal Commission on Health Services in its exhaustive study of existing health services and future needs addressed issues related to the supply of nurses. In 1969, the Task Force Reports on the Costs of Health Services in Canada opened discussion of manpower utilization by underlining the importance of more efficient use of registered nurses, suggesting specific ways of assigning certain tasks to less-qualified personnel. In October 1970, the Canadian Nurses' Association issued an official statement that manpower needs can be met effectively and economically by expanding the role of the nurse.[14]

Provincial commissions and committees, established in several provinces to consider problems of health services and health manpower, have urged expanded roles for nurses. In Ontario, the Committee on the Healing Arts gave extensive consideration to the practice of nursing, the relations of nurses with other health workers, and the functions of different kinds of nurses.[15] A study prepared for the Committee on the Healing Arts urged that nursing recognize its role as interdependent with that of medicine and strengthen cooperation with the medical and hospital associations, rather than concerning itself solely with those functions not shared with physicians.[16] Perhaps in response to this suggestion, one of the recommendations of the Committee on the Healing Arts was that a definition of the practice of medicine be developed incorporating the idea of interdisciplinary team practice. Provincial commissions in Quebec[17] and Nova Scotia[18] stressed the role of community health centers and of community nurses working in association with physicians in provision of primary care. The movement for community health centers in Canada received strong impetus from the Hastings report on that subject, and community health centers now assume a central role for the nurse in the provision of ambulatory care.[19]

In 1971, a national conference was convened to discuss the question of assistance to the physician. Consensus was reached at this conference that the registered nurse is the most logical worker to fill the role of physician's assistant.[20] In effect, the decision was reached not to go the route that had been followed in the United States—perhaps because Canada had no returning military veterans, but more likely because of Canada's exceptionally high supply of nurses (active and inactive)—a ratio of one nurse per 182 people.[21] Instead, the decision was made to look for assistance in primary care to professional nurses who have thorough scientific grounding, experience in working in close relationships with physicians, and a portable qualification.

In 1972, the Report of the Committee on Nurse Practitioners to the Department of National Health and Welfare of Canada recommended guidelines for developing educational programs for nurse practitioners to serve as initial contact for entrance into the system of care, to assess the individual's health status, and to determine the need for medical, nursing, and other intervention.[22] The Committee recommended that the development of nurse practitioners be regarded as the highest priority in meeting primary health-care needs; that the nurse practitioner function as part of a multidisciplinary health team; and that educational programs to train nurse practitioners be developed—as indeed they had already begun to develop at McMaster University and other places. The position was taken that since widespread acceptance of nurse practitioners depends on attitudinal change, the rate of development should be gradual.

Finally, a joint statement of the Canadian Nurses' Association and the Canadian Medical Association endorsed expanding roles for nurses, particularly for primary health care in appropriate forms of team practice.[23] The role and responsibilities proposed include well-child care and prenatal and postnatal care.

In the absence of a physician, the nurse would perform triage and initial evaluation, and also deal with emergencies. (The Northern Outpost nurse would have particularly broad functions, as in the past.) In association with a physician, the nurse would carry out procedures, provide health supervision for stable patients with chronic illness, and be responsible for supportive and social services. Training programs for nurses with extensive experience or university preparation could be short-term training, whereas nurses from two- or three-year programs might require more extensive additional training for these roles. Educational programs would be developed jointly by nursing and medical faculties. Supervised clinical practice would be a key aspect of these educational programs.

A number of Canadian studies have documented the effectiveness of nurse practitioners in providing health care. One study deserves special mention. From July 1971 to July 1972, in a large suburban Ontario practice of two family physicians who had been unable to accept new patients for two years, a randomized, controlled trial was conducted to assess the effects of substituting nurse practitioners for physicians in providing primary care.[24] In this carefully designed study involving nearly 5,000 patients, the care provided by nurse practitioners was found to be safe and effective. Not only could increased numbers of patients be seen, but the participation of nurse practitioners contributed to improved physician care because of the stimulating interchange between physicians and nurses. The study suggested, further, that if appropriate financial arrangements were made these might serve as an inducement to physicians to employ nurse practitioners and, at the same time, result in lower overall costs of care. Acknowledging that neither the concept of the nurse practitioner nor its evaluation is new, the Canadian study pointed to Outpost nurses who "have established an enviable record of clinical accomplishment in isolated areas in the Canadian North and Maritime provinces."[25]

Despite the thorough consideration given by health policy makers to developing a nurse practitioner in Canada along the lines of the American nurse practitioner, and despite the favorable experience with nurse practitioners in team practice with physicians in Ontario, the nurse practitioner movement has not grown in Canada. Saskatchewan undertook some demonstration projects involving nurse practitioners in rural areas, and Manitoba stationed a few specially trained nurses in rural clinics, but a few swallows do not make a summer. Except for the Outpost nurses in the Far North, Canadian nurses have not assumed the functions of diagnosis and treatment in primary care. Rather the Canadian strategy has been to expand the role of the nurse in performing a wide variety of *procedures* and to rely on doctors for the functions of diagnosis and treatment. In line with this approach, Departments of Family or Community Medicine in Canadian medical schools have been strengthened to increase the numbers and qualifications of family physicians.

NURSING FUNCTIONS IN BELGIUM

There are two levels of basic nursing education in Belgium.[26] The higher-level nurse, called a "technical" nurse, is prepared in a three-year program leading to a diploma. The lower-level nurse, called a "vocational" nurse, is trained in a two- or three-year program leading to a certificate. The higher-level nurse must meet the conditions for university entrance and takes two years of general nursing study and then a third year specialized in various fields—midwifery, hospital nursing, pediatric nursing, psychiatric nursing, and social nursing. Postbasic education is available for both levels, and in 1975 the first advanced degree program in nursing in Western Europe (except for the United Kingdom and Poland) was started in Belgium.

The issue of nursing functions and law became quite a live issue in Belgium in 1971, when Belgian nurses organized themselves to conduct an inquiry among doctors on the subject of nursing functions. In interviews with doctors, nurses asked whether they could properly perform certain specific procedures. The doctors replied, in essence, that nurses could do all these procedures perfectly, that they did them every day, and, in fact, that without nurses' doing these procedures the hospitals would not be able to function.[27] But the tasks listed were all functions that nurses were not legally authorized to do. For example, the Belgian law authorized nurses to do intramuscular injections but not intravenous injections; but nurses actually did intravenous injections commonly.

In 1974 a new law on the practice of nursing was enacted, which, together with regulations under the law, authorizes nurses to perform a broader scope of functions than in the past.[28] These broadened functions, however, are all procedures—some of them highly technical and sophisticated, but still procedures, not diagnosis and treatment. There is no nurse practitioner movement in Belgium in the American sense, since doctors have resisted even expanded procedural nursing functions, and a relatively large supply of family doctors meets the need for primary care.

NURSING FUNCTIONS IN NORWAY

All registered nurses in Norway are prepared in three-year nursing schools independent of hospitals, but usually adjacent to the hospitals where the clinical training is provided.[29] Highly advanced nursing specialists are trained in public health nursing, nurse midwifery, nurse anesthesia, clinical fields, administration, and teaching.

Although nurses play many roles in most countries, in Norway they perform roles that would generally be performed by physicians in the United States, as illustrated by the considerable use of nurse anesthetists in hospitals and of nurse midwives, who handle all normal deliveries. The public health nurse works with the District Doctor (who serves both as public health officer paid by the government and as general practitioner reimbursed from the health insurance system), doing maternal and child health services, school health work, communicable disease control, follow-up of discharged mental patients, and other public health activities. District nurses are engaged in home nursing and care of the aged, disabled, and chronically ill.

Norway assigns great responsibility to highly trained clinical nurses in pediatrics, geriatrics, and medicine-surgery and places great reliance on nurse-midwives and nurse-anesthetists. The development of health and social centers for providing ambulatory care is expanding nursing functions in the community as well. Despite this recognition of the importance of nursing in many spheres, Norway has rejected the idea of nurse practitioners and holds the view that doctors must be responsible for the primary-care functions of diagnosis and treatment, even for so-called "simple" cases. The Norwegian Nurses' Association is opposed to having nurses make medical decisions on the ground that nurses lack the requisite medical training. The Norwegian approach, therefore, is to encourage rigorous postgraduate training for general practitioners, after which a special title, "General Practitioner, D.N.L.F.," is authorized. General practitioners with this special qualification in family medicine are entitled to higher fees under the health insurance scheme as partial compensation for the time spent in postgraduate training.

NURSING FUNCTIONS IN POLAND

Poland has only one level of nurse—the fully qualified graduate nurse, trained either in a five-year lyceum program that combines nurse's training with secondary education or in a two-year postmatriculation program for students who have completed university entrance requirements.[30] Poland no longer trains any assistant or second-level nurses, and most of the assistant nurses trained in the past are enrolled in educational programs to become fully qualified nurses. In line with its efforts to improve nursing education, Poland has established four-year master's degree programs for academic training of graduate nurses for administration, teaching, and clinical nursing. The first program was established in 1969, Poland being the first nation on the European continent to provide graduate training in nursing.

While the functions of Polish nurses in hospitals and the community are very broad, nurses are not involved in diagnostic and therapeutic decisions, and there is no plan to assign them these functions, which are considered medical functions. In the years following World War II, when the country was devastated and the supply of doctors and nurses decimated, Poland trained a second-level doctor—the *feldsher*—to bring care to its suffering urban and rural people.

Feldshers were trained in two- or three-year programs (following grade 11 or grade 9, respectively) in public health prevention, general medicine, obstetrics, pediatrics, and minor surgery, and they filled an important gap until Poland succeeded in training thousands of new doctors. By 1958, however, the supply of doctors was adequate, and training of *feldshers* was ended. Just as Poland determined that all nurses should be fully qualified, so it rejected continued training of a second-level doctor. This experience explains the lack of any movement in Poland corresponding to the nurse practitioner movement in the United States.

INSIGHTS FOR THE UNITED STATES

In all five countries studied, the functions of the fully trained nurse have expanded over the years. As medical and surgical procedures have become increasingly complex, the nurse has assumed responsibility for certain clinical procedures formerly carried out by doctors in all countries. Nurses have also taken on a large role in ambulatory care in the community, providing public health, psychosocial, and curative ambulatory services on a broader scale than in the past. The countries in the study also train and place great reliance on nurses for specialized functions. They serve as nurse-midwives, nurse-anesthetists, psychiatric nurses, and nurses specially qualified for the routine and preventive examination of babies and for counseling of mothers.

This expansion in functions and use of nurse specialists is in substantial accord with developments in the United States, where nursing functions have been expanding with improved education and higher technology over the years. Although we do not use nurse-midwives and nurse-anesthetists as widely as the countries in the study do, our highly sophisticated nurses in the clinical specialties, public health, rehabilitation, and geriatrics reflect the same trend toward increased responsibility for technical and psychosocial functions in patient care.

The significant difference between these countries and the United States, however, is that the expanded role for nurses in the countries in the study relates to nursing *procedures* and does not include responsibility for diagnostic and therapeutic decisions. In the United States, on the other hand, development of the nurse practitioner—and the amendment of the nursing and medical practice acts to authorize functioning of the nurse practitioner—expands the role of the nurse to include diagnosis and treatment of patients in primary care. The rationale is that the nurse is trained to diagnose and handle "simple" diagnoses, but also works under protocols and with supervision.

The explanation for this important difference lies primarily in the supply of primary-care physicians in the other countries as opposed to that in the United States. In the countries of the study, 40 to 50 percent of the doctors engaged in clinical practice are generalists, as compared with fewer than 20 percent in the United States. This single fact may well explain the impetus in the United States to develop nurse practitioners as doctor substitutes, while the other countries have placed their emphasis on increasing the numbers and quality of their general practitioners.

With enactment of the Health Professions Educational Assistance Act of 1976, the United States took a deliberate step to use federal funding for medical education to encourage training of physicians for primary care. A medical school's eligibility for capitation grants is conditional on its having a certain and increasing percentage of filled first-year positions in direct or affiliated medical residency programs in the primary-care fields of internal medicine, family medicine, or general pediatrics.

While it is too early to know whether the proportion of physicians in primary care can be substantially increased by this and other measures, this change in policy to use financing of medical education not simply to increase the number of doctors but to change the proportion of generalists and specialists will very likely have a bearing on the future of the nurse practitioner. Already there is some question about the future of the pediatric nurse practitioner, for example. Although the first training program was launched more than a decade ago, in 1965, a review of the experience concludes that

> there is insufficient evidence to date that the public's health needs have been served better by the PNP. No study is available that outlines the PNP's work history beyond the early period of exciting pioneering and adaption.[31]

Serious questions have been raised about the soundness of the nurse practitioner approach in the United States on the ground that it tends to create a second-class system of care for the poor.[32] It is well known that nurse practitioners work in substantial numbers in rural areas and serve the poor and minority groups in these settings.[33] In fact, the Rural Health Clinic Services Act of 1977 encourages the employment of nurse practitioners and physicians' assistants in rural areas by authorizing reimbursement by Medicare and Medicaid for rural health services provided by physicians' assistants and nurse practitioners in accordance with state laws.[34] This policy is justified as compensating for physician shortages in rural areas. By implication, physicians are thereby relieved of social responsibility for care of the disadvantaged—a concept that may not be socially or politically tolerated for very long.

Evidence is also emerging that nurse practitioners are used to a significant degree to provide medical care to minority groups in urban locations and in public clinics.[35] (Actually, the Rural Health Clinic Services Act authorizes reimbursement of nurse practitioners and physicians' assistants in urban areas on a demonstration basis.) In a nationwide study of 8,905 patients seen by 356 family nurse practitioners during three months of 1977, half of the FNPs were located in public clinic settings, where they saw proportionately more minority groups than FNPs in private clinic settings. These findings led the authors to conclude that "there is a strong likelihood that a high percentage of FNPs will continue to find employment in publicly financed settings."[36]

It should be emphasized here that criticism of using nurse practitioners as physician substitutes in primary care applies to industrialized countries and not to impoverished less-developed countries. Industrialized countries presumably have the resources to train more physicians for primary care, whereas developing countries generally regard physician substitutes as a "transitional solution" until the number of doctors can be increased.[37]

In this connection, it is noteworthy that in the report of the world's first international conference on primary care, held at Alma-Ata, U.S.S.R., in September 1978, there was no reference to nurse practitioners. It was recognized that developing countries had to make use of personnel less fully trained than physicians, but the Alma-Ata conference apparently gave no attention to the use of nurse practitioners and physician's assistants in industrialized countries for providing primary care.

While there is growing concern about the equity and soundness of using nurse practitioners as physician substitutes for diagnosis and treatment in primary care, there is general agreement that the nurse practitioner is thoroughly qualified to perform many technical procedures requiring a high degree of skill. These functions of the nurse practitioner may be performed in clinical association with a physician or may be independent functions—for example, in family planning services.[38] The consensus in the United States on this point is shared by the countries in the study, where great responsibility for performance of highly sophisticated technical procedures is assigned to nurses.

It was sound, therefore, to amend American nursing practice acts to authorize nurses to perform expanded functions for which they are well qualified. The various methods used to modernize nursing practice acts in the United States, and to authorize delegation of expanded functions to nurses, described so effectively by Bonnie Bullough elsewhere in this volume, were a response to this urgent need. Changes in nursing legislation were long overdue.

Is it sound, however, to use nurse practitioners in the country with the world's greatest resources to provide primary care (essentially for the poor) because of insufficient numbers of primary doctors and geographic maldistribution of those whom we do have? This movement to use nurse practitioners for diagnosis and treatment in primary care may well represent a social philosophy contrary to the goal of equity in health services and a serious departure from the principles of American democracy.

REFERENCES

1. See N. Hershey, *Expanded Roles for Professional Nurses,* 3 J. NURS. ADMIN. 30 (November–December 1973).
2. See J. C. H. Dewdney, AUSTRALIAN HEALTH SERVICES (1972).

3. See J. E. F. Hastings, *Federal-Provincial Insurance for Hospital and Physician's Care in Canada*, 4 INT. J. HEALTH SERV. (November 1971).
4. See Jozef Van Langendonck, *The European Experience in Social Health Insurance*, SOCIAL SECURITY BULLETIN 21–30 (July 1973).
5. Karl Evang, HEALTH SERVICES IN NORWAY (1969).
6. Milton I. Roemer and Ruth Roemer, HEALTH MANPOWER IN THE SOCIALIST HEALTH CARE SYSTEM OF POLAND, Ch. I (1977).
7. Milton I. Roemer and Ruth Roemer, HEALTH MANPOWER IN THE CHANGING AUSTRALIAN HEALTH SERVICES SCENE, Chs. III and IV (1976).
8. Royal Australian Nursing Federation and the National Florence Nightingale Committee of Australia, SURVEY REPORT ON THE WASTAGE OF GENERAL TRAINED NURSES FROM NURSING IN AUSTRALIA (1967).
9. See, for example, Nurses' Board of Western Australia, *Policy on the Role of the Nurse*, 3 AUS. NURS. J. 4, at 43–44 (October 1973).
10. S. Sax, MEDICAL CARE IN THE MELTING POT, AN AUSTRALIAN REVIEW 50 (1972).
11. Dewdney, *supra*, 255–56.
12. EXPANSION OF MEDICAL EDUCATION, Report of the Committee on Medical Education to the Australian Universities Commission (Peter Karmel, Chmn, 1973).
13. Milton I. Roemer and Ruth Roemer, HEALTH MANPOWER POLICY UNDER NATIONAL HEALTH INSURANCE—THE CANADIAN EXPERIENCE, Chs. III and IV (September 1977).
14. See D. Morgan, *The Future Expanded Role of the Nurse*, CAN. HOSP. 75(1972).
15. REPORT OF THE COMMITTEE ON THE HEALING ARTS (Ontario), Vol. 2 (1970).
16. V. V. Murray, NURSING IN ONTARIO, A STUDY FOR THE COMMITTEE ON THE HEALING ARTS (1970).
17. REPORT OF THE COMMISSION OF INQUIRY ON HEALTH AND SOCIAL WELFARE, Vol. IV (Government of Quebec, 1970).
18. HEALTH CARE IN NOVA SCOTIA, A NEW DIRECTION FOR THE SEVENTIES, THE REPORT OF THE NOVA SCOTIA COUNCIL OF HEALTH 73–76 (1972).
19. THE COMMUNITY HEALTH CENTRE IN CANADA, REPORT OF THE STUDY ON COMMUNITY HEALTH CENTRES PRESENTED TO THE MINISTERS OF HEALTH (John E.F. Hastings, Study Director, July 1972).
20. MINISTRY OF NATIONAL HEALTH AND WELFARE NATIONAL CONFERENCE ON ASSISTANCE TO THE PHYSICIAN, THE COMPLEMENTARY ROLES OF THE PHYSICIAN AND THE NURSE (1972).
21. *Nursing in Canada: From Pioneering History to a Modern Federation*, 15 INT. NURS. REV. 1 at 29 (1968). This ratio compares with the ratio of one nurse per 300 population in the United States. See U.S. Dept. of Health, Education, and Welfare, HEALTH RESOURCES STATISTICS, HEALTH MANPOWER AND HEALTH FACILITIES, 1971 (1972).
22. REPORT OF THE COMMITTEE ON NURSE PRACTITIONERS TO THE DEPARTMENT OF NATIONAL HEALTH AND WELFARE, CANADA (April 1972).
23. *The Expanded Role of the Nurse: A Joint Statement of CNA/CMA*, CAN. NURSE 23–25 (May, 1973).
24. W. Spitzer, D. Sackett, J. Sibley, R. Roberts, D. Kergin, B. Hackett, and A. Olynich. The Burlington Randomized Trial of the Nurse Practitioner, 290 NEW ENGL. J. MED. 251 (January 31, 1974); see W. Spitzer, D. Kergin, M. Yoshida, W. Russell, B. Hackett, and C. Goldsmith, *Nurse Practitioners in Primary Care III. The Southern Ontario Randomized Trial*, 108 CAN. MED. ASSOC. J. 1,005 (April 21, 1973).
25. Spitzer *et al.*, *supra*, 251; see also C. Keith, *What is Outpost Nursing?* 41 CAN NURSE (September 1971).

26. Milton I. Roemer and Ruth Roemer, HEALTH MANPOWER POLICIES IN THE BELGIAN HEALTH CARE SYSTEM, Chs. III and IV (1977).
27. Personal communication from Dr. Josef Van Langendonck, Institute of Social Security, Catholic University of Leuven, Belgium.
28. *Loi relative à l'art de soigner,* December 20, 1974.
29. Milton I. Roemer and Ruth Roemer, MANPOWER IN THE HEALTH CARE SYSTEM OF NORWAY, Chs. III and IV (1977).
30. Milton I. Roemer and Ruth Roemer, HEALTH MANPOWER IN THE SOCIALIST HEALTH CARE SYSTEM OF POLAND, Chs. III and IV (1977).
31. Bernard P. Schachtel, *The Pediatric Nurse Practitioner: Origins and Challenges* 16 MEDICAL CARE 121 at 1,025 (December 1978).
32. Milton I. Roemer, *Primary Care and Physician Extenders in Affluent Countries,* 7 INT'L. J. HEALTH SVCS. 4 at 545–55 (1977); Milton Terris, *False Starts and Lesser Alternatives,* 53, BULL. N.Y. ACAD. MED. 1 at 129–140 (January–February 1977).
33. Judith Sullivan, Christy Z. Dachelet, Harry A. Stultz, and Marie Henry, *The Rural Nurse Practitioner: A Challenge and a Response,* 68 AM. J. PUB. HEALTH 10 at 972–76 (October 1978).
34. P.L. 95–210.
35. Betty L. Pesznecker and Mary Ann Draye, *Family Nurse Practitioners in Primary Care: A Study of Practiced and Patients,* 68 AM. J. PUB. HEALTH 10 at 977–80 (October 1978).
36. *Ibid,* 979–80.
37. Milton I. Roemer, *Primary Care . . . , supra,* 550.
38. Ruth Roemer, *The Nurse Practitioner in Family Planning Services: Law and Practice,* 6 FAMILY PLANNING/POPULATION REPORTER 3 at 28–33 (June 1977).

12 Nurses in Private Practice

PATRICIA J. LEWIS

In isolated parts of the country it has not been unusual to find a nurse practicing alone. With no health-care agencies readily available, the nurse has taken on the responsibility of providing nursing care for the people in the community. In 1971, M. Lucille Kinlein hung out her shingle in an area where there were physicians and other health-care agencies.[1] That was the first recorded instance of a nurse in an urban area who practiced on a fee-for-service basis and was responsible only to herself and her clients, not to a doctor or an organization, for the care she gave. Since that time an increasing number of nurses have also opened their own practices, either alone or in groups with other nurses.

The reasons the nurses give for taking that step center primarily around the frustrations of trying to work within an institutional framework, and, for many of them, a desire to work in a more expanded role.[2] The nurses feel that institutional work requires too much time and energy to keep the organization running, with too little left for working directly with clients. A feeling of powerlessness results from their lack of influence on policies that govern nursing care delivery and from giving nursing care within the confines of a rigid structure.

At the present time it is difficult for many people to enter the health-care system because the point of entry is through physicians and many physicians are too busy to accept more patients. However, an even greater barrier is created by the physician's role: the diagnosis and treatment of illness. Many health-care consumers do not need these services, but do need health-maintenance services, information about life events, or education about illnesses which have already been diagnosed and are under treatment. This problem could be greatly lessened by having as the point of entry into the health-care system primary-care nurses working in an expanded role. As early as 1969, Charles Lewis predicted the possibility of nurses serving this function by going into private practice and using physician services as a backup.[3]

There are also some sociological factors that have influenced the movement of nurses toward private practice. The first private nursing practices started in the early 1970s—about the same time the feminist movement made great strides toward greater independence and recognition of women as individuals. Because the nursing profession is made up primarily of women, the status of nurses as professionals closely paralleled that of other women in our society. As women demanded legal and cultural equality, they began to reach out more into areas that had been thought of primarily as men's areas—such as opening an independent business or practice. At the same time, nursing was rejecting its image of "assisting" the medical profession and asserting its position as a profession capable of making independent decisions for which members were willing to be held accountable. The frustration of not being able to do this within an institutional framework has contributed to some nurses' desire to work outside that restrictive structure.

Although in the past physicians tended to come from the higher social classes and nurses from the middle and working classes, this is less true today.[4] It can be observed that nurses from upper-middle- and upper-class backgrounds are becoming very prevalent. Many physicians are not aware of this change and continue to relate to nurses as social, as well as professional, subordinates, causing discomfort and anger in the nurses. This may be another factor in nurses' desire to work less closely with physicians.

THE EXPANDED ROLE

The expanded role many nurses are seeking can be defined in the terms formulated by a committee of the Wisconsin Nurses' Association:

> The expanded role refers to enlargement of one's role in utilizing all aspects of problem-solving processes: delineation of the field of the problem, assessing and implementing care, and evaluating outcomes. The result is a qualitative change in the nurse's delivery of patient care services.
>
> Role expansion is based on theory, utilizing natural and behavioral sciences which give direction to nursing action. Knowledge and skill are applied to decision-making, as well as to performance.
>
> A nurse functioning in an expanded role acts on knowledge that reflects theory, e.g., determining the need for a pap smear and dealing constructively with the behavioral factors which inhibit the patient from taking the recommended action.
>
> The nurse assumes or shares responsibility for the health care services delivered to the patient. Plans and goals are established by the nurse or in consultation with other health care professionals.[5]

Nurses in private practice have expressed satisfaction about having full authority over their practices and assuming all the responsibility for the quality of the care they give. Their acceptance of that responsibility has earned them respect from many other professionals, who treat them as equals.

THE PATTERNS OF PRACTICE

Most nurses in private practice follow similar patterns in providing care to their clients. They see clients in a variety of settings—office, home, hospital, nursing home. The nurse constructs a data base using a health history and a complete or partial physical examination, then, with the client, compiles a problem list and formulates a plan for nursing care or referral to another health-care provider. On following visits the nurse will check on progress and discuss ways to solve problems that may have come up. If the need is indicated, some nurses will recommend over-the-counter drugs and initiate laboratory tests. Most nurses receive few, if any, referrals from physicians, but other professionals, friends, and clients spread the word.

A few nurses work only as consultants. However, many of them also act as health-care providers or educators of other health-care providers.

There are several ways of organizing the business structure of a practice. The commonest are briefly described below.

In an individual or *sole proprietorship*, one individual (or a married couple, considered one person for this purpose by the government) has complete responsibility for the business, but may hire employees or associates on salary. The owner is responsible for management, policy determination, and financial matters but may let employees share in the decision-making process and profits. All income from the business belongs to the owner (rather than to the business) and is taxed by the federal government at the same rate as individual income from any other job would be. This is not always a disadvantage, because business loss, which is to be expected in the first years, is also passed on to the owner, who may use it to offset income from other sources and thus lower income tax liability. The owner is personally liable for all aspects of the business, including the actions of its employees. If a successful lawsuit is filed against the practice or if the practice has other financial problems, the owner could lose not only the business property but also personal property. The sole proprietorship ends when the owner dissolves the practice or dies, i.e., it cannot be passed on to another person.

A *general partnership* comprises two or more individuals who agree to share ownership in a business for profit. Each co-owner is responsible for his or her share of the management and liabilities of the practice. The partnership may also employ others who are not partners. This form of organization has the advantage of informal structure and flexible management. Additional professionals in the practice increase the potential for greater income. This structure also has some disadvantages. Each partner may be required to use personal assets to cover liabilities if the partnership assets are inadequate to meet the business obligations. If any partner is found by the courts to be guilty of a negligent act performed while practicing in the partnership, all of the partners are responsible to the injured party. The profit is shared by the partners and is taxed as personal income. Any partner has the authority to sign contracts which will then bind all of the partners. The partnership dissolves if one partner leaves.

A *limited partnership* has "general partners," who have the same risks as those in a general partnership, and "limited partners," who are sheltered from personal liability except to the extent of their investment in the practice. Limited partners are not permitted to participate in the management of the business affairs of the partnership.

A *business corporation* is a legal entity which has the same power as a natural person to perform acts within its stated purpose. It is managed by a board of directors and a group of shareholders. All persons working in the corporation are employees. Recognition of the corporation by the law as a separate entity gives this organizational structure several advantages. The corporation can engage in legal transactions, e.g., owning property, contracting to do consulting work, etc. The members (shareholders) have limited liability, so if the corporation is successfully sued, the individual shareholders would not lose more than they have invested in shares. (However, it should be kept in mind that in a malpractice suit *both* the corporation and the nurse could be sued as separate individuals.) The corporation has perpetual existence even though individual members may leave the practice.

Unlike other forms of business, the corporation has an income which is recognized as being separate from that of the individual members. Consequently, the corporation is taxed on its profits (at a lower rate than an individual would be), and the individual members are taxed only on the money they take out of the corporation. When the profits are distributed, they are divided among the shareholders based on the number of shares each owns. A corporation is allowed to offer tax-free fringe benefits to its members, including profit-sharing plans, sick pay, medical reimbursement, and pension plans.

The corporation also has some disadvantages. The rules and regulations specified by law lead to a more formal organization with less flexible management. (However, this can be minimized by careful planning in the organizational stages.) The income of the corporation is taxed, and the dividends are also taxed when they are reported as income on the individual shareholder's income tax return. This means that tax is being paid twice on the same money; this can be avoided by having the corporation's income and losses passed through to its shareholders by a process called Subchapter S election.

Another type of corporation is the *professional* or *service corporation*. This has many of the same characteristics as a business corporation, but all members are licensed as members of the same profession. All members are jointly liable for practice errors made by employees of the corporation, but in matters not connected with the professional aspects of the practice the liability of the shareholder is limited to the amount he or she has invested in the practice. The professional corporation is dissolved when there are no corporate members licensed to practice its profession in the state.

The *unincorporated association* is not as popular as it was in the years before professional corporations existed. This form of business structure is used mostly in states where there are legal barriers restricting the use of professional corporations. An unincorporated association is organized without a charter or process of incorporation for the pursuit of some specific purpose. It is formed according to articles of association, which are signed by the original associates and acknowledged by future members.[6]

An association has many of the features of the corporation, such as centralized management, continuity of organization, and transferability of interests. As in a partnership, each member is personally liable for both the professional and business obligations of the association. Unlike a corporation, the association is not considered a separate legal entity distinct from the members. Usually, its contracts cannot be held in the name of the association and the members must join together in pursuing any legal action for the association.[7]

The type of business organization chosen by nurses depends on how the characteristics of that form meet their needs. The wisest course of action to take when forming any type of business is to become familiar with the advantages and disadvantages of the different forms of organization and then to obtain the services of a good attorney and certified public accountant. There are many legal and practical aspects of the business that can make their assistance important.

There are relatively fewer nurse practitioners than other types of nurses in private practice. This is probably because intrinsic job satisfaction is high for nurse practitioners.[8] They find their jobs challenging and rewarding because they are encouraged to use a greater percentage of their skills in working with clients. This is particularly true for those who follow a caseload of patients over an extended period and have a practice which focuses more on nursing than on delegated medical tasks.

Nurse practitioners state that they prefer to work closely with physicians for several reasons. They need the legal protection the physician can provide, because they often work in the areas of diagnosis and treatment, which have been designated as medical practice by law in many states and can legally be done only under a physician's supervision. By working closely with physicians who treat them as colleagues as they learn and practice, many nurse practitioners achieve prestige, challenge, and opportunity for creativity similar to what nurses in private practice are seeking.

FACTORS LIMITING PRIVATE PRACTICE

Although the number of nurses engaging in private practice is increasing, a number of factors tend to inhibit this movement. First, there are the difficulties associated with running a business—balancing books, paying rent and taxes, completing government forms, hiring help, etc.—involving business knowledge that many nurses do not have and do not want to have. If their practice is not large enough to support ancillary help, nurses find themselves functioning in secretarial and housekeeping roles as well as nursing. Most nurses find it much easier to let someone else worry about the mechanics of making the practice run so that they can concentrate on client care.

There are also risks involved, which some nurses are not willing to accept. One of these is the risk of rejection by other health-care professionals (nurses as well as physicians) who believe that private practice is not an acceptable way for nurses to work. Many believe that it is not legal for a nurse to work independently, but none of the nurse practice acts require a nurse to work under supervision.

Another risk is the financial one. In addition to the initial expense involved in establishing a business, nurses must support their practice as it slowly grows to the point where it can be self-supporting. This frequently takes years. Nurses in private practice would find the financial going easier if health insurance companies, Medicare, and Medicaid would cover their fees. In many instances government agencies and insurance companies will not cover nursing fees unless the service has been ordered by a physician. There have been some encouraging changes in this area in the last few years. An increasing number of private insurance companies are covering services provided by nurses in private practice. A few states have passed legislation requiring insurance companies to make third-party payments directly to nurses.

Changes in federal Medicare regulations now make it possible for nurse practitioners in rural, under-served areas to be reimbursed for many of their services. To qualify, nurse practitioners must arrange for a physician to provide or supervise medical services for the clients, but they may own the rural health clinic in which they work.[9] While this legislation does not cover nurses in urban areas, it does indicate a possible move in that direction.

Institutions and physicians who employ nurses offer them some legal assistance under the *respondeat superior* law, which states that employers are responsible for the wrongful acts of their employees, in certain cases, so that both can be sued by an injured person.[10] Consequently, for their own protection, most employers set up strictly defined limits within which nurses can practice. If they work within these limits, many nurses feel, their chances of getting into trouble for practicing outside the legal definition of nursing are minimized. All nurses must become very familiar with the nurse practice act in their state and the court's interpretation of it, if any. As long as they practice within the limits outlined by the law, their risk of being accused of practicing in areas not legally open to nurses is minimized.

Many hospitals have no mechanism (or desire) for allowing nonemployee nurses access to their patients or charts. Some hospitals will not even permit nurses in private practice to talk about the cure of their patients to staff nurses. This presents a barrier to the comprehensive, continuing care the nurse in private practice is trying to offer. The hospital's administration is concerned about its liability for the actions of the nurse. Although the number is small, an increasing number of hospitals are developing a procedure for granting staff privileges to nonemployee nurses. These privileges frequently do not allow the nurse to admit clients, but will allow them access to their clients, the clients' records, and the staff nurses providing the clients' care.

Solo practice can be professionally stifling for the nurse. The knowledge that is gained from the informal give-and-take in practice with other professionals is not there. It is not as easy to get information when the nurse is unsure about what to do with a client or wants some one to audit the practice. Private practitioners find it difficult to get someone to cover their practice when they are away. These problems are virtually eliminated by a group practice.

THE FUTURE OF PRIVATE PRACTICE

Changes in state and federal law make it increasingly easy for nurses to work in private practice in an expanded role. Consumers are becoming increasingly knowledgeable and curious about health care. They are also becoming aware of their right to continuous, personalized care offered in an atmosphere that encourages them to ask and to learn about what is right and wrong with their health. When they become aware of it, they are accepting of nurses offering this service. I believe that this tendency will encourage nurses to continue to go into private practice in increasing numbers. In addition, since nurses recognize the need for patients to receive care provided by other disciplines as well, I predict that they will be forming multidisciplinary group practices. The broad orientation these practices can provide increases their chances of success.

REFERENCES

1. M. L. Kinlein, *Independent Nurse Practitioner*, 20 NURS. OUTLOOK 22–24 (January 1972).
2. Kinlein, *supra;* B. Agree, *Beginning an Independent Nursing Practice*, 74 AM. J. NURS. 636–42 (April 1974); R. Rafferty & J. Carner, *Nursing Consultants, Inc.—A Corporation*, 21 NURS. OUTLOOK 232–35 (April 1973); J. Greenidge, A. Zimmern, & M. Kohnke, *Community Nurse Practitioners—A Partnership*, 21 NURS. OUTLOOK 228–31 (April, 1973); C. Koltz, Personal correspondence (October 29, 1973); V. Sheward, *A New Long Island Concept: Independent Nurse*, NEWSDAY (August 13, 1973); A. Robinson & M. L. Kinlein, *Independent Nurse-Practitioner*, 35 RN 40–44 (January 1972).
3. C. Lewis, *The Team Is in the Doctor's Bag*, paper presented at the meeting of the National League for Nursing in Detroit (May 21, 1969).
4. E. Rosinski, *Social Classes of Medical Students*, 193 J. AM. MED. ASSOC. 89 (July 12, 1965); C. Hughes et al., *Twenty Thousand Nurses Tell Their Story* (1958).
5. Wisconsin Nurses' Association Ad Hoc Committee to Define and Promote the Extended and or Expanded Role of the Nurse in the State of Wisconsin.

6. Center for Research in Ambulatory Health Care Administration, THE ORGANIZATION AND DEVELOPMENT OF A MEDICAL GROUP PRACTICE (1976).
7. *Ibid*.
8. B. Bullough, *Is the Nurse Practitioner Role a Source of Increased Work Satisfaction?* 23 NURS. RES. 25 (January–February 1974).
9. Health Care Financing Administration, HEW, *Rural Health Clinics: Conditions for Certification*, 43 FEDERAL REGISTER 5,373–77 (February 8, 1978).
10. H. Creighton, LAW EVERY NURSE SHOULD KNOW (1975); R. Zahourek, D. Leone, & F. Lang, CREATIVE HEALTH SERVICES (1976); A. Jacox & C. Norris, eds., ORGANIZING FOR INDEPENDENT NURSING PRACTICE (1977).

13 The Evolving Mental Health Clinical Nurse Specialist in Private Practice

CORRINE L. HATTON

One of the earliest evolving roles for nurses was that of the clinical nurse specialist, also known as nurse clinician and clinical nurse, which developed in the early 1960s in response to needs expressed by both patients and nurses. Traditionally, as nurses advanced in the hierarchy of nursing they entered more and more into administration or teaching, drawing further and further away from patients. Even those who tried to remain at the bedside found that under the economics of hospital administration, bedside care was often given over to aides or others not particularly skilled in meeting the medical-psychosocial needs of the patients. Inevitably, patients complained about the hierarchical structure of nursing, while nurses expressed frustration about pushing paper and attending committee meetings.

In an effort to deal with some of these criticisms, several schools of nursing worked out graduate curricula designed to give special training in the clinical specialties to nurses who would then work with patients and their families as well as teaching and consulting with staff nurses, in the process enhancing and increasing the quality of nursing care.

The clinical nurse specialization was designed as a master's-level position, though not all such specialists at first held master's degrees. In 1974, however, the ANA Congress for Nursing Practice, at the ANA Convention, presented a definition of the clinical nurse specialist which required that such specialists hold a master's degree. Subsequently various divisions have adopted similar definitions. The ANA Division on Psychiatric and Mental Health Nursing Practice, for example, has published a "Statement on Psychiatric and Mental Health Nursing Practice," clearly delineating the differences between the generalist and specialist and requiring as a minimum for the specialist a master's degree in psychiatric and mental health nursing.[1]

Though clinical nurse specialists have had difficulty in establishing a special identity, the problems for those in psychiatric and mental health seem to have been less severe than those in medical-surgical or maternal-child health. One possible explanation for this is that the practice of psychiatry is less "absolute" than the rest of medical practice and there is an overlapping of roles, with psychiatrists, psychologists, nurses, and social workers using similar if not identical treatment modalities, especially in community mental health centers, where the same kind of expertise is expected from everyone.

Another possible explanation is that in the mental health field it is not always clear who is in charge of the patient. Since psychiatrists cannot be on duty constantly, much of the actual therapy has to be left to others who have greater contact with the patient. Nurse specialists in the mental health field have been able to expand their role to the extent that some have independent practices.

Change has been rapid; as late as 1960 there was considerable concern over whether psychiatric nurses should engage in psychotherapy* and whether they would still be nurses if they did so. In a 1962 article, J. A. Schmahl claimed that

> in the competition for autonomy and prestige and in fear of being plunged into therapeutic nihilism, everyone, i.e., psychiatrists, psychologists, social workers, and now psychiatric nurses—is scrambling to practice psychotherapy.

He added that

> psychotherapy is an autonomous specialty, as is nursing, and I believe it is impossible for the psychiatric nurse to become a practicing psychotherapist and at the same time retain her identity as a nurse—in attempting to do so, she becomes a kind of two-headed creature who is neither nurse nor therapist and thereby relegates herself to the position of second-class citizen.[2]

The controversy continued for several years [3]

Even while the controversy raged, education institutions included a greater emphasis on psychotherapy in their graduate nursing programs, and more and more nurses began to function as psychotherapists. By 1972 Terrence Calnen could conclude that

> because of their improved education, their ongoing contact with the patient, and their capacity to intervene in his interpersonal conduct and manipulate his environment, psychiatric nurses have joined other professionals as therapists.[4]

Others such as Suzanne Lego[5] and Gertrude B. Ujhely[6] emphasized the role of psychiatric nurses by pointing out their differences from and similarities to other psychotherapists. Psychiatric nurses with advanced degrees began to set up

---

*The definition of "psychotherapy" as used here is from the ANA "Statement on Psychiatric and Mental Health Nursing Practice" and refers to "all generally accepted and respected methods of therapy, specifically including individual therapy (e.g., insight therapy, brief goal-oriented therapy, behavioral therapy), group therapy, and family therapy. Psychotherapy denotes a formally structured, contractual relationship between the therapist and client(s) for explicit purpose of effecting change in the client(s). (p.15)

private practices as counselors and therapists, and the literature dealing with mental health clinical nurse specialists changed its focus from attempts to justify the presence of nurses in psychotherapy to such issues as responsibility and accountability,[7] transition,[8] organization,[9] and even survival as independent practitioners.[10] Changes have been rapid.[11]

Though the nurses could deal with the question of their capability to practice, their legal right to do so required legislative intervention. In 1969, Marcia Stachyra urged nurses to "begin legislative reform" which would "explicitly sanction qualified nurses doing psychotherapy."[12] In the meantime she urged the national organization to develop a certification program for clinical specialists in mental health. She warned in 1973 that

> certification by a professional association does not legally prevent uncertified persons from performing the functions, since professional associations do not have legal regulatory power.

Nonetheless, she felt, certification was a first step toward self-regulation.[13]

The ANA Council of Advanced Practitioners of Psychiatric and Mental Health Nursing held its first meeting at the 1974 ANA Convention, and one of its first orders of business was to work out specialist certification standards and examinations.[14] The Council gave its first examination in 1977 and has been giving them regularly since. Even before the 1974 meeting of the ANA, state nursing associations had begun independently to act in the field; in New Jersey, for example, certification has been carried out through the New Jersey Society of Certified Clinical Specialists in Psychiatric Nursing since 1972.[15]

But there are still many problems. One major question is how clinical nurse specialists in mental health should be differentiated from nurse psychotherapists. Gertrude Ujhely, one of the pioneers in the private practice movement, wrote in 1973 that "we shall have to differentiate the nurse psychotherapists from nurses in general and from the clinical specialist in psychiatric nursing in particular."[16] She stated that the rigorous training, supervision, and personal analysis undergone by psychotherapists could be in conflict with the education and training of clinical nurse specialists or even antithetical to their theoretical beliefs.

> I have the feeling that the reason we are not proceeding any faster with clinical specialist certification has to do with this conflict. I think we may well need two kinds of certification—one for clinical specialists in mental health-psychiatric nursing, and one for the clinical specialist who wants to practice psychotherapy.[17]

This issue has not yet been resolved.

Also not resolved is the basic legal issue; certification does not make a practice legal. It is given for expertise and excellence, but it is not a legal document, like a license, which authorizes individuals to practice psychotherapy in any state. In recent years many states have updated and revised their practice acts, but most of these laws need further revision if society is to realize the full potential for service of well-prepared clinical nurse specialists. For example, the 1974 revision of the California nurse practice act includes the following statement:

> The practice of nursing within the meaning of this chapter means those functions helping people cope with difficulties in daily living which are associated with their actual or potential health or illness problems or the treatment thereof which require a substantial amount of scientific knowledge or technical skill, and include all of the following:
>
> (a) Direct and indirect patient care services that insure the safety, comfort, personal hygiene and protection of patients; and the performance of disease prevention and restorative measures.[18]

This statement was thought to be sufficient sanction for a private practice in mental health, but more than implied sanction is needed. A specific statement in the law spelling out a nurse's right to practice counseling and psychotherapy is a necessity. Nurses who have been practicing in a psychotherapeutic role for some years have come to feel strongly that they are handicapped by not being licensed to practice counseling and psychotherapy. Psychologists and social workers have fought this battle, and nurses will have to do the same.

State licensure is needed not only for legal protection but also to enable third-party reimbursement to practitioners for counseling and psychotherapy. Currently, nurse therapists are not always able to collect reimbursement because they have no clearly specified authorization to provide these health services under the current licensure system.

Obviously there is still a lot of legislative work to be done, but there has been progress. In 1974 I wrote:

> There is a general trend among psychiatric nurses to feel that "we must get out of hospitals and into the community." Now I have no desire to tell people where they must practice. Surely many people are being seen these days outside the hospital walls. However, if we all abandon the hospitals, who, may I ask, will be left to take care of patients? And if another discipline or less trained nursing personnel take over, where does that leave patients and nurses? Let's face it—right now there is not a demand for nurse therapists, but there is an enormous demand for quality, conscientious, and concerned nursing care. Patients are crying desperately to be heard—they are shocked if they get taken care of by an RN for a whole day, but they desire that kind of strength and reassurance that an RN can give.[19]

Conditions and attitudes change; I would not make that same statement today. Quite clearly not all specialists are abandoning the hospital, and there is room for a variety of specialists, of whom psychotherapists are only one group. Those who enter psychotherapy through nursing know the physiological as well as the psychological aspects of illness and have special expertise for making home visits and for helping clients who have difficulty adjusting to chronic illness. There is a growing need for such nurse-therapists.

Legal and political problems remain. We need organization and political knowhow; we need to educate ourselves, other professionals, and the general public about changing roles, functions, and areas of expertise in nursing. This will impose considerable strain on us, but it can be done. In a few short years the mental health specialization has moved from infancy to adolescence; with perseverance it might soon enter into young adulthood.

REFERENCES

1. American Nurses' Association Division on Psychiatric and Mental Health Nursing, STATEMENT OF PSYCHIATRIC AND MENTAL HEALTH NURSING PRACTICE (1976).
2. J. A. Schmahl, *The Psychiatric Nurse and Psychotherapy,* 10 NURS. OUTLOOK 460–65 (July 1962).
3. C. R. Hartman, *The Role Fusion of Psychiatric Nursing with Psychiatry,* 7 PSYCHIATR. OPINION 7 (October 1971); J. Churchill, *An Issue: Nurses and Psychotherapy,* 5 PERSPECT. PSYCHIATR. CARE 4 at 160–62 (1967); *The Nurse as a Therapist v. Her Role in the Medical Model* and *Psychiatric Nurse v. Mental Health Worker,* 6 PERSPECT. PSYCHIATR. CARE 271–72, 288–89 (1968); J. S. Hays, *The Psychiatric Nurse as Sociotherapist,* 62 AM. J. NURS. 64–67 (June, 1962); M. S. Zaslove, J. T. Ungerleider, & M. Fuller, *The Importance of the Psychiatric Nurse: Views of Physicians, Patients, and Nurses,* 125 AM. J. PSYCHIATRY 482–86 (October, 1968).
4. T. Calnen, *Whose Agents?: A Re-evaluation of the Role of the Psychiatric Nurse in the Therapeutic Community,* 10 PERSPECT. PSYCHIATR. CARE 211–19 (1972).
5. S. Lego, *Nurse Psychotherapists: How Are We Different?* 11 PERSPECT. PSYCHIATR. CARE 144–47 (1973).
6. G. B. Ujhely, *The Nurse as Psychotherapist: What Are the Issues?* 11 PERSPECT. PSYCHIATR. CARE 155–60 (1973).
7. Laura J. Ryan, Max K. Gearhart, & Susan Simmons, *From Personal Responsibility to Professional Accountability in Psychiatric Nursing,* J. PSYCHIATR. NURS. 19–24 (June 1977).
8. Norma Alhon, *Preparing to Individuate from Team Member to Independent Practitioner,* J. PSYCHIATR. NURS. 31–32 (June 1977).
9. Ada K. Jacox, & Catherine M. Norris, eds., ORGANIZING FOR INDEPENDENT NURSING PRACTICE (1977).
10. Harriett E. Goodspeed, *The Independent Practitioner—Can It Survive?* J. PSYCHIATR. NURS. 33–36 (August 1976).
11. Sr. M. Frances Smalkowski, *A Year Later: An Independent Practitioner Looks Back,* J. PSYCHIATR. NURS. 35–36 (August 1976).
12. M. Stachyra, *Nurses, Psychotherapy and the Law,* 7 PERSPECT. PSYCHIATR. CARE 200–13 (1969).
13. M. Stachyra, *Self-Regulation through Certification,* 11 PERSPECT. PSYCHIATR. CARE, 148–54 (1973).
14. *Report of Convention,* AM. J. NURS. 1,272 (July 1974).

15. S. Rouslin, *On Certification of the Clinical Specialists in Psychiatric Nursing,* 10 PERSPECT. PSYCHIATR. CARE 201 (editorial, 1972).
16. G. B. Ujhely, *The Nurse as Psychotherapist: What Are the Issues?* 11 PERSPECT. PSYCHIATR. CARE 155–60 (1973).
17. *Ibid.*
18. CALIFORNIA BUSINESS AND PROFESSIONS CODE, Ch. 6, Art. 2, §2725.
19. C. L. Hatton, *The Mental Health Clinical Nurse Specialist in Private Practice,* in THE LAW AND THE EXPANDING NURSING ROLE, ed. B. Bullough (1975), 118–24.

14 Physician's Assistants and The Law

BONNIE BULLOUGH AND CAROL WINTER

Nurse practitioners and physician's assistants are clearly linked in the minds of most people outside those two occupations. The literature of medical sociology and public health uses such terms as "physician extenders" or "middle medical workers" to refer to the two groups collectively. Moreover, the linkage is often accepted by governmental bodies. The 1972 amendments to the Social Security Act gave the Secretary of Health, Education and Welfare the right to carry out experimental programs aimed at developing methods to reimburse nurse practitioners and physician's assistants for their services.[1] When the secretary failed to use this power, Congress moved again in 1978 to pass the Rural Health Clinics Bill (H.R. 8422), authorizing payments under Medicare and Medicaid to nurse practitioners and physician's assistants in rural clinics which met certain standards as well as in urban demonstration clinics.[2] Precedent for linking the two occupations has also appeared in state reimbursement packages. The California Department of Consumer Affairs, for example, has gone beyond the federal government with its Career Mobility Project. A task force has proposed that the state certify a new occupation called "middle-level practitioner," which would include nurse practitioners, physician's assistants, nurse midwives, and clinical pharmacists.[3]

Neither physician's assistants (P.A.s) nor nurse practitioners (N.P.s) are completely happy with this linkage. Physician's assistants tend to think of themselves as having higher status than nurse practitioners; in one attitudinal study, physician's assistants described themselves as more intelligent, aggressive, and competent than registered nurses. They saw themselves as more like the physician than the nurse.[4] On the other hand, nurse practitioners perceive themselves as better educated and more holistic in their approach to patient care than physician's assistants. Probably both are right. Physician's assistants are more likely to be men, and men tend to be accorded more status than women. Moreover, their closeness to physicians allows them to borrow more status from their physician colleagues. Nurse practitioners tend to have more years of formal schooling than physician's assistants and are better prepared to deliver the social-psychological aspects of patient care. But, in spite of these differences in the objective reality and self-image, the two occupations remain politically and practically linked, and it therefore seems prudent for both groups to learn more about each other and to be prepared to work together in the practice setting as well as on the political front. Hence this chapter on physician's assistants in a book addressed primarily to nurses.

HISTORY

The physician's assistant movement started in 1965, when Eugene Stead established a training program at Duke University. His first class included four students, all ex-corpsmen. The two-year program included basic sciences and the less complex medical skills the assistants would need in the specific practices of their prospective employers. These skills were taught in a nine-month didactic component and a 15-month clinical rotation. Although Stead's first motivation was to relieve overworked doctors of some of the simple repetitive tasks they carried out each day, in order to give them time to attend continuing education programs, he soon realized the potential of the new occupation for extending health care.[5]

The second major training program was the one-year Medex course for ex-independent-duty corpsmen, first set up in Washington State in 1969. This project was established, with federal financing, to provide high-level technical assistants for primary physicians working in the rural areas of the state, where the shortage of doctors was acute.[6] As other Medex projects were funded, the focus on primary care remained, but some were established in urban poverty areas, the other area of physician shortage. A hallmark of the Medex programs was pre-employment placement of students with preceptors who later became employers. This not only secured the student a job but allowed the projects some control over area of practice.

Shortly after the first Medex program was established, Stanford University set up a two-year physician's assistant program; a four-year program was established at Alderson-Broaddus College in West Virginia; and the University of Colorado established its five-year child associate program. By 1972, 31 programs had been started with a variety of governmental and private funding. From that time on, the Comprehensive Health Manpower Training Act became the most important source of funding for physician's assistant training. Contracts were given to programs that would (1) recruit students from medically underserved areas; (2) train them to deliver primary ambulatory care; and (3) place graduates in medically underserved areas.[7] Although it was less publicized, one of the motivations for the passage of the act seems to have been to provide a useful role for corpsmen returning from the Vietnam battlefields with a significant body of medical knowledge and skill.

However, from the beginning much of that skill was not used. The new occupation was conceptualized as limited and dependent. Physician's assistants were to perform routine technical tasks under close supervision. They were to give primary care in rural or low-income areas where there was a doctor shortage, or specialized care in those practices, such as urology and orthopedics, which included a significant component of routine tasks. Under no circumstances was this conceptualized as an occupation that might be competitive with medicine.[8] This intention to keep the occupation limited and dependent was clearly spelled out in the definition adopted by the American Medical Association House of Delegates in December 1971:

> The assistant to the primary care physician is a skilled person qualified by academic and clinical training to provide patient services under the supervision and responsibility of a Doctor of Medicine or Osteopathy, who is, in turn, responsible for the performance of that assistant. The assistant may be involved with patients of the physician in any medical setting for which the physician is responsible. The assistant will not supplant the doctor in the sphere of decision making required to establish a diagnosis and plan therapy. He will assist in gathering the data necessary to reach decisions and in implementing the therapeutic plan for the patient . . . the application of his [M.D.] knowledge toward a logical and systematic evaluation of the patients' problems and planning a program of management and therapy can only be performed by the physician.[9]

Growth of the occupation was supported by the media, which showed a lively interest in the concept. Physician's assistants appeared in several medical shows; *Time* and *Life* magazines ran articles; and newspapers around the country ran feature stories.

The medical profession organized itself to sponsor the occupation but control it in many ways. In 1972 a Joint Review Committee under the sponsorship of the Council on Medical Education developed guidelines to accredit training programs. In the same year the National Board of Medical Examiners developed a certifying examination, which was first given to 880 candidates in 1973. In 1975 this examination was turned over to the National Commission on the Certification of Physician's Assistants, a group controlled by a coalition of 14 organizations, most of them medical.[10] The examination is now administered annually to about 1,500 physician's assistants and nurse practitioners, either graduates of formal programs or informally trained.[11]

The relatively short time span from the inception of the new occupation to its entrenchment was analyzed by Sadler, who concluded that the conditions present at the beginning of the movement contributed to its remarkable success. A manpower pool—the returning corpsmen—was readily available and in need of civilian jobs; the movement was viewed as a creative solution to the health manpower shortage; and physician's assistants could provide manpower in primary and preventive medicine at a cost to the consumer considerably less than physician training and utilization.[12]

CURRENT PATTERNS

As of this writing, there are more than 50 physician's assistant training programs in operation.[13] A survey of the 1977 graduates of these programs indicates that they are predominantly male (69 percent) and from a variety of social class origins. The majority of the recruits had previous experience in some other health occupation: 54 percent were corpsmen, 22 percent medical technologists, 5 percent nurses; only 22 percent had no previous medical occupation.[14] These factors (sex, social class origin, and previous occupation) tend to vary significantly between programs; since the individual programs have unique ideologies and missions they attract different student populations.[15]

Although physician's assistants are employed in all 50 states, over a third are in the South, where many of the early training programs developed. They provide care in a variety of settings: 44 percent work in private physicians' offices (with 16 percent of this group in remote satellite clinics); 33 percent are attached to hospitals; 11 percent are in the military corps; 12 percent in clinics; and the remaining few in nursing homes, administration, industry, prisons, emergency rooms, and other health-care settings. The range of salaries was wide, with an average of $15,391 for the 1975 graduates in 1977. Less than ten percent made more than $20,000 annually. In general, the medical specialties paid more than general practice settings, and rural salaries were higher than urban ones, probably reflecting a higher level of responsibility in the rural practices.[16]

A review of the descriptive articles about the practice of physician's assistants suggests that there are two major types of practice settings which employ them. One is the primary ambulatory care setting, where they function in a role similar to that of a family nurse practitioner or a family physician, caring for patients with ordinary episodic illnesses, following patients with chronic problems, and referring cases beyond their scope of function to their physician supervisor or an appropriate specialist. Increasingly, however, P.A.s are employed in specialized medical practice settings, particularly orthopedics, urology, surgery, and emergency rooms.[17] In the specialty practices their roles overlap those of interns and technicians. For example, in one hospital neurological service, physician's assistants do admission work-ups, make daily rounds, and alternate call with the junior neurosurgical residents. They write up progress notes and discharge summaries. Their use in this role has enabled the service to reduce the number of residents in training and improve the educational experience of the remaining group by relieving them of many routine chores.[18] Another article describes the work role of a P.A. on a thoracic surgery service. In addition to routine hospital tasks, he also serves as first or second assistant in thoracic surgery, and remains in the hospital on nights when patients have had open heart surgery.[19] In one university, a P.A. is a facilitator of clinical competence in a neurosurgery course. He works in a practice laboratory with medical students who are learning to perform a neurological history and physical examination. When the course was evaluated, 97 percent of the medical students reported that he was helpful, even though his salary is only one-third that of a physician clinical faculty member.[20]

LEGAL STATUS

The problem of providing legal sanction for physician's assistants was somewhat different from the task of expanding existing nursing licensure to accommodate nurse practitioners. Nurses were already licensed, while P.A.s entered the field without a historical legal base. Moreover, they arrived at a time when licensure for all health professionals was under attack, so individual licensure was out of the question politically. In 1970 the American Medical Association and the American Hospital Association, with the support of the American Nurses Association and National League for Nursing, suggested a two-year moratorium.[21] The moratorium concept gained momentum and came out as a formal Department of Health, Education and Welfare request in 1971.[22] It undoubtedly aimed at blocking physician's assistants, although it was rationalized as a holding action in order to allow the states an opportunity to review their total credentialing policy before any further proliferation of licensed health occupations occurred. The Department of Health, Education and Welfare also urged the professions and the states to formulate criteria for defining those occupations that actually required licensure and to examine alternatives to individual credentialing, including institutional licensure. This agenda may have been as salient as any move against the new professionals. Another two-year moratorium was requested in 1973.[23] By 1975, the move toward institutional licensure was waning, so the moratorium failed to achieve institutional licensure, but it probably did serve as a deterrent to the establishment of individual licensure for physician's assistants.

Given this deterrent, two main laws were utilized to give legal status to physician's assistants: the general delegatory statute and the regulatory statute. The delegatory statutes amended state medical practice acts to permit physicians to delegate tasks to other workers. In some cases these statutes are very broad, allowing physicians to delegate to whomever they choose, while others specifically indicate that delegation can be only to a physician's assistant or a nurse practitioner. The regulatory statutes authorize a specific organizational entity, ordinarily the Board of Medicine, to establish rules and regulations governing the education and practice of P.A.'s.[24]

The general delegatory statutes were most congruent with the moratorium philosophy of not rushing to license new categories of health workers. Proponents of this approach, including most notably the American Medical Association, even wanted nurse practitioners to be covered in this way. They argued that the patient is best safeguarded by leaving all the important decisions to the physician, including what will be delegated and to whom.[25] In addition to the problematic advantage of augmenting or preserving the power of physicians, the approach had the real advantage of allowing more experimentation with new health roles. Its disadvantage was that it gave P.A.s no clear legal status, and it failed to protect the public by establishing standards for education or practice.

Consequently, the trend now seems to favor the regulatory approach. Most of the 38 states that had passed a physician's assistant law by 1975 used this mechanism.[26] The regulatory statute gives a clearer status to P.A.s, particularly in those states where the practitioner is individually certified. Most of the regulations outline a scope of function and specify a minimum training period, with two years seeming to be the modal time span. Thus there seems to be more consumer protection built into this approach.

But this approach is not without major problems. Since the regulatory authority is ordinarily delegated to state medical boards, and they carry responsibility for protecting medical "turf," the scope of functions of physician's assistants is often overly restricted.[27] Other protectors of their areas, including optometrists and dentists, have also come forward to lobby to protect their own functions; performance optometric services is forbidden to P.A.s in ten states and of dentistry in six. Winston Dean suggests that the optometrists' vigorous political activities stem from recent technological breakthroughs which permit eye refractions and eyeglass prescriptions to be carried out by minimally trained persons who can rely on sophisticated mechanical devices.[28]

Another disadvantage to the regulatory route is the fact that delays of two or more years in the regulation writing process are not uncommon. However, since nursing boards have on occasion taken that long to write nurse practitioner regulations, it is difficult to place blame on the medical establishment for the delay. It may be that public regulation writing is a necessarily slow process

Because of the moratorium, there seems to have been no serious consideration given to individual licensure for physician's assistants, although the Colorado Child Health Assistant law comes closest to this status. It requires candidates to pass written and oral examinations and allows the child health associate to "practice pediatrics."[29] Health personnel planners may need to give this option more serious consideration in the future if the occupation is to remain viable.

RELATIONSHIPS BETWEEN NURSES AND PHYSICIAN'S ASSISTANTS

While physician's assistants were probably a major factor stimulating the growth of the nurse practitioner concept (as outlined in Chapter 4), relationships between the two occupations have been stormy. The physician's assistant movement emerged at a time when nursing was involved in a major internal struggle about its future direction. The 1965 position paper of the American Nurses' Association suggested that nurses with advanced preparation at the baccalaureate and graduate levels should have a social-psychological rather than a technical medical focus.[30] Yet here was a new occupation ready to move in between nursing and medicine, claiming more power, status, and income than nursing because it was willing to take over technical medical tasks. Such a situation was threatening to nursing.

Relationships were further strained in 1970 when the American Medical Association announced that it planned to make 100,000 office nurses into physician's assistants.[31] The AMA made the statement without any consultation with the American Nurses' Association, which quickly deplored the announcement, arguing that nursing practice was much more than the performance of delegated medical tasks. This response also suggests that nursing's major grievance against physician's assistants is their name, especially when it applied to nurses. Obviously, this is a quarrel with medicine rather than with physician's assistants, although this differentiation has not always been clear. Medicine's tendency to argue that all nonphysicians look alike denied nurses their own roots and their own unique supportive functions. Not surprisingly, relationships deteriorated further when the American Academy of Pediatrics developed guidelines for pediatric nurse associates (practitioners) without consulting with the American Nurses' Association.[32] Various position papers issued by state and national nursing bodies express this ambivalence toward physician's assistants.[33]

More recently an issue has arisen which is more clearly related to the relationship between nurses and physician's assistants. The Washington State Nurses' Association brought suit after an attorney general's opinion said that it was legal for nurses to carry out orders written by physician's assistants. A 1978 ruling has held that these orders are not legal until countersigned by a physician. The Florida Nurses' Association is seeking a similar ruling.[34] Probably these efforts will be harmful to nursing in the long run, because they build a legal case for conceptualizing order writing as an exclusive physician function, rather than looking at the orders as a shared treatment plan drawn up collectively by the various members of the health-care team. This seems to be a situation where more cooperation between nurses and physician's assistants is called for.

However, in spite of all of these problems, relationships between nurses and physician's assistants seem to be improving. Individual practitioners are working well together in many settings. In California, the Stanford physician's assistant program and the Davis nurse practitioner program have merged many of their didactic and clinical teaching functions.

Before there is any great rejoicing over this verification of the ultimate friendliness of mankind, however, it is important to point out that the détente is probably due to the fact that nursing no longer views physician's assistants as a threat. At the inception of the P.A. and the N.P. movements, both programs were financed by grants from private and federal sources. Now that both occupations have proven their worth, the granting agencies feel their job is done and money for demonstration projects is becoming less plentiful. Consequently, nurse practitioner training is moving into the mainstream of nursing education, where it is being incorporated into baccalaureate and master's programs. No broad-scale comparable movement is occurring in medical schools. The P.A. programs in medical schools were usually supported by a few visionaries who saw them as a way to improve the health-care delivery system, but visionaries are seldom powerful tenured medical professors. Medical schools have not moved to institutionalize physician's assistant education, and the number of training programs is beginning to diminish. The twin barriers of limited legal sanction and lack of a solid institutional educational base means that the occupation will probably remain limited. The next decade will be crucial in its development.

REFERENCES

1. B. Bullough, *The Medicare-Medicaid Amendments,* 73 AM. J. NURS. 1926–29 (November, 1973).
2. *Rural Health Bill Signed: Payments to NPs Authorized,* 78 AM. J. NURS. 8, 15 (January, 1978).
3. Roger Lee Carrick, Project Director, AN INTERIM STAFF REPORT: CAREER MOBILITY IN PRIMARY CARE, (Career Mobility Project, Department of Consumer Affairs, State of California, 1979).
4. G. Engel, *The Birth of an Occupation: Perspectives of Physician's Assistants,* (paper read at American Sociological Association meeting, 1976).
5. E. A. Stead, Jr., *Training and Use of Paramedical Personnel*, 277 N. ENG. J. MED. 800–1 (October 12, 1967); A. M. Sadler, B. Sadler, & A. Bliss, THE PHYSICIAN'S ASSISTANT: TODAY AND TOMORROW 25–26 (1975).
6. National Center for Health Services Research and Development, FOCUS 8–9 (Summer 1970).
7. D. W. Fisher & S. M. Horowitz, *Physician's Assistant: Profile of a New Health Profession,* THE NEW HEALTH PROFESSIONALS NURSE PRACTITIONERS AND PHYSICIAN'S ASSISTANTS 40–54, ed. A. A. Bliss & E. D. Cohen (1977).
8. Engel, *supra;* FOCUS *supra;* E. Schneller, THE PHYSICIAN'S ASSISTANT (1978).
9. Sadler, Sadler & Bliss, *supra,* 25–26.
10. B. J. Andrew, *National Examination for Assistants to the Primary Care Physician*, in Bliss & Cohen, *supra,* 93–105; D. L. Glazer, *National Commission on Certification of Physician's Assistants; A Precedent in Collaboration,* Bliss & Cohen, *supra,* 86–92.
11. W. Bicknell *et al., Physician's Assistants and Nurse Practitioners in the U.S.: Roadblocks to Success,* 6 PHYSICIAN ASSISTANT JOURNAL 130–37 (Fall, 1976).
12. FOCUS, *supra,* 3–4, 15.
13. Fisher & Horowitz, *supra,* 42.
14. B. Perry, *Physician's Assistants: An Overview of an Emerging Health Profession,* 52 MEDICAL CARE 982–90 (December 1977).
15. Schneller, *supra,* 57.
16. Perry, *supra.*

17. A. A. Bliss & E. D. Cohen, *Issues and Conclusions: The Next to Last Word*, in THE NEW HEALTH PROFESSIONALS 371–82, ed. Bliss and Cohen (1977).
18. V. K. Sonntay, *Neurosurgery and the Physician Assistant*, 8 SURG. NEUROL. 3 at 207–08 (September, 1977).
19. J. Miller et al., *Use of Physician's Assistants in Thoracic and Cardiovascular Surgery in the Community Hospital*, 44 AMER. SURG. 162–64.
20. R. Macket et al., *Physician's Assistants as Facilitators of Clinical Competence in a Neurosciences Course*, 51 J. MED. EDUC. 428 (May 1976).
21. H. S. Cohen and L. K. Miike, DEVELOPMENTS IN HEALTH MANPOWER LICENSURE: A FOLLOW-UP TO THE 1971 REPORT ON LICENSURE AND RELATED HEALTH PERSONNEL CREDENTIALING 3 (1973).
22. REPORT ON LICENSURE AND RELATED HEALTH PERSONNEL CREDENTIALING (1971).
23. Macket et al., *supra*, 1–21.
24. W. J. Dean, *State Legislation for Physician's Assistants: A Review and Analysis*, 88 HEALTH SERVICE REPORTS 3–12 (January 1973); A. Sorkin, HEALTH MANPOWER (1977).
25. *Licensure of Health Occupations*, prepared by the AMA Council on Health Manpower and adopted by the AMA House of Delegates, December 1970; cited in P. C. Kissim, *Physician's Assistant and Nurse Practitioner Laws for Expanded Medical Delegation;* Bliss & Cohen, *supra*, 116–49.
26. NATIONAL NEW HEALTH PRACTITIONER PROGRAM: PROFILE, 1976–77, Association of Physician Assistant Programs, Washington (1977).
27. AMA Council on Health Manpower, *supra*, 146.
28. Dean, *supra*, 8.
29. Kissim, *supra*; Colorado Revised Statutes, § 12-31-101(2)–103(2) (1974).
30. *Educational Preparation for Nurse Practitioners and Assistants to Nurses: A Position Paper*, American Nurses' Association (1965).
31. G. Andreoli, *Physician Assistants and Nurse Practitioners: A Harmonious Future*, 6 PA J. 126–29 (1976).
32. Andreoli, *supra*, A. M. Sadler, *New Health Practitioner Education: Problems and Issues*, 50 J. MED. EDUC. 67–73 (1975).
33. Massachusetts Nurses' Association, *Position Statement on the Physician's Assistant* (March 1971); ANA Board of Directors, *The American Nurses' Association Views The Emerging Physician's Assistants* (1971); New York State Nurses' Association, *Statement on the Physician's Associate and Specialist's Assistant* (1972).
34. *Judge Rules PA Orders Not Legal until Countersigned*, 78 AM. J. NURS. 1143 (1978).

15 Constructing and Adapting Protocols

MARTHA A. SIEGEL AND BONNIE BULLOUGH

The term "protocol" becomes ever more important to nurses. This is particularly true for those who work in expanded roles in acute or primary care. Use of the term to describe outlined steps to diagnose and treat given conditions apparently started with members of the Ambulatory Care Project at Beth Israel Hospital in Boston. Starting in 1969, BIH physicians and other researchers wrote and field-tested protocols for managing such conditions as upper respiratory infection, headache, low-back pain, diabetes, and hypertension.[1]

In a parallel project at the Dartmouth Promis Laboratory, the phrase "clinical algorithms" was used to describe its product. The simple term "protocols," however, seems to be the more popular. Both projects originally had physician's assistants in mind, but the focus has shifted to nurse practitioners.

If professionals decide to use protocols, sometimes published ones that have been developed by experts, tested, and validated are appropriate. Often, however, these protocols do not meet agency needs without revision and new ones must be prepared.

Whether an agency staff adapts existing protocols or writes new ones, much of the work takes place before the multidisciplinary committee actually writes them.

The composition of the committee is an important early consideration. Since, in practice, nurses often have the major responsibility for initiating and writing protocols, they may want to study the formal and informal power structure of the organization in order to identify key people. These persons should be consulted or be represented on the committee. Their involvement will provide information, support change, and smooth the path to adopting and using the protocols.

After the committee is constituted, members need to discuss some issues, and their decisions about these issues become the basic assumptions on which

Reprinted from 77 AM. J. NURS. 1616 (October 1977).

they write the protocols. These issues can be summarized as (a) salient legal constraints and requirements, (b) patterns of personnel use in the agency, (c) characteristics of the patient population, and (d) agency and community resources.

The committee's first task is to determine the user's legal scope of practice. Since state laws vary, the nurse practice act and related regulations must be consulted.

Legislative mandate supports the growing use of protocols. For example, the 1974 California nurse practice act allows registered nurses to alter patients' treatment regimens or perform other traditionally medical acts when the acts are covered by policies and protocols. The law specifies that an agency committee with representatives from administration, nursing, and medicine must draw up the protocols.[2]

The Tennessee Board of Nursing specifies that nurses who manage the medical aspects of patient care must follow written medical protocols that have been developed by a nurse and a sponsoring physician. When the TBN issued the ruling, it indicated that it expected protocols to vary with the complexity of the patient problem and the preparation of the practitioner.[3]

Under Idaho regulations, the joint boards of nursing and medicine call for standard procedures and standards of performance rather than protocols. The Idaho committee charged with writing the procedures is like California's. The committee could vary from one nurse and one physician, in a private office, to a fairly large group that includes pharmacists and dietitians, in complex agencies.[4]

In most states, the laws and regulations for all registered nurses are the same, but in a growing number of states, new categories of nurses are being defined. For example, while the legal scope of practice of all registered nurses in Washington State is broad, the board of nursing there now designates two special groups: "advanced registered nurses" and "specialized registered nurses."[5] Nurses in these categories may manage drug therapy in accordance with protocols. Therefore, protocols for drug therapy would be appropriate for them but not for other Washington nurses.

Probably the most controversial issue in expanded nursing practice is the administration, prescription, and dispensing of drugs. Related state laws should always be studied.

In California, all registered nurses can use protocols. California requires protocols for the administration of traditionally medical treatment but not for nursing therapy or diagnostic data collection. The Idaho law stipulates that diagnostic procedures should be a part of the standard procedures of the agencies where they are drawn up.

Decisions about the amount of structure and the specificity of directions in the protocol depend on the patterns of personnel use in the agency. The users' levels of preparation and experience are important. Obviously, an experienced nurse with practitioner preparation could have more latitude in decision making than a paraprofessional worker.

The availability of physician consultants is another consideration. A protocol for a rural nurse practitioner may need to cover more contingencies than one for a nurse in a large teaching institution where many medical specialists are available for consultation. In all situations, the agency staff must clearly define the work parameters of the nurse using the protocol and clearly state where the responsibilities of the nurse practitioner and physician begin and end.

Another question is who is authorized to sign prescriptions; X-ray, laboratory, and consultation requests; referrals to occupational therapy and physical therapy; and so forth. While prescription signing may be specified in state licensing regulations, responsibility in other areas is likely to be a matter of agency policy. The committee must make these decisions with members of the involved departments after joint exploration of responsibilities, professional boundaries, and sharing of feelings. To prevent later confusion and inefficiency, these decisions should be made an explicit part of agency policy.

Data about the patient population are also useful. The age, sex, cultural and educational background, and economic level of the patients influence data collection and treatment. For example, family practice clinics would need protocols covering all age groups, while pediatric clinics or geriatric centers would not. Protocols on treatment of diabetics would cover teaching that is appropriate to the patients' cultural background, education, and income. Studying the frequency of presenting complaints, specific patient problems, and complications helps the committee decide which protocols they need to write and in what order to write them.

Assessment of agency and community resources is important. Resources determine whether the protocols should call for the practitioner to act alone or to refer. A nurse practitioner in a small rural clinic might prescribe a diabetic diet or counsel an alcoholic. Protocols for an urban comprehensive clinic might indicate that the nurse is to refer patients to a dietitian, a social worker, or Alcoholics Anonymous.

If the decision is to use a published protocol, the task is relatively simple. The committee reviews the protocol to see if it is consistent with the basic assumptions that they have identified. Sometimes changes are needed to respond to laws, agency policy, the characteristics of the patient population, and community resources. Sometimes differences arise as to which treatment modality is preferable. After the alterations, the protocol should be tried for a specified time. Some agencies with a research orientation may want to formalize the clinical trial and compare patient outcomes in control and experimental groups. Other agencies merely look at the patient care process to see if it seems reasonable.

Whatever approach is used, the committee should agree on how and when to review the clinical trial to see whether the protocol needs further modification or can now be adopted. After adoption, periodic review and alterations are needed to reflect research developments related to the condition and to changes in agency assumptions.

The patient conditions covered by protocols can be of two types: presenting complaints, such as headache or low-back pain or previously diagnosed conditions, such as diabetes. Protocols focused on presenting complaints address both diagnosis and treatment. Protocols for managing diagnosed illnesses are more likely to include guidelines for monitoring the condition, modifying treatment within specified parameters, consultation, and referring. (Steps for the actual writing are detailed below.)

Changes in health care and in the laws related to nursing and medicine point toward the increased use of protocols in primary care. Not all nurses are happy about this trend; some believe that protocols reduce patient care to cookbook medicine. These critics see the development of protocols as an attempt by physicians to limit the scope of practice of nurse practitioners and hamstring their legitimate use of clinical judgment.

On the other hand, supporters of the concept believe that protocols can provide models for clinical practice and facilitate care evaluation through peer review. The process of developing protocols forces clinicians to survey the literature and think through the basis for their clinical decisions. Furthermore, the process encourages interdisciplinary communication and cooperation.

HOW TO WRITE A PROTOCOL

You are on a committee that is to write protocols for nurse practitioners to use in evaluating or managing patients' conditions. You have done the preparatory work and are ready to write a protocol for managing headache as a presenting symptom. The protocol will be used by a nurse practitioner who treats adults in the outpatient department of an agency that has an emergency room, physician consultation, and laboratory and X-ray facilities.

Take the following steps:

Review assumptions. Refer to the committee's previously developed assumptions and policy.

Review the literature. Master current knowledge about the condition, including related anatomy and physiology, pathophysiology, signs and symptoms, and treatment modalities.

List conditions. Using the literature, list the conditions that may cause headache as the presenting complaint: allergy, anxiety, aneurysm—nonruptured or ruptured—arteritis, basilar-artery insufficiency, brain tumor, cardiovascular accident, depression, encephalitis, fever/systemic illness, glaucoma, hypertension, meningitis, migraine (vascular), muscle tension, nasal congestion/sinus infection/allergy, organic brain syndrome, refractive error, subdural hematoma, and trauma.

Constructing and Adapting Protocols   183

Select the most probable condition(s). Decide which of these possible conditions to include in the protocol. Criteria for making this judgment, suggested by Greenfield (Chapter 16), include its frequency and the importance of identifying it.

Include migraine and muscle tension because they are common, accounting for 90 percent of headaches in one study.[6]

Include arteritis, basilar-artery insufficiency, brain abscess, brain tumor, cardiovascular accident (CVA), encephalitis, glaucoma, meningitis, nonruptured and ruptured aneurysm, subdural hematoma, and trauma. These are less common but must be included because missing them leads to extremely serious consequences.

Include conditions that may easily be screened for. Examples: hypertension and refractive error. Include allergy/nasal congestion/sinus infection because, if found, they can be managed by the nurse practitioner.

Consider but probably exclude such systemic disorders as fever, infectious diseases, anxiety, depression, and organic brain syndrome. The associated headache, as one of many presenting symptoms, might be included as a symptom in protocols dealing with those disorders.

Define diagnostic points. Specify the attributes—critical diagnostic points—for each condition that may present with headache. For example, the headache caused by a brain tumor often is severe and persistent. The patient has no history of headache or this headache is different from previous headaches. The pain interferes with sleep, is not relieved by analgesics, is recent in onset, often at a time pinpointed by the patient, or is associated with vomiting not preceded by nausea. Often the patient has papilledema, signs of central nervous system involvement, and stiff, painful neck muscles.

Patients with refractive errors often present with a vague frontal headache. It usually occurs late in the day and is associated with a different use of the eyes, as in job changes.

Translate critical points into questions. Suggest the asking of informational questions, such as "When does your headache begin?" "What time of day (or night) does it occur?" "What makes it better?" "Do you have nausea with it?" "Do you vomit?"

Decide what to do. Explain what the nurse is to do. Is the nurse to refer immediately, consult, collect further data, or treat? Base your answers on the seriousness of the suspected conditions and the time available or justifiable for study before referral.

Specify for emergencies and "do-not-miss" conditions. Code the data that suggest any of these conditions so that the nurse will immediately refer, for example, brain tumor, aneurysms, trauma, encephalomeningitis, brain abcess, subdural hematoma, CVA, and basilar-artery insufficiency.

Items related to changes in sensorium or central nervous system abnormalities should be coded for immediate referral because they often characterize these serious conditions.

Note the serious conditions that nonetheless might allow the nurse more time for history taking, physical examination, and laboratory and screening tests before referring to a physician. Examples: arteritis, glaucoma, and refractive error. A patient with a headache may be in the early months of cranial arteritis before the headache becomes severe. Specify the key indications for referral: middle age or older, a history of malaise, anorexia, and burning pain in the temporal region; a tender and distended temporal artery, fever, and elevated sedimentation rate.

List the indicators for referral for glaucoma; pain in the eyes, increasing tearing, visual-field disturbances, and increased intra-ocular tension as evidenced by tonometry or history. The Snellen test might reveal refractive error. Code these responses to indicate referral to the appropriate specialist.

Some findings should direct the nurse to another protocol. For example, specify that headache with elevated blood pressure and no other significant headache-related findings calls for the use of a hypertensive-screening protocol.

Provide guidelines. Cover the nurse's treatment of those patients with headache whom he or she alone will see: patients with migraine, muscle tension, and nasal/sinus allergy disorders. Initial treatment is within the nurse practitioner's capability.

Specify the appropriate medications, patient education, counseling, and exercise programs, including options for individuals.

Specify criteria that will help the nurse and patient evaluate the treatment. Specify instructions to patients about complications, danger signs, indications for notifying the nurse or physician immediately, and directions for reaching them. Spell out the criteria for the nurse's re-evaluation of the patient's condition and decision to continue, discontinue, or modify treatment, or refer the patient to a physician.

REFERENCES

1. A. Komaroff et al., *Protocol for Physician Assistants: Management of Diabetes and Hypertension,* 290 N.ENG. J. MED. 307–12 (February 7, 1974); S. Greenfield et al., *Nurse Protocol Management of Low Back Pain,* 123 WESTERN J. MED. 350–59 (1975).
2. CALIFORNIA (STATE) BUSINESS AND PROFESSIONS CODE, §2725.
3. Tennesee Board of Nursing, RULES AND REGULATIONS CONCERNING THE LICENSURE AND EDUCATION OF REGISTERED NURSES, Ch. IV, *Nsg, RN* 32.
4. Idaho State Board of Nursing and Idaho State Board of Medicine, MINIMUM STANDARDS, RULES AND REGULATIONS FOR THE EXPANDING ROLE OF THE REGISTERED PROFESSIONAL NURSE (1972).

5. Washington State Board of Nursing, RULES/REGULATIONS, WAC 308–120–190 to 230.
6. A.P. Friedman, CHRONIC RECURRING HEADACHE (1973).

PROTOCOLS AVAILABLE

A number of protocols are available from Beth Israel Hospital, Boston, Mass. Each includes two documents, an Introduction and a Training Manual. For information about titles and prices, write to Anthony L. Komaroff, M.D., Ambulatory Care Project, Beth Israel Hospital, 330 Brookline Avenue, Boston, Mass. 02215. See also A. L. Kamaroff, R. N. Winikoff, eds., COMMON ACUTE ILLNESSES: A PROBLEM-ORIENTED TEXTBOOK WITH PROTOCOLS (Boston, Little, Brown, 1977).

Other collected protocols are published by Patient Care FlowChart Service, 16 Thorndal Circle, P.O. Box 1245, Darien, Conn. 06820. Readers may order the whole collection, part of it, or a single FlowChart. Complete service includes 205 FlowCharts, cross-indexed according to code numbers of the International Classification of Diseases, updated quarterly. The cost is $95 for the two volumes and one year of updating; $25 per year for renewals. A FlowChart "100" Book, soft bound and with 100 FlowCharts, not updated, costs $15. Single FlowCharts cost $1.00, prepaid.

Other protocols appear in Carolyn M. Hudak et al., *Clinical Protocols: A Guide for Nurses and Physicians*. Philadelphia, J. B. Lippincott, 1976, 461 pp, $8.75.

16 Protocols as Analogs to Standing Orders

SHELDON GREENFIELD

A *protocol,* as the term will be used here, is an instrument that guides a practitioner in the collection of data and recommends specific action based on that data. [1] Because adequately validated protocols represent a proven strategy in the workup and management of specific problems, they insure both high standards of quality of medical care and careful audit. As an explicit set of directions, constructed and approved by licensed physicians, their relation to the law as analogs to standing orders is a tantalizing subject.

This chapter will explore the relation of protocols to the law, discussing first the conceptualization of the protocol as an instrument in medical care, then the development and validation of protocols, and finally their potential for widespread use in the practice of medicine. The focus here is on the protocol systems for primary care developed by the Ambulatory Care Project, Beth Israel Hospital, Boston.

THE PROTOCOL CONCEPT

The protocol concept originated in response to the national call for nonphysicians to compensate for the physician shortage. If used to guide and audit performance, it was thought, protocols not only could assure certain high standards of quality of care but also could conserve physician time by facilitating the delegation of clinical care responsibilities to other health-care providers and practitioners. The conceptual framework for the protocol is that an instrument representing the sequential decision-making process of the physician allows a person with minimal medical knowledge to collect data appropriate for a particular patient. Further, because the protocols are far more explicit and individualized for the particular patient than "guidelines" would be, they allow a nurse or other practitioner to take independent action where indicated. The combination of

---

This chapter is a revised version of "Protocol Management of Dysuria, Urinary Frequency, and Vaginal Discharge," by Sheldon Greenfield, Gerald Friedland, Sally Scifers, Arthur Rhodes, W. L. Black, and Anthony L. Komaroff, which originally appeared in *Annals of Internal Medicine* 81:451–52 (1974).

Protocols and Standing Orders   187

specificity for the individual patient and standardization of patient care justify delegation of responsibility from the initiation of data collection through disposition, including the decision to send the patient home without seeing a physician.

If protocols are to possess these capabilities, several conditions must be met. (1) A significant percentage of complaints in a primary-care clinic or facility must fall into a relatively small number of categories. A practitioner using protocols must be able to handle the majority of patients' problems with a relatively small number of protocols. Prior studies of primary-care practice have supported this contention,[2] and our own data, collected at the Kaiser facility at Inglewood, California, confirm these analyses (Table 1).[3] It is generally held that between eight and 12 chief complaints or problems will represent from 50 to 80 percent of primary-care practice. (2) Once the critical protocols are constructed, the practitioners must be able to collect the data indicated by performing adequate histories and physical examinations and be able to follow the logic inherent in each sequential step with minimal error. We do not assume that past medical training is helpful; rather, we define and delimit the job to be done, select the group of skills necessary to accomplish the job, and test whether the selection of skills is appropriate and whether these skills can be performed by nurses with no experience apart from basic nurse training. (3) If the data are collected properly, the deductive logic must lead to the proper decision or series of decisions, and hence to a proper outcome of the encounter. Both the second and third conditions must be determined experimentally by validation trials.

Table 1. Distribution of Presenting Complaints
Kaiser–Inglewood Clinic, March 1973

Complaint	Number
URI	797
Abdominal pain	289
Headache	237
Back pain	182
Chest pain	175
Legs/feet	165
Return to work slip	158
Rash, skin	127
Dizziness, etc.	118
Return visit	113
Arms/hand	98
Gynecologic	94
Side pain	88
Urinary	87
Blood pressure	85
Ears (no other URI)	85
Nausea, vomiting, diarrhea	73
Total patients	2909
Total complaints	3842
Protocol coverage by complaint	2422 (63%)

DEVELOPMENT AND VALIDATION
OF PROTOCOLS

The last twenty years of medical research has by and large, focused on the mechanisms of disease. Very little work has gone into the scientific basis for the solving of clinical medical problems as patients present these problems to physicians. Thus, the data on which to base most of the decisions made in medical practice are not available. For example, how high must a fever be in combination with sore throat and tender enlarged lymph nodes to make a diagnosis of streptococcal pharyngitis? Does pain in the groin accompany a backache often enough so that groin pain need not point to a gastrointestinal or genitourinary condition in a patient complaining of back pain? Will patients with certain serious back diseases be detected by a single question attempting to ascertain whether the pain is relieved by bed rest? How often are the symptoms dysuria and frequency caused by vaginitis rather than urinary tract infection? Such clinical questions go on and on. The strategies for solving clinical problems are not, by and large, taught in medical school, either because not enough is known about them or because it is assumed that after a physician has spent many years on the wards as a medical student and house officer, he or she can easily integrate organ system pathophysiology and patient problems.

Protocols attempt to standardize diagnostic and management strategy explicitly and concisely. Beginning with a complaint, the intellectual processes of the practitioner unfold, each step dependent on preceding responses or physical findings. Decisions about what historical and physical information to collect and what action to take are generally based on two considerations: the frequency of a condition or a diagnosis sought and the importance or value placed on making the diagnosis, or, more precisely, defining the condition.[4] For example, diphtheria is so rare in adults in the northern United States that it is not unreasonable to leave it out of the differential diagnosis of a person with sore throat. On the other hand, although bacterial meningitis is very rare in patients with the chief complaint of headache alone, it is easy to diagnose and is treatable; thus great importance is placed on its detection.

One of three outcomes is chosen as the protocol comes to a final decision about an individual patient. One outcome is to refer the patient to the physician because of potential complexity of diagnosis or management. For example, a patient with backache who is found to have a high fever should be worked up by a physician for osteomyelitis, epidural abscess, or other serious infectious processes. Another outcome is that the physician reviews the protocol data, having the option of examining one of the physical findings or checking over part of the history. A third outcome is the protocol recommendation that a patient can safely be sent home without seeing a doctor. This latter possibility, which obviously has great value in conserving physician time, makes it mandatory for protocols to be adequately validated.

Our protocol for dysuria, urine frequency, vaginal discharge, and vaginal irritation will serve as an illustration for protocol development. The major logical pathways are shown diagramatically in Figure 1. A patient presenting with dysuria and/or frequency has the relevant history taken by the nurse administering the protocol. Pertinent parts of the physical examination are performed, including palpation for costovertebral tenderness, temperature, and blood pressure. Next, a urinalysis is performed and a urine sample cultured. If the urinalysis shows at least 20 or more white cells or 2+ bacteria per high power field in a centrifuged sediment, the patient is treated for presumptive urinary tract infection. If the urinalysis is negative, a pelvic exam is done to determine whether the urinary tract symptoms are due to vaginitis. If vaginitis is not present, the patient is considered to have urethral syndrome or urethritis, is informed about the nature of the condition, and is not treated with antibiotics pending culture results. A patient complaining of either vaginal discharge or irritation of the vulva receives a pelvic exam, which includes examination for gross abnormalities, inspection and palpation of the cervix for purulent discharge and tenderness, and examination of a wet mount of the vaginal discharge. The patient is treated for monilia or trichomonas if present. If neither is detected on wet mount, the patient is treated for nonspecific vaginitis.

Patients are automatically referred to the physician if they are on a return visit for any of the above symptoms, are older than 45, have had a recent gynecologic procedure, are pregnant, or have diabetes, severe abdominal pain, back pain, incontinence, hypertension, significant fever, or any vaginal abnormalities on observation. A history of recurrent urinary tract infection or chronic kidney disease and a history of medications recently inserted vaginally are reasons for verbal consultation with the physician after the workup is completed, but in these instances the physician need not see the patient.

Urinary tract infections are treated with sulfisoxazole. In the presence of sulfonamide allergy, tetracycline or ampicillin is used. Mycostatin suppositories are prescribed for monilia infection and metronidazole for trichomonas infection. Sulfonamide vaginal suppositiories are used in the treatment of nonspecific vagnitis.

The accuracy of the initial diagnosis is checked when the culture returns, and treatment is modified if necessary. Patients are advised to return if rash, fever, chills, or vomiting develop, or if the symptoms continue for more than three days in the case of urinary tract infection or seven days in the case of vaginitis.

As might be expected, the decisions made during a history and physical exam are extremely complicated. The actual logic pattern of the urinary tract infection–vaginitis protocol is shown in Figure 2. Every attribute or data bit is included for a specific reason; it follows that the answer to every question must be linked to a decision, such as pursuing a symptom or sign further, initiating treatment, referral to the physician, and so forth. W. L. Black has taken this branching logic tree and combined it with a data collection sheet, as shown in Figure 3. This form allows the nurse to check off the presence or absence of an

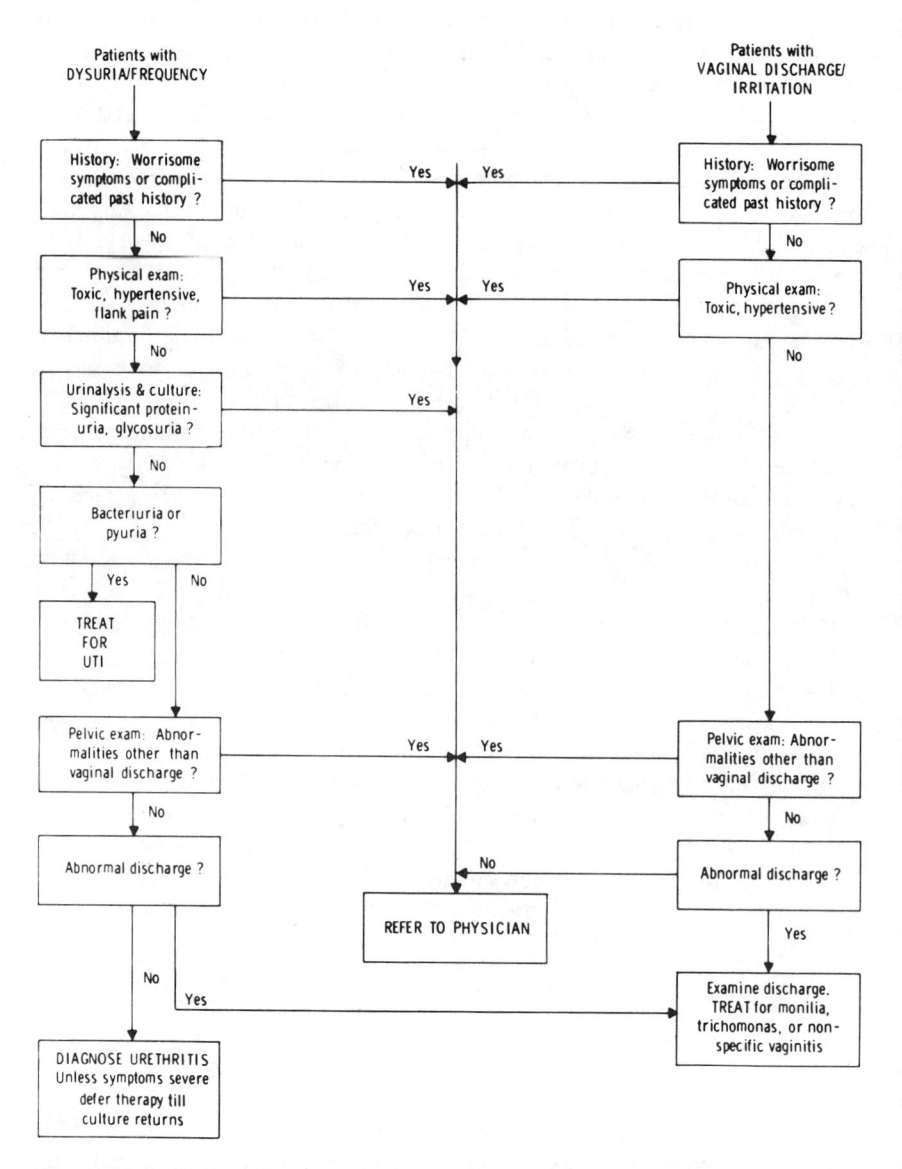

190   Practitioners, Specialists, and Assistants

```
Patients with                                              Patients with
DYSURIA/FREQUENCY                                          VAGINAL DISCHARGE/
                                                           IRRITATION
        ↓                                                         ↓
┌──────────────────┐                                    ┌──────────────────┐
│ History: Worrisome│    Yes         Yes                │ History: Worrisome│
│ symptoms or compli│───────►    ◄────────────────────── symptoms or compli│
│ cated past history?│                                   │ cated past history?│
└──────────────────┘                                    └──────────────────┘
        │ No                                                    │ No
        ↓                                                       ↓
┌──────────────────┐                                    ┌──────────────────┐
│ Physical exam:   │    Yes         Yes                 │ Physical exam:   │
│ Toxic, hypertensive│──────►    ◄──────────────────────│ Toxic, hypertensive?│
│ flank pain?      │                                    └──────────────────┘
└──────────────────┘                                            │ No
        │ No                                                    ↓
        ↓
┌──────────────────┐
│ Urinalysis & culture:│   Yes
│ Significant protein- │─────►
│ uria, glycosuria?    │
└──────────────────┘
        │ No
        ↓
┌──────────────┐
│ Bacteriuria or│
│ pyuria?       │
└──────────────┘
   Yes      No
    ↓
┌────────┐
│ TREAT  │
│ FOR    │
│ UTI    │
└────────┘

┌──────────────────┐                                    ┌──────────────────┐
│ Pelvic exam: Abnor-│   Yes         Yes                │ Pelvic exam: Abnor-│
│ malities other than│──────►    ◄──────────────────────│ malities other than│
│ vaginal discharge? │                                   │ vaginal discharge? │
└──────────────────┘                                    └──────────────────┘
        │ No                                                    │ No
        ↓                                                       ↓
┌──────────────────┐              No                    ┌──────────────────┐
│ Abnormal discharge?│        ◄──────                   │ Abnormal discharge?│
└──────────────────┘                                    └──────────────────┘
                           ┌──────────────────┐                 │ Yes
                           │ REFER TO PHYSICIAN│                ↓
                           └──────────────────┘        ┌──────────────────┐
        │ No                                           │ Examine discharge.│
        │ Yes                                          │ TREAT for monilia,│
        └─────────────────────────────────────────────►│ trichomonas, or non│
                                                      │ specific vaginitis │
┌──────────────────┐                                   └──────────────────┘
│ DIAGNOSE URETHRITIS│
│ Unless symptoms severe│
│ defer therapy till    │
│ culture returns       │
└──────────────────┘
```

Fig. 1. Major logic pathways through the UTI/Vaginitis Protocol. The protocol itself specified what is meant by phrases such as "worrisome symptoms" and "toxic." In addition to the logic shown above, the protocol contains many other minor pathways and logic branch points.

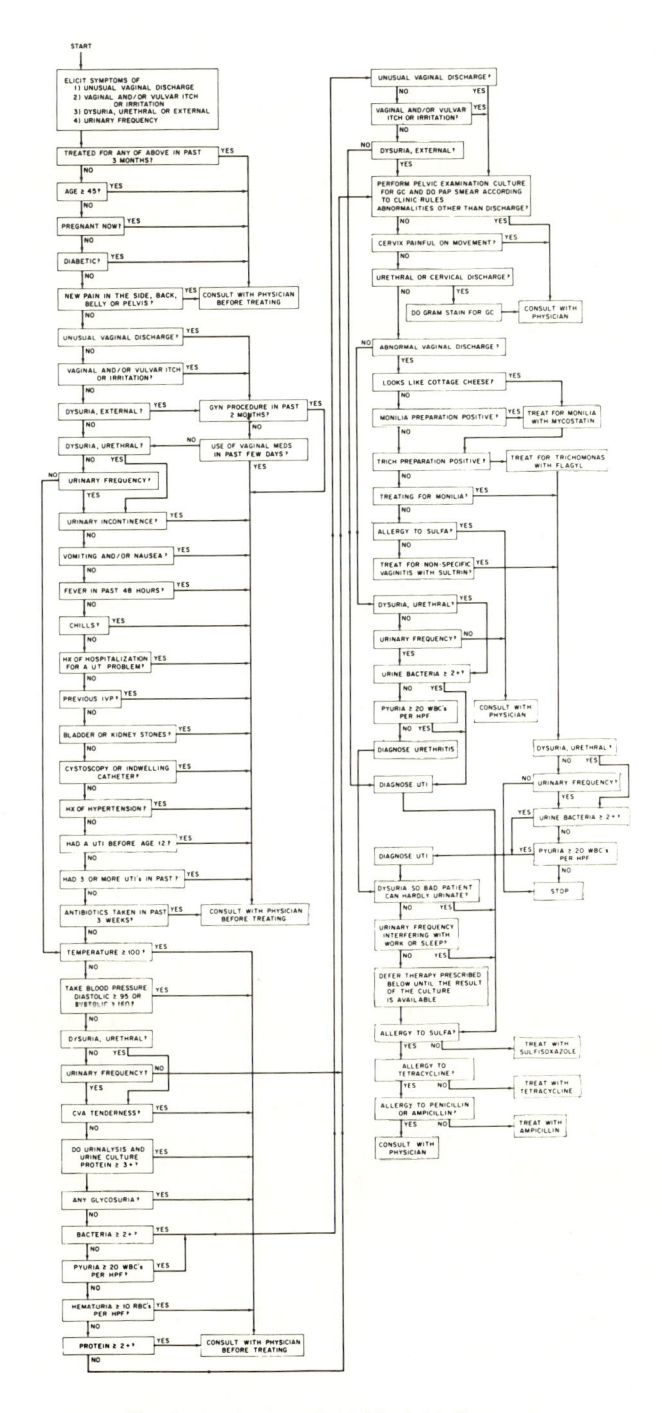

Fig. 2. Logic tree of UTI/Vaginitis Protocol.

U.T.I./VAGINITIS PROTOCOL© (12/73)   Unit #:   Date:
                                          Name:
Chief complaint(s) _____   Birthdate: Phone:
                                          Provider:

yes no SUBJECTIVE
☒☐   Vaginal discharge, unusual   ☐ ■ Any blue boxes checked
        Days duration _____   A Stop   ☐ ☐ Any red boxes checked? *Consult MD*
☒☐   Vaginal/vulvar itch/irritation   *Do Pelvic (Pap & GC culture)*
        Days duration _____   ☐ ☐ Abnormalities-not discharge
☐ ■   Pain/burning on urination   ☐ ☐ Cervix painful on movement
☒☐   Inside urethra   ☐ ☐ Urethral/cervical discharge?
☒☐   Outside on a raw area   *Do GC gram stain* _____
        Days duration _____   ☐ ■ Abnormal vaginal discharge
☒☐   Unusually frequent urination   ☐ ☐ Looks like cottage cheese? *Dx monilia*
        Days duration _____   ☐ ☐ Monilia prep positive? *Dx monilia*
☐ ☐   Rx for any of above in past 3 mo   ☐ ■ Trich prep positive? *Dx trichomonas*
☐ ☐   Age ≥ 45   ☐ ☐ Any vag dx? *Dx non-specific vaginitis*
☐ ☐   Pregnant now
☐ ☐   Diabetic   ☐ ☐ Any dx yet?
☐ ■   New pain side/back/belly/pelvis   ☐ ☐ Any greys? *Dx urethritis*
☐ ☐   Severe
                                             Stop   ☐ ☐ Any reds? *Consult MD*
☐ ■   Any blue boxes checked   Stop   ☐ ☐ Will consult MD for other reasons
☐ ☐   Gyn procedure in past 2 mo
☐ ☐   Meds inserted into vagina   PLAN (also see back of protocol)
        in past few days   ☐ ☐ Dx of trichomonas? *Rx Flagyl*
☐ ■   Any grey boxes checked   ☐ ■ Dx of monilia? *Rx Mycostatin*
☐ ☐   Incontinence (prior to UTI Sx)   ☐ ■ Dx of non-specific vaginitis?
☐ ☐   Vomiting/too nauseated to eat   Stop   ☐ ☐ Sulfa allergy? *Consult MD Rx Sultrin*
☐ ☐   Fever by Hx in past 48 hrs
☐ ☐   Chills, teeth chatter   Stop   ☐ ☐ Dx of UTI/urethritis
☐ ☐   Hx of hospitalization for UT prob.   ☐ ■ Dx of urethritis/vaginitis
☐ ☐   Kidney X-ray (IVP)   ☐ ☐ Dysuria so bad pt can hardly urinate
☐ ☐   Bladder/kidney stones   ☐ ☐ Frequency interfering with work
☐ ☐   Cystoscopy/in-dwelling catheter   or sleep? *Rx as below but tell pt*
☐ ☐   High blood pressure   *to wait for culture result before*
☐ ☐   Had a UTI before age 12   *beginning med*
☐ ☐   Past UTI's ≥ 3
☐ ☐   Antibiotic taken in past 3 weeks   ☐ ■ Sulfa allergy? *Rx Sulfisoxazole*
                                                     ☐ ■ Tetracycline allergy? *Rx Tetracycline*
        OBJECTIVE   ☐ ☐ Penicillin/Ampicillin allergy?
☐ ☐   Temperature ≥ 100 _____   *Consult MD   Rx Ampicillin*
☐ ☐   Systolic BP ≥ 160 or Diastolic ≥ 95
        BP: _____   _____
☐ A   Any grey boxes checked
☐ ☐   CVA tenderness   _____

        Do urinalysis and culture

        Bact ____ WBC ____ RBC ____   _____
☐ ☐   ≥ 3+ protein _____
        Any sugar _____
■ ☐   Bact ≥ 2+ or WBC ≥ 20? *Dx UTI*
■ ☐   ≥ 10 RBC
   A   ≥ 2+ protein

        © The Beth Israel Hospital Association and Massachusetts Institute of Technology 1974

Fig. 3. UTI/Vaginitis Protocol.

INSTRUCTIONS TO PATIENTS	
If Dx vaginitis: Tell patient to return in 1 week if no relief. Give patient information sheet.	Ampicillin 250 mg #40 1 QID X 10 Flagyl 250 mg #30 TID X 10 (Consult MD about also treating consort.) Mycostatin vag. tabs 100,000 U #30 1 BID X 15 - - even during period Sulfix Sulfisoxazole 0.5 gm #80 2 QID X 10 with full glass of water Sultrin triple sulfa vag. supps. #20 1 BID X 10 - - even during period Tetracycline HC1 250 mg #40 1 QID X 10 on an empty stomach
If Dx UTI/urethritis: Tell patient to return if rash, fever vomiting or chills occur. Give patient information sheet.	
If urine culture done: Tell patient to call back for culture results in 3 days.	
The chart below indicates what the patient should be told at that time.	

CULTURE POSITIVE	CULTURE NEGATIVE

If no UT Rx given:
  Arrange for therapy.
 	
If UT Rx given; pt told to wait
  Begin med; return in 3 days if Sx persist and in 3 weeks for reculture.
 	
If UT Rx given; pt told to start:
  Return if Sx still present; otherwise continue meds and return in 3 weeks for reculture.
	If no UT Rx given:
	  Continue vaginitis meds as directed.
	
	If UT Rx given; pt told to wait:
	  Don't take med. Return in 1 week if Sx persist.
	
	If UT Rx given; pt told to start:
	  Stop UTI/urethritis med. Return if dysuria/frequency still present or if they recur.

For the most recent edition of this protocol and/or further information, write:
Ambulatory Care Project, Beth Israel Hospital, 330 Brookline Ave., Boston, Ma. 02215

NOTE:
On actual hospital form...
- will be red
- will be yellow
- will be blue
- will be grey

attribute, guided by a set of internal instructions based on color-coding and special symbols. For example, a dot means to skip the following questions and go on to the next set of questions.

It is apparent that making the intellectual process of the practitioner explicit is a difficult task. Not only must the decisions be clearly made for each data bit or attribute, but the presence of each must be justified in some way by whatever literature is available, or by personal practice experience in the absence of supporting data. For example, if there is no known level of fever at which a decision to treat or not to treat with an antibiotic is made, we require the protocol developer to say that a temperature level of 102 F is chosen arbitrarily, so that other practitioners can address themselves concretely and specifically to that piece of information.

Therefore, the initial construction of the protocol can take as long as several weeks, or even months. In the Beth Israel Hospital Ambulatory Care Program, protocols have been initially constructed by general physicians rather than by specialists. An expert on backache who might be an orthopedic or neurologic surgeon or a rehabilitation physical medicine specialist has expert knowledge in the disease causing backache, but a specialist is more inclined to be disease-oriented that a generalist, and is less likely to do an examination appropriate for primary care. For example, a specialist almost always orders an X-ray of the lumbar spine in a person with backache; a general practitioner might well not order the X-ray, knowing that of 400 or 500 patients presenting with backache, only one or two will have a serious disease that would be detected by X-ray and not by history or physical exam.[5] Moreover, many back X-rays will show minimal to moderate osteoarthritis, which may not actually be the cause of the patient's backache but only a coincidental finding. Some surveys have shown that as many as 40 or 50 percent of patients of middle age or older may have some minimal degenerative joint disease changes apparent on spinal X-ray. Therefore, from the point of view of the general practitioner, an X-ray may not be a cost-efficient test to order, even though the specialist might consider it to be mandatory.

Once the protocols have gone through the intial development by the generalists, they are then reviewed by experts in the field and finally by a larger panel of general physicians. It is not enough, however, to construct an "armchair" strategy for the workup of a complaint. Too few of the decisions necessary in clincial practice are supported by data to make those decisions. Therefore, to be valid a protocol has to be field tested. Adequate field testing to validate the protocol has been one of the major thrusts of the Beth Israel Hospital Ambulatory Care Program, and we have undertaken to devise methodology for the validation of protocols as we validate a critical number of protocols for use in practice. At the time of this writing, protocols adequately validated now include those for urinary tract infection,[4] vaginitis,[4] upper respiratory tract infection,[2] low-back pain,[16] and headache. Chronic disease protocols for diabetes and hypertension have also been validated.[3]

What is adequate validation? How are we to be satisfied that a protocol can be used safely and with highest quality available medical care? At first glance it would seem to be enough if the nurses administering the protocols could be found to have done the proper workups as certified by physicians seeing the same patients. That would be what we call a validation of process. However, we know that many of the steps physicians take are not necessarily related to a proper outcome; thus it is also necessary to test for the outcome of the encounter. Further, even if outcomes are determined, how are we to know whether the achieved outcome represents good medical care? If, upon testing a protocol for low-back pain, the nurses found that 80 percent of their patients experienced symptomatic relief, how are we to know that physician-provided care could not have achieved 90 percent? The literature does not tell us what to expect about the relief of symptoms for chief complaints, because most of the studies in the literature deal with diseases rather than complaints. Therefore, we have decided to compare ourselves to physicians in practice. If nurses using a protocol are as effective as physicians in a well-controlled trial, we can say that the protocol administered by a nurse is an adequate mode of delivery of care.

As a concrete example of adequate validation of protocol, I will briefly describe the protocol validation study for the complaints of dysuria, frequency, and vaginitis in women. The study, conducted at the UCLA Student Health Service, was designed to compare the performance of a protocol-guided nurse to the performance of a group of physicians with respect to history taking, physical examination, simple laboratory observations, and management. The study design is depicted in Figure 4. Women presenting with either dysuria, urinary frequency, vaginal discharge, or vaginal irritation were randomly allocated to one of two groups. One group was seen first by the nurse—an RN without prior

STUDY DESIGN

All Patients (Random) → Nurse-protocol → Physician → Physician Treatment

Blind Comparison of Data Collection

Physician → Nurse-protocol → Nurse-protocol Treatment

Comparison of Outcome

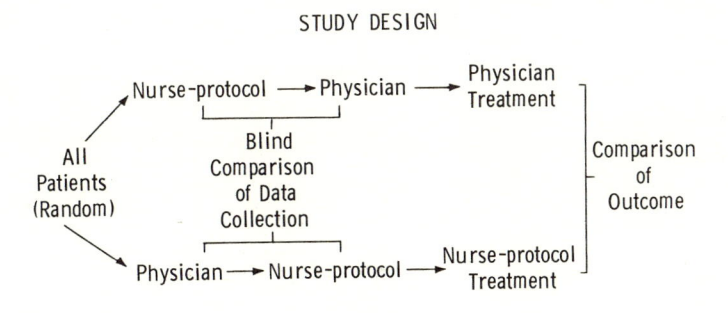

Fig. 4. A randomized crossover study design to compare both process and outcome. The patients followed the treatment recommendations of the practitioner they saw last.

practitioner experience—and then by one of a group of 13 participating physicians. The physicians were advised of the study goals and design, and all inquiries were answered; however, the protocol decision logic was not reviewed with any physician. Patients assigned to the other group were seen first by a physician and then by the nurse. Neither the physician nor the nurse knew the other's findings. The nurse performed her own examination of urine sediment and vaginal smear without knowledge of the Student Health Laboratory examination of the same specimens.

The nurse on the protocol form, and the physician on a similar form that did not include any decision logic, recorded their respective histories and physical findings; after ascertaining the laboratory results, they committed themselves on paper to a presumptive diagnosis and plan. The group of patients seen last by physicians followed the physician's recommendations (physician group). The other group, those seen by the nurse, followed the protocol disposition and therapy (nurse–protocol group). In this group, the nurse presented to the physician the protocol recommendations regarding treatment or the need for referral to a physician, and requested that the physician indicate on a special sheet his or her judgment about these protocol decisions. The physician was asked, in effect, whether the protocol action was reasonable, not whether it corresponded exactly to what he or she had recommended or would recommend. If the physician was opposed to the nurse–protocol disposition or therapy in this group of patients seen last by the nurse, the physician's decision prevailed, and these patients were removed from the analysis of outcome results.

The patients were asked to telephone two days later for the results of the urine culture. If the urine culture was positive, the patient was asked to return for a repeat culture one week after termination of therapy. Within a week following the clinic visit all patients were contacted by telephone to ask about presence, absence, or alleviation of symptoms, and to inquire about complications.

The results showed favorable comparison between physicians and the nurse–protocol. Concordance between physicians and the nurse with respect to history is recorded in Table 2. Of the 146 histories, 139 were essentially identical. Of the seven discrepancies, six were cases in which the physician made

Table 2. Data Collection Concordance Between Physicians and Nurse–Protocol (N–P)

	Identical	Physician Error	N–P Error
History	139	6 (4)	1 (0)*
Physical exam	137	0	9 (0)

*( ) Resulting in altered diagnosis or management.

an error. In four cases, the physicians agreed that they had erred in not pursuing symptoms suggestive of either vaginitis or urinary tract infection, and management was altered upon discovery of the other condition. In two cases, physicians agreed that they had not acquired a presumptive history of past urinary tract problems. There was one patient in whom the nurse did not detect a past history of significant urinary tract infection.

Concordance was similar with respect to physical examination. Of the 146 cases, 137 had virtually identical physical examination. In nine cases the nurse was considered to have made an error, based on concurrent physician assessment. These were not independently verified. In no case did any of these physical exam errors result in a different management decision. In five cases the nurse did not recognize the cheesy character of vaginal discharge, but monilia was seen on wet mount; in four cases physicians noted costovertebral angle tenderness, which the nurse had not noted, but did not specifically diagnose pyelonephritis, and did not alter management of routine urinary tract infection.

Evaluation of nurse laboratory work indicated that the laboratory findings agreed with the nurse's findings in 54 of 58 urinalyses performed. In the four cases where there was disagreement, the physician who had seen the patient examined the sediment himself and confirmed the nurse's observation. With respect to wet mounts of vaginal secretions, in nine cases of 39 in which the nurse detected monilia, the laboratory failed to note the presence of monilia. In all these cases, the nurse findings were confirmed by the physician upon review. The nurse failed to note monilia on one specimen that was found to be positive by the laboratory. There was no independent judgment made on the specimens reported negative by both nurse and laboratory.

The protocol's diagnostic accuracy was evaluated in those cases in which the patient would have gone home without seeing a physician. The nurse using the protocol made the decision to refer the patient to the doctor in 16 cases, or 11 percent. Concordance of diagnosis in the remaining 130 patients is seen in Table 3. The diagnoses were made after review of the laboratory work in the case of both physicians and nurse. It can be seen that agreement was virtually complete. In two cases the diagnosis of vaginitis was pursued and confirmed by the nurse when the physician had noted only urinary tract infection to be present; in both instances, upon review, the physician agreed with the nurse–protocol diagnosis and therapy. In one case the laboratory found monilia on a gram stain of vaginal discharge; this woman had been diagnosed by the nurse as having nonspecific vaginitis.

There was virtually complete agreement with regard to therapy as well. In one case the physician agreed with the nurse–protocol diagnosis but preferred another treatment. In the other 129 cases, physicians judged the protocol treatment plan to be "reasonable." In all, physicians concurred with the nurse–protocol diagnosis and management (specific therapy or referral) in 144 of 146 cases.

Table 3. Diagnosis Concordance Between Nurse–Protocol and Physician for 130 Patients

N–P Diagnosis	Urinary tract infection	Urethral syndrome or urethritis	Monilia	Nonspecific vaginitis	Trichomonas	Urinary tract infection and vaginitis	Other*
Urinary tract infection	28						
Urethral syndrome or urethritis		6					
Monilia			37				
Nonspecific vaginitis			1	41			
Trichomonas					1		
Urinary tract infection and vaginitis	2					8	
Other*							6

*Includes no pathology found, trichomonas and monilia together, suspect allergic reactions to vaginal insertions.

In addition to prescribing specific treatment, the protocol recommended review of the record in consultation with the physician in 11 cases. Nine of these were reviewed for a suspect past history of urinary tract disease. Two were reviewed for recently having taken medication that might potentially interfere with diagnosis and therapy. There was agreement on the need for review of all these 11 records.

All 16 patients referred to the physician by the protocol were referred appropriately, according to the physician. Of the 16 referrals, seven were due either to a return visit for the same complaint or for medication recently taken that would interfere with the diagnosis and therapy, three were for symptoms and signs of generalized toxicity, and the remainder were for miscellaneous reasons. The protocol did not fail to refer any patient whom the physicians felt should be examined by a physician.

Symptomatic outcome was evaluated in the nurse–protocol group and the physician group. A total of 76 patients was allocated to the nurse treatment group; of these, eight did not receive nurse–protocol management because of referral (six cases), physician disagreement (one case), or no identifiable pathology (one case). Similarly, five patients of the 70 assigned to the physician group were excluded from analysis of specific therapy because of referrals to subspecialists or other complications. Symptomatic outcome for the remaining 68 patients treated by nurse–protocol and 65 patients treated by physicians are recorded in Table 4. Of the 65 patients who received physician treatment, all but two reported alleviation or improvement of symptoms. Similarly, only two of the 68 nurse–protocol patients reported no improvement. The three patients with vaginitis who did not improve were thought to have nonspecific vaginitis on the first visit, and were later treated for monilia infection. One patient who had a urinary tract infection (treated by the physician) had an allergic reaction to sulfisoxazole.

Table 4. Symptomatic Outcome by Treatment Group and Diagnosis

	UTI/US*		Vaginitis		Both	
	Total	Improved	Total	Improved	Total	Improved
Nurse–protocol	16	16	49	47	3	3
Physician	23	22	35	34	7	7

*Urinary tract infection/urethral syndrome.

Results of antibiotic treatment for urinary tract infection are shown in Table 5. Nine of the physicians' 15 culture-positive patients had repeat cultures one week after termination of treatment. Eight out of nine cultures were sterile. Similarly, of the 14 positive cultures in the nurse–protocol patients group, 12 were recultured and ten of these were sterile in three weeks.

Table 5. Culture Results of Antibiotic Treatment for Urinary Tract Infection

Patients	Positive before Treatment	Total Recultured	Culture Sterile 3 weeks
Physician	15	9	8
Nurse-protocol	14	12	10
Totals	29	21	18

This study supported the hypothesis that the nurse could accurately collect the relevant clinical data and that, using the protocol, she could make appropriate diagnostic, therapeutic, and disposition judgments. Thus the protocol was both efficient in conserving physician time and effective in delivering medical care. The outcome of an encounter would always appear to be the best criterion for its success or failure; however, for the complaints studied here, culture and symptomatic outcome are not sufficient to validate protocol decisions, because urinary tract symptoms, vaginitis symptoms, and bacteriuria can be self-limited. This particular study design permitted independent evaluation of both process and outcome.

Safety, one of our major considerations, was found to be adequate. Those patients who would have been sent home by the protocol rules without seeing a physician had no complications, at least as ascertained by a followup by concurrent physician estimation of the conplexity of the problem. All potential complications were referred to the physicians, and we anticipate that the protocol decision logic is conservative enough to continue this degree of safety with even larger numbers.

Similar kinds of results have been obtained with the validation studies of backache, upper respiratory infection, and headache. These results reinforce our concept that a registered nurse using materials that allow for intensive training in well-defined skills with definite rules for referral can perform as well as a physician.

Before discussing the implications of protocol usage in relation to the law, the final aspect of the protocol movement—use and barriers to use in practice—must be considered. There is growing acceptance of protocols in the United States. Validation studies are being published in the major medical journals. Requests for protocols have exceeded the supply, and a nationwide survey to determine the extent of usage in various situations is in progress. The major barriers to their use, which are being examined at the present time, fall into two major areas. One is that nurses who have had general nurse practitioner training in addition to working with protocols are motivated to make more and more independent decisions as their knowledge and skills develop. They are often anxious to go further than the protocol or to deviate from it, and they may find the protocol limiting. We have stressed repeatedly that a protocol represents minimum standards—a floor rather than a ceiling. Once the minimum workup has been done, insuring minimum quality of care, then other aspects of the workup can be added.

The second concern is that nurses, like physicians, often feel that the protocol workup calls for too much. It is said that the workup is too compulsive, too lengthy, too cumbersome. This criticism reflects the tension between exigencies of daily practice and the high quality workup of patient complaints. For example, of all patients that present with headache to a family practice or general practice office, only a vanishing small fraction will have stroke as the cause of headache. While headache is a common concomitant of stroke, most patients with stroke have other signs or symptoms that are serious enough to take them to the emergency room. However, there is no question that a few patients with stroke present initially with headache alone. Therefore we feel it incumbent to include some attributes to investigate the possibility of stroke causing headache. How far should we go? The doctor in practice might say that if a person does not appear to be having a stroke, i.e., no obvious paralysis or difficulty walking, that is good enough. However, because we are explicitly committing ourselves in print to sets of standards for practice for nonphysicians, we feel it necessary to be conservative and have required more than a casual look at a patient with only a remote possibility of a stroke. Nurses, like physicians, are anxious to be as efficient as possible and want to eliminate what they feel from their own experience is an unnecessary section on stroke. Many parallels to this example exist; practitioners are constantly "pruning" their workups according to their experience and their time constraints. The development at the Beth Israel Hospital of a single form allowing both the logic to be followed and the data to be recorded has been shown in preliminary time–motion studies not to slow down the practitioner's pace. Moreover, if a physician in a practice wants to eliminate some attributes from the protocol, this can be done quite easily and the attendant risks and benefits will be spelled out clearly. On the other hand, major modifications of the protocol, leading to different kinds of decisions and different kinds of outcomes, should probably be tested more formally (as in our trials). We feel that once the bulk of a protocol workup has been adequately tested in field trials with hundreds of patients, minor modifications and cutbacks can be done without harm to the patients.

Like standing orders, protocols must constantly be changed and revised according to new discoveries in medical science. If a new diagnostic test eliminates a considerable part of a workup, it should be incorporated into the protocol. If we adhere to the principle that a protocol should always represent, in the most parsimonious exacting form, the intellectual processes of the physician kept up to date, then it can be used as a safe and reliable instrument. There is no reason why a protocol should be fossilized like a medical textbook after three to four years of use.

The protocol's relation to the law will become clearer once the concepts as well as the problems of protocol development, validation, and use in clinical practice become known. If protocols in fact represent what the doctor thinks and does, if the development of protocols includes widespread peer review, if the protocols are validated in a way that allows them to have proven therapeutic efficacy, then protocols can conceivably stand as analogs to standing orders. Protocols can ensure a minimum standard of quality of care based on current standards for practice, and as such could have considerable legal support. To the extent that the protocol workups include the approval and support of local physicians in a community or in a health-care unit, this approval would further strengthen their potential for replacing standing orders. In this regard it must be emphasized that it is the protocol which directs the nurse to order additional diagnostic tests or specific therapy and to either discharge patients or refer them to a physician.

The role of protocols in relation to the law will necessarily be limited by the extent of their ability to cover a large fraction of patient visits with standardized and well-validated protocols. Locally constructed protocols, not subject to complete validation studies but incorporating local peer review, could supplement protocols available from large medical centers that have been clinically validated. The use of protocols may introduce a useful approach to normalizing the relationship between the law and the delegation of clinical tasks to nurses in the practice of primary care.

REFERENCES

1. A. Komaroff, G. Reiffen, & H. Sherman, *Problem-Oriented Protocols for Physician-Extenders,* in APPLYING THE PROBLEM ORIENTED SYSTEM 186–96, W. Hurst, H. Walker & N. Woody, eds. (1973); S. Greenfield, F. Bragg, D. McCraith, et al., *An Upper Respiratory Complaint Protocol for Physician-Extenders,* 133 ARCH. INTERN. MED. 294–99 (1974); A. Komaroff, W. Black, M. Flatley, et al., *Protocols for Physician Assistants: Management of Diabetes and Hypertension,* 290 N. ENGL. J. MED. 307–12 (1974); S. Greenfield, G. Friedland, S. Scifers, et al., *Protocol Management of Dysuria, Frequency and Vaginal Discharge,* 81 ANNALS INTERN. MED. 452–57 (1974).
2. O. Peterson, L. Andrews, R. Spain, et al., AN ANALYTICAL STUDY OF NORTH CAROLINA GENERAL PRACTICE (1956); J. Dingle, *The Ills of Man,* 229 SCI. AM. 77–84 (1974); S. Bain & W. Spaulding, *The Importance of Coding Presenting Symptoms,* 97 CAN. MED. ASSOC. J. 1953 (October 14, 1967); M. Budd, B. Reiffen, M. Rodman, et al., A PROGRAM FOR AN AMBULATORY CARE SERVICE (1969); L. Goodstine, K. Streiff, & F. Bragg, EVALUATION OF AIDE TRIAGE OF AMBULATORY PATIENTS (1971); Lincoln Laboratory, Commission on Chronic Illness, CHRONIC ILLNESS IN A LARGE CITY: THE BALTIMORE STUDY (1957); H. Schonfeld, J. Heston, & I. Falk, *Number of Physicians Required for Primary Medical Care,* 286 N. ENGL. J. MED. 571 (1972); G. Goldberg, M. Grady, & M. Budd, APPLICABILITY OF PROTOCOL MANAGEMENT OF CHRONIC DISEASE TO AN AGED POPULATION (1970); ACP-7 Lincoln Laboratory & Beth Israel Hospital; NATIONAL DISEASE AND THERAPEUTIC INDEX, SPECIALTY PROFILE, D. Kozlow, ed. (1970).
3. H. Sherman & A. Komaroff, PROGRESS REPORT 9A (1974).
4. W. Schwartz, G. Gorry, J. Kassirer, et al., *Decision Analysis and Clinical Judgment,* 55 AM. J. MED. 459–72 (1973).
5. S. Greenfield, H. Anderson, R. Winickoff, et al., *Management of Low Back Pain by a Protocol and a Physician-Extender* 22 CLINICAL RESEARCH 378A (1974).

17 Emerging Trends in Nursing Practice and Law

BONNIE BULLOUGH

Nursing practice is affected by statutes written at both the state and federal levels as well as by court decisions. The state laws relating to nursing, known as *state nurse practice acts*, are the major statutory control over nursing practice. The federal influence is felt primarily through the power of the government to grant or withhold funds as, for example, to finance nursing education or, more recently, to pay nurse practitioners employed in rural health-care and demonstration urban clinics.

In this work the history of the state nurse practice acts has been traced through three phases. During the first phase, from 1903 to 1938, laws to register nurses were passed in all of the states. Registered nurses were ordinarily defined as persons who had finished three years of training, passed state board examination, possessed good health, and had good characters. During the second phase of nursing licensure, from 1938 to 1971, the emphasis in the definition of nursing changed from a focus on the personal attributes of nurses to an emphasis on their scope of function. That scope was necessarily limited in this period by the power of the medical profession as well as the timidity of the nursing profession. As a result, acknowledged definitions excluded diagnosing and treating patients, even though nurses in this period actually carried out these functions in *sub rosa* fashion. The second phase was also marked by two other major events. Mandatory licensure was sought to protect both the profession and the public from untrained persons who were also called nurses, and the nursing role was stratified into the professional (or registered) and practical levels.

The third phase in the history of nursing licensure began in 1971. It has been characterized by rapid changes in licensure as nurses have sought to expand their written scope of function. There are some emerging trends that suggest that further changes will follow.

STATE CERTIFICATION OF NURSES IN SPECIALTIES

The major new trend in nursing licensure is the development of state certification for specialized nurses. To date this certification has focused on nurse-midwives, practitioners, and anesthetists, but it could probably be extended to include clinical specialists if the profession chooses to lobby for such an extension.

The history of midwifery in the United States has been traced in a recent book by Litoff. Prior to the last century, midwives performed all deliveries, but during the later part of the nineteenth century obstetrics developed as a medical specialty, tending to focus on difficult deliveries and/or well-to-do patients. Concerned with the oversupply of physicians that developed in this period, medicine moved to phase out midwifery and turn over all obstetric care to doctors.[1] Organized nursing seems to have accepted this effort; at least there is no record of nurses' fighting the legislative revisions in medical practice acts calculated to outlaw midwifery. Nurses were apparently convinced that women would be better served by skilled physician care and hospital deliveries. During this period, however, nurse midwifery grew in most other countries where informally trained lay midwives were replaced with formally trained midwives or more often by nurse-midwives. In the United States, nurse-midwives were allowed to practice only in a few scattered "outposts." By 1965 nurse midwifery was legal only in New Mexico, the eastern counties of Kentucky, New York City, and the Virgin Islands.[2]

Spurred on by the women's movement and encouraged by a growing revolt against the technical orientation of the all-physician obstetric work force, both lay midwifery and nurse-midwifery have again emerged in this country. Even in states where they are illegal lay midwives have a significant underground following. Nurse-midwives, who can furnish the same personal support as the lay midwives, have the advantage of better scientific backgrounds. Consequently, nurse-midwifery has gained most from the revolt. A survey done by the American College of Nurse Midwives in 1976 indicated that twenty jurisdictions had passed specific legislation recognizing nurse-midwives. Most other states were sanctioning them either with permissive legislation or by allowing them to practice under the more blanket extensions in the scope of practice acts for registered nurses enacted since 1971.[3] Updating these figures to the present, 27 states plus the District of Columbia and the Virgin Islands have special laws or regulations mentioning midwives; in 20 of these jurisdictions a certificate is granted by the state.

The development of state certification for nurse practitioners is even more recent. Although the current phase in nursing started in 1971, regulations to set up mechanisms for certification of nurse practitioners were not drawn up in any of the states until 1975. Since that time, 19 states have started certifying nurse practitioners.

Anesthesia as a specialty for nurses dates from the nineteenth century when Edith Graham and Alice Magaw started administering anesthesia at the Mayo Clinic.[4] Until recently anesthesia involved only a small group of nurses; but it has now started to expand, and some nurse-anesthetist training programs are moving into nursing school master's programs. Nine states have now developed a certification mechanism for nurse-anesthetists, although the practice is probably also legal under the general provisions of expanded nurse practice acts.

Some states certify nurse-midwives, anesthetists, and practitioners while some deal with only one or two of these specialties. Whether or not the certification mechanism is extended to include hospital-based clinical specialists remains to be seen. To date only the Washington State law calls for certification of "specialized registered nurses." Certainly, the need for certification is more clear for nurse practitioners who give ambulatory care and need the title to facilitate third-party payments, but certification for institutionally employed clinical specialists would probably encourage recognition of the advanced talent of these nurses as well as afford some consumer protection.

Although the states often use the term *certification* to describe this credentialing process, *licensure* may actually be a more accurate term since previous usage has reserved "certification" for credentials granted by a professional body rather than by the state. What seems to be happening is the development of a second level of licensure for registered nurses. The first level is the basic registered nurse, including graduates of associate, baccalaureate, and other diploma programs, while the second level is the advanced specialty. If current trends in nursing education continue, the rapidly expanding associate degree programs may emerge as the primary source of preparation for the first level.

The second level will probably be the master's rather than the baccalaureate level, which is now being discussed in professional circles as the projected entry into practice requirement. This is partly because nurse practitioner preparation is moving to master's degree programs. This movement will gain momentum as grant funds to prepare nurse practitioners in short-term certificate programs disappear. In some areas, practitioner education is being institutionalized at the master's level since the content is sufficiently complex to warrant this move. Similar trends in midwifery, anesthesia, and clinical specialist preparation also make the master's degree the emerging specialty level. Thus, the future licensure pattern for registered nurses will probably include stopping points at two and six years, with a degree but no licensure marking the baccalaureate level.

ENTRY-INTO-PRACTICE RESOLUTIONS

Other alternatives, however, are possible. For example, if nursing unites behind the entry-into-practice resolutions this pattern could change. This movement started in 1974 when the New York State Nurses' Association passed a resolution calling for the baccalaureate degree as the minimum preparation for entry into professional practice by 1985.[5] This resolution quickly became the focus of a national discussion and in 1976 the Council of Baccalaureate and Higher Degrees of the National League for Nursing passed a similar resolution. The idea gained further when a package of three entry-into-practice resolutions was passed by the American Nurses' Association in 1978.[6] Subsequently, various other nursing organizations have debated the issue and some, including most notably the American Association of Operating Room Nurses (AAORN), have supported the movement. The resolutions are emerging as one of the major issues facing the profession today, although there are differences of opinion as to what they mean, whether or not they should be implemented, and what their implementation would accomplish for the profession. The major deterrent to implementation seems to be the problem of what to do about the current registered nurse work force, 80 percent of whom do not hold a baccalaureate degree. Obviously, either a career-ladder plan for easier mobility through the educational system or some sort of "grandparent" clause, which protects current license holders, is needed to deal fairly with this group if the resolutions are to be seriously considered.

It seems clear that the New York State Nurses' Association did not have a career ladder in mind when it passed the original resolution. Rather, it seemed to have conceptualized the baccalaureate graduate as the registered nurse, while nurses with associate degrees were to be technical or practical nurses. Articulation between the two groups of nurses was not spelled out in the original resolution, although there was considerable sentiment in favor of some type of grandparent clause that would allow existing registered nurses the right to retain their current titles. Only new graduates would be required to earn the baccalaureate degree. The resolution passed by the Council of Baccalaureate and Higher Degrees of the NLN used similar wording, but members of the council were less certain about a grandparent clause. Possibly more of them knew that such a clause is not a popular concept in the political arena. Legislators tend to argue that the additional education is either needed for patient safety or it is not. They see inequity in allowing present practitioners to hold out with less education than entering candidates are required to have. The other argument against a grandfather clause is that it delays implementation for up to 45 years while the current licensees continue practicing. Thus the fair and politically prudent grandparent clause is not without problems.

The 1978 ANA resolutions, which are compiled in an appendix to this chapter, are quite different in focus from the original New York proposal. They called for "increased accessibility to high quality career mobility programs which utilize flexible approaches for individuals seeking academic degrees in nursing," thus addressing the problem of the existing work force by advocating continued education rather than the grandparent clause. The ANA package of resolutions carefully avoided the issue of titling the entry-level nurse since, if the baccalaureate nurse is titled "professional" or "baccalaureate," a battle over the current title of "registered nurse" might be avoided.

Supporters of the resolution argue that this step would bring order to a disorderly educational system. Patients, the public, and colleagues within the health-care delivery system would be less confused if nursing settled on one standard program for the preparation of registered nurses. They feel that the growing complexity of patient care necessitates the baccalaureate rather than the associate degree level as the first nursing preparation.

The arguments against the resolutions are practical rather than ideological. Since 80 percent of the registered nursing workforce do not hold the baccalaureate degree, the struggle to achieve legislation—which would seriously threaten the livelihood of most nurses—could cost more than it is worth. If the struggle to upgrade the workforce to the baccalaureate level were to be mounted seriously, the American Hospital Association would probably enter the fight against the resolutions. In the process, the credibility of nursing in the state legislatures and Congress would undoubtedly be damaged.

The present status of the resolutions suggests that it is indeed the practical problems that are the important ones. The New York State Nurses' Association has been unsuccessful in getting its proposed legislation through the necessary legislative committees. While there does not seem to be a significant internal struggle within the nursing organization, the dissidents have probably left the association, and the real struggle will come when and if the bill is seriously considered in Albany.

The Ohio Nurses' Association is also seriously considering trying to get the legislature to pass an entry-into-practice bill. They have, in fact, delayed expanding their basic nurse practice act in order to give priority to this issue. In the meantime the Buckeye Nurses' Association has been organized to represent diploma nurses who are opposed to change. This weakens the ONA. Nurses in other states are watching these two states with anxiety, but even with the difficulties of New York and Ohio before them the supporters of entry-into-practice resolutions are not depressed. They see the resolution of support by the AAORN as a magnificient step forward, particularly since few operating-room nurses hold advanced degrees.

If the supporters of these resolutions are successful, licensure would move to a four- and six-year pattern instead of the one outlined above which jumped from the two-year to the six-year level. The baccalaureate would become the first registered nurse and the master's would comprise the specialty levels. These changes would no doubt have an influence on practical nursing which would probably merge with associate degree nursing.

THE CREDENTIALING STUDY

The other recent event which could have consequences for the statutory status of nursing is the publication of the credentialing study. In 1974 the House of Delegates of the ANA passed a resolution calling on the association to investigate the possibility of accrediting schools of nursing. The resolution led to the formation of a study committee and a major research project at the University of Wisconsin. After assessing the current status of all of the governmental and professional credentialing mechanisms in operation, the study group decided that the current system is much in need of reform: it is fragmented and marked by both gaps and overlaps. The study group recommended that a single credentialing body be set up and directed by a coalition of nursing organizations. This body could accredit nursing programs run by schools of nursing or other institutions, license nurses, and certify all of the advanced specialties that are now handled by a variety of large and small nursing organizations as well as the state governments.[7]

While this proposal might be perceived as merely an attempt to reform the system, it can also be seen as an attempt to move toward professionalization by increasing the control over nursing by its members. As the latter, it becomes obvious that the recommendations will have difficulty being adopted. The trend described earlier in this chapter, the development of state licensure for nursing specialists, is clearly a move in the opposite direction. It implies greater control over nursing by state governments (or, broadly conceived, by consumers). Thus, there is a significant potential for conflict with the states if the credentialing study is vigorously supported by the profession. Unfortunately, nursing has arrived at this position of seeking more professional autonomy at a later time than most other professions. Law, medicine, education, and social work have already achieved professional status and in the process they often gave the concept a bad name by stretching their span of control a bit too far, robbing consumers of legitimate decision-making power. Thus, nursing is in the position of making its move for greater control at the height of the consumer movement. This will make implementation of the credentialing study difficult.

COURT DECISIONS AND THE EXPANDING NURSING ROLE

As discussed in Chapters 6 and 10 the decisions of the courts also have an impact on nursing. The trend is clearly in the direction of expecting more from nurses. The landmark case in the field is the 1965 Darling case. The plantiff, who broke his leg while playing football, was taken to a local hospital where he was treated with traction and a plaster cast. The cast was apparently too tight since his toes became swollen, painful, and dark. His physician notched his cast, but soon blood and eventually a foul-smelling drainage was noted by the nursing staff. Eventually, he was taken to another hospital where his leg was amputated.

The case was vigorously defended by both the physcian and the hospital. The hospital argued that it was not responsible for what happened to the patient since it merely housed and supported him while doctors made all of the diagnostic and treatment decisions. This line of reasoning failed to impress the court. The hospital and its nurses were held negligent primarily because the nurses did not test the circulation in the patient's foot frequently enough, did not realize that the developing symptoms were dangerous, and did not call hospital authorities when the attending physician failed to act.[8]

A recent West Virginia case reiterates these findings. In this case the patient entered the hospital suffering from a comminuted fracture of his wrist. During his hospital stay an infection developed; his arm became swollen and black, with a foul smelling drainage. He became feverish, unable to retain oral antibiotics, and finally delerious. He survived, but his arm had to be amputated. The nursing staff reported these symptoms to the treating physician but he failed to act. The jury found and the appelate court upheld the finding that the hospital was negligent because the nurses did not report the failure of the attending physician to his department chairman. The nursing procedure manual called for this further reporting, so simply accepting the patient's deteriorating condition was considered negligent.[9]

These cases suggest that more judgment is being called for by nurses. They are not only being held accountable for their own actions; they are also responsible for monitoring the care given by other health professionals. This trend toward demanding more accountability means that nurses will probably be involved in more malpractice suits. Nurses are responding to this threat by purchasing malpractice insurance, yet insurance itself can also be a factor supporting law suits since, in the past, the traditional reputation of nurses for near-poverty income and their lack of insurance acted as deterrents to malpractice suits. Now that they have insurance they are good candidates for suits. It would seem that every silver lining has a cloud attached.

MANDATORY CONTINUING EDUCATION

The realization that all nurses, and not just the specialists, are expanding their scope of function and being held accountable for the quality of their practice is resulting in at least one other emerging trend. Mandatory continuing education has been legislated in California, Minnesota, Florida, Kansas, and Massachusetts. State boards of nursing in Oregon, Colorado, Louisiana, and South Dakota have also been given the power to set up mandatory continuing-education requirements if they choose. In Oregon and Nebraska, nurses who have been inactive for five or more years are required to take a refresher course before re-entering the job market.[10]

In spite of its rapid spread, mandatory continued education remains controversial. Some nurses argue that they should not be forced to attend courses because keeping up within one's field is a private professional responsibility, while others vigorously support the idea as one method to achieve continued competency.[11] California, which was the first state to pass such a law, has been requiring 30 contact hours of education for all nurses relicensed after January 1, 1978. While most nurses have complied with this requirement without too much difficulty, the two nursing boards (separate boards for registered and vocational nurses) have found controlling the quality and cost of the courses an almost impossible task. Still, in spite of this, mandatory continuing education laws are being considered in at least 16 other states as of this writing.

CONCLUSION

These emerging trends are a part of the ferment that accompanies rapid social change. Nursing is in such a period of change. The scope of function of all nurses is expanding; nurses are more honestly admitting their roles in diagnosis and the treatment of patients; specialities are developing and nurses are demanding their rightful place on the scales of salary, power, and prestige. Consequently, the costs of increased responsibility are being leveled on the profession; legal liability is increasing and it is becoming apparent that nurses need more education. It is a challenging era in which to nurse.

REFERENCES

1. J. Litoff, AMERICAN MIDWIVES: 1860 TO THE PRESENT (1978).
2. E. H. Fogotson, R. Roemer, R. W. Newman, *Legal Regulation of Health Personnel in the United States,* in REPORT OF THE NATIONAL ADVISORY COMMISSION ON HEALTH MANPOWER, vol. 2 (1967).
3. A. M. Forman, E. M. Cooper, *Legislation and Nurse-Midwifery Practice in the USA.* 21 J. NURSE-MIDWIFERY (1976); R. Roemer, *The Nurse Practitioner in Family Planning Services: Law and Practice.* 6 FAM. PLAN. POPULAT. REPORTER (1977).
4. H. Clapesattle, THE DOCTORS MAYO 362–63, 429 (1943); S. Thatcher, A HISTORY OF ANESTHESIA WITH EMPHASIS ON THE NURSE SPECIALIST (1952); A. Magaw, *A Review of Over 14,000 Surgical Anesthetics* 3 SURG. GYNECOL. OBSTET. 795 (1906).
5. New York State Nurses' Association, *Resolution on Entry into Professional Practice,* (Albany 1974).
6. *American Nurses' Association Convention '78,* 78 AM. J. NURS. 1230 (1978); *A.N.A. Convention* 26 NURS. OUTLOOK 500 (1978).
7. American Nurses Association, THE STUDY OF CREDENTIALING IN NURSING: A NEW APPROACH (1979); *Credentialing in Nursing: A New Approach,* Report of the Committee for the Study of Credentialing in Nursing 79 AM J. NURS. 674 (1979); *Positions, Conclusions and Recommendations from the Study of Credentialing in Nursing: A New Approach.* 27 NURS. OUTLOOK 263 (1979).
8. Darling vs Charleston Community Hospital. 200 NE 2d 145 (1964), 211 NE 2d 253 (1965); A.R. Holder, MEDICAL MALPRACTICE LAW (1975); *The Darling Case.* 206 J.A.M.A. 1875 (1968); *The Darling Case Revisited.* 206 J.A.M.A. 1665 (1968).
9. Utter vs. United Hospital Center Incorporated. 236 SE 2d 213 (West Virginia 1977); *Hospital Liable for Nurses' Failure to Report Questioned Patient Care.* 36 CITATION 1 (1977).
10. *The Status of Continuing Education: Voluntary and Mandatory.* 77 AM. J. NURS. 410 (1977); *Continuing Education to Become Mandatory in Massachusetts in 1982 Under New Law.* 78 AM. J. NURS. 183 (1978).
11. J. G. Whitaker, *The Issue of Mandatory Continuing Education.* 9 NURS. CLIN. N. AM. 475 (1974).

Appendix: Entry-Into-Practice Resolutions

RESOLUTION 56: IDENTIFICATION AND TITLING OF ESTABLISHMENT OF TWO CATEGORIES OF NURSING PRACTICE

Whereas, ANA for the past 13 years has upheld the position that the "minimum preparation for beginning professional practice at the present time should be baccalaureate degree education in nursing," and the "minimum preparation for beginning technical nursing practice at the present time should be associate degree education in nursing,"

Therefore be it resolved that: ANA ensure that two categories of nursing practice be clearly identified and titled by 1980,

And be it further resolved that: By 1985 minimum preparation for entry into professional nursing practice is the baccalaureate degree in nursing,

And be it further resolved that: ANA, through appropriate structural units, work closely with SNAs and other nursing organizations to identify the two defined categories of nursing practice,

And be it further resolved that: National guidelines for implementation be identified and reported back to ANA membership by 1980.

RESOLUTION 57: ESTABLISHING A MECHANISM FOR DERIVING COMPETENCY STATEMENTS FOR TWO CATEGORIES OF NURSING PRACTICE

Whereas, ANA for the past 13 years has upheld the position that the "minimum preparation for beginning professional practice at the present time should be baccalaureate degree education in nursing," and the "minimum preparation for beginning technical nursing practice at the present time should be associate degree education in nursing," and

Whereas, Nursing groups throughout the country have developed, or are in the process of developing, competency statements of two categories of nursing practice, and

Whereas, There is a need for statements to clearly differentiate the competencies for associate and baccalaureate degree prepared nurses,

Therefore be it resolved that: ANA establish a mechanism for deriving a comprehensive statement of competencies for two categories of nursing practice by 1980.

RESOLUTION 58: INCREASING ACCESSIBILITY OF CAREER MOBILITY PROGRAMS IN NURSING

Whereas, Since 1965 ANA has supported the position that all nurses obtain educational preparation in colleges and universities, and

Whereas, The Commission on Nursing Education has developed standards to ensure quality educational programs, and

Whereas, The overwhelming majority of registered nurses currently do not hold a baccalaureate degree in nursing and vocational nurses do not hold an associate degree, and

Whereas, Future employment of nurses undoubtedly will be based on academic preparation as well as licensure, and

Whereas, There are limited educational opportunities for large numbers of non-degreed nurses in many geographic areas, and

Whereas, flexible and non-traditional programs in nursing education can be developed while ensuring academic integrity,

Therefore be it resolved that: ANA actively support increased accessibility to high quality career mobility programs which utilize flexible approaches for individuals seeking academic degrees in nursing.

Bibliography

Abdellah F: Nursing practitioners and nursing practice. Am J Public Health 66:245, 1976
Agree BC: Beginning an independent nursing practice. Am J Nurs 74:636, 1974
Agree BC: The threat of institutional licensure. Am J Nurs 73:1758, 1973
Aiken L: Primary care: the challenge for nursing. Am J Nurs 77:16, 1977
Alhon N: Preparing to individuate from team member to independent practitioner. J Psychiatr Nurs 15:31, 1977
Amendment of the Arizona nursing practice law broadens definition of professional nursing. Am J Nurs 72:1203, 1972
American Academy of Nursing: Primary Care by Nurses: Sphere of Responsibility and Accountability. Kansas City, Mo., American Nurses' Association, 1977
American Academy of Pediatrics: Executive board initiates child health care manpower training program in major effort to improve pediatric care. AAP Newsletter 20:1, 1969
American Hospital Association: Special committee on provision of health service. Policy Statement. Chicago, 1971
American Hospital Association: Statement on licensure of health care personnel. Hospitals 45:82, 1971
American Hospital Association: A patient's bill of rights. Chicago, 1973
AMA calls for NP and PA supervision by MD's, wants practitioner reimbursement through MD's. Am J Nurs 77:1248, 1977
American Law Institute: Model Penal Code. Philadelphia, ALI, 1962
American Medical Association, Council on Health Manpower: Licensure of health occupations. Mimeographed, December 1970
American Medical Association: Accredited Educational Programs for the Assistant to the Primary Care Physician. Chicago, AMA, 1974
American Medical Association, Committee on Nursing: Medicine and nursing in the 1970's: a position statement. JAMA 213:1881, 1970
American Nurses' Association: Resolution on institutional licensure. Am J Nurs 72:1106, 1972
American Nurses' Association: Code for nurses. Kansas City, Mo., 1976
American Nurses' Association: Model Practice Act. Kansas City, Mo., ANA, 1976
American Nurses' Association: The Scope of Nursing Practice: Description of Practice: Nurse Practitioner/Clinician, Clinical Nurse Specialist. Kansas City, Mo., ANA, 1976
American Nurses' Association: Facts about Nursing: A Statistical Summary 1976–7. Kansas City, Mo., ANA, 1977

American Nurses' Association: The Study of Credentialing in Nursing: A New Approach. New York, ANA, 1979
American Nurses' Association, Division on Psychiatric and Mental Health: Statement of Psychiatric and Mental Health Nursing Practice. Kansas City, Mo., ANA, 1976
American Nurses' Association, Education Committee: First position paper on education for nursing. Am J Nurs 65:106, 1965
American Nurses' Association, Maternal and Child Health Nursing Practice Division, and American Academy of Pediatrics: Guidelines on short-term continuing education programs for pediatric nurse associates. Am J Nurs 71:509, 1971
American Nurses' Association Convention '78. Am J Nurs 78:1230, 1978
American Nurses' Association, Board of Directors: The American Nurses' Association views the emerging physicians' assistant. Kansas City, Mo., December 1971
ANA Board approves a definition of nursing practice. Am J Nurs 55:1474, 1955
ANA Convention 1978. Nurs Outlook 26:500, 1978
Anderson, BE: Facilitation of the Interstate Movement of Nurses. Philadelphia, Lippincott, 1950
Andreoli G: Physician assistants and nurse practitioners; a harmonious future. Phys Assist J 6:126, 1976
Andrews, PM, Yankauer A: The pediatric nurse practitioner: growth of the concept. Am J Nurs 71:505, 1971
Andrus LH, Fenley MD: Educational evolution of a family nurse practitioner program to improve primary care distribution. J Med Ed 51:317, 1976
Annas, GJ: The Rights of Hospital Patients: The Basic ACLU Guide to a Hospital Patient's Rights. New York Avon Books, 1975
Bain S, Spaulding W: The importance of coding presenting systems. Can Med Assoc J 97:953, 1967
Bates B: Twelve paradoxes: a message for nurse practitioners. Nurs Outlook 22:686, 1974
Barbee GG: Special procedures: I.V.'s, blood transfusions and skin testing. In Proceedings: Institute on Medico-Legal Aspects of Nursing Practice. Santa Monica, California Nurses' Association, 41, 1961
Barbee G: When is the nurse held liable? Am J Nurs 54:1343, 1954
Benne KD, Birnbaum M: Principles of changing. In Bennis G et al (eds): The Planning of Change, 2nd ed. New York, Holt, Rinehart and Winston, 1969
Bergman A: Physician's assistants belong in the nursing profession. Am J Nurs 71:975, 1971
Berwind A: The nurse in the coronary care unit. In Bullough B (ed): The Law and the Expanding Nursing Role. New York, Appleton, 1975
Besch LB: Informed consent: a patient's right. Nurs Outlook 27:32, 1979
Bickne W et al: Physician's assistants and nurse practitioners in the United States: roadblocks to success. Phys Assist J 6:130, 1976
Black D: The Behavior of Law. New York, Academic Press, 1976
Bliss AA, Cohen ED (eds): The New Health Professionals: Nurse Practitioners and Physician's Assistants. Germantown, Md., Aspen Systems, 1977
Bonham-Carter H: Is a general register for nurses desirable? Nursing Record, September 6, 1888, p 301
Booth A: Legal accommodation of the nurse practitioner concept, the process in North Carolina. Nurse Practitioner 2:13, 1977
Boyd LC: State Registration for Nurses, 2nd ed., Philadelphia, Saunders, 1915
Breckinridge M: An adventure in midwifery. Survey 57:25, 1926
Breckinridge M: Midwifery in the Kentucky mountains, an investigation in 1923. Q Bull Front Nurs Serv 17:29, 1942
Brief history and current provisions of the law to regulate the practice of nursing in Maine. Maine Nurse 4:10, 1973

British Medical Association: Memorandum on the bills for state registration of nurses prepared respectively by the Association for the State Registration of Trained Nurses and the Royal British Nurses Association. Br J Nurs June 11, 1904, p 472

Brown vs. Board of Education, 347 U.S. 483 (1954)

Browne HE, Issacs G: The frontier nursing service; the primary care nurse in the community hospital. Am J Obstet Gynecol 124:14, 1976

Browning, MH, Lewis E: Expanded Role of the Nurse. New York, American Journal of Nursing Co., 1973

Budd M, Reiffen B, Rodman M, et al: A program for an ambulatory care service. Cambridge, Massachusetts Institute of Technology, January 1969

Bullough B: Social-psychological barriers to housing desegregation. Los Angeles, University of California Housing, Real Estate and Urban Land Studies Program, 1969

Bullough B: Alienation in the ghetto. Am J Sociol 72:469, 1967

Bullough B: The Medicare-Medicaid amendments. Am J Nurs 73:1926, 1973

Bullough B: Is the nurse practitioner role a source of increased work satisfaction? Nurs Res 23:25, 1974

Bullough B: Barriers to the nurse practitioner movement: problems of women in a woman's field. Int J Health Serv 5:225, 1975

Bullough B: The law and the expanding nursing role. Am J Public Health 66:249, 1976

Bullough B: Influences on role expansion. Am J Nurs 76:1476, 1976

Bullough VL: The Development of Medicine as a Profession. Basel, Karger, 1966

Bullough VL: The Subordinate Sex, with a final chapter by B. Bullough. New York Penguin, 1974

Bullough V, Bullough B: Sin, Sickness and Sanity. New York, New American Library, 1977

Bullough VL, Bullough B: The Care of the Sick: The Emergence of Modern Nursing. New York, Prodist, 1978

Burg CD, Brand TS, Hinman MC, Alan-Vaughn GG: Acts of diagnosis by nurses and the Colorado professional nursing practice act. Denver Law 45:467, 1968

Calnen T: Whose agents?: a re-evaluation of the role of the psychiatric nurse in the therapeutic community. Perspect Psychiatr Care 10:59, 1972

Cambridge Research Institute: Trends Affecting the United States Health Care System. DHEW Publication 4RA 76-14503, January 1976

Carnegie Commission on Higher Education: Higher Education and the Nation's Health: Policies for Medical and Dental Education. Special Report and Recommendations. New York, McGraw-Hill, 1970

Carnegie Commission on Higher Education: Less Time, More Options: Education Beyond the High School. Special Report and Recommendations. New York, McGraw-Hill, 1971

Carrick RL: Interim Staff Report: Career Mobility in Primary Care. Sacramento, Career Mobility Project, Department of Consumer Affairs, State of California, 1979

Cazalas MW: Nursing and the Law. Germantown, Aspen Systems, 1978

Center for Research in Ambulatory Health Care Administration: The Organization and Development of a Medical Group Practice. Cambridge, Mass. Ballinger, 1976.

Central Committee for the State Registration of Nurses: Deputation to the home secretary. Br J Nurs, August 8, 1914, p 115

Central Committee for the State Registration of Nurses: State legislation and the college of nursing (negotiations between the committee and the college of nursing to join a bill). British Journal of Nursing 238–40, September 16, 1916

Central Committee for the State Registration of Nurses: Correspondence between the committee and the college of nursing on the nurses registration bill. Br J Nurs, December 2, 1916, p 447

216 Bibliography

Child Abuse and Treatment Act, Public Law 93-247, 88 Stat 4 (1973)
Christensen vs. State of Iowa, 563 F.2d 353, 8th Cir. (1977)
Churchill J: An issue: nurses and psychotherapy. Perspect Psychiatr Care 5:160, 1967
Clapesattle H: The Doctors Mayo. Garden City, N.Y., Garden City Publishing, 1943
Clark and Fin: 200, 210, 8 Eng. Rep. 718, 722 (1843)
Clarke AR: Editorial: Legislation—news and views. RN 12:39, 1949
Cohen HS, Miike LK: Developments in Health Manpower Licensure: A Follow-up to the 1971 Report on Licensure and Related Health Personnel Credentialing. DHEW Publication number HRA 74-3101, 1973
Cohen HS, Dean WJ: To practice or not to practice: developing state law and policy on physicians assistants. Milbank Mem Fund Q, Fall, 1974
College of Nursing: Conference on state registration. Br J Nurs, April 1, 1916, p 292
Commission of Inquiry on Health and Social Welfare: Report. Quebec City, Province of Quebec, 1970
Committee on the Healing Arts. Report 2. Ontario, 1970
Committee on Nurse Practitioners: Report. Ottawa, Department of National Health and Welfare, April 1972
Committee for the Study of Credentialing in Nursing: Credentialing in nursing: a new approach. Am J Nurs 79:674, 1979
Conference on State Registration of Nurses: Conference between representatives of various nursing bodies and the Parliamentary Bills Committee of the B.M.A. held on 14th January 1896, report of proceedings. Nursing Record, January 18, 1896, p 55
Continuing education to become mandatory in Massachusetts in 1982 under new law. Am J Nurs 78:183, 1978
Corning PA: The Evolution of Medicare: From Idea to Law. DHEW, Social Security Administration, Research Report No. 29, Washington, U.S. Government Printing Office, 1969
Cayne DW: Hospital liability: Implications of recent physician's assistant statutes. Clev St Law Rev 21:98, 1972
Crawford JA: The reasons for the state registration of trained nurses. Nursing Record, August 25, 1900, p 149
Creighton H: Changing Legal Attitudes: The Effect of the Law on Nursing. New York, NLN Council of Hospitals and Related Institutional Nursing Service, 1974
Creighton H: Law Every Nurse Should Know, 3d ed. Philadelphia, Saunders, 1975
Curran WJ, Harding TW: The law and mental health. Int Dig of Health Legis 28:725, 1977
Curran WJ: New paramedical personnel—to license or not to license. N Engl J Med 282:1085, 1972
Dahl RA: Who Governs? Democracy and Power in an American City. New Haven, Yale University Press, 1961
Daniels AK: How free should the profession be? In Freidson E (ed): The Professions and Their Prospects. Beverly Hills, Sage 1971
Darling vs. Charleston Community Hospital. 200 NE 2d 145 (1964); 211 NE 2d 253 (Illinois 1965)
The Darling case. JAMA 206:1665, 1968
The Darling case revisited. JAMA 206:1875, 1968
Davidson MH et al: A short-term intensive training program for pediatric nurse practitioners. J Pediatr 87:315, 1975
Davis AJ, Aroskar MA: Ethical Dilemmas and Nursing Practice. New York, Appleton, 1978

Dean WJ: State legislation for physician's assistants: a review and analysis. Health Serv Rep 88:3, 1973
De Maio D: The born-again nurse. Nurs Outlook 27:272, 1979
Dent vs. West Virginia, United States Reports: Cases Adjudged in the Supreme Court, 129:114–128, 1888
Deputation of anti registrationists at the privy council office. Br J Nurs June 23, 1905, p 499
Derbyshire RC: Medical Licensure and Discipline in the United States. Baltimore, The Johns Hopkins Press, 1969
deSilva EB: Jurisprudence for nurses. Hosp Prog 14:23, 1933
deTornyay R: State board member. Am J Nurs 69:570, 1969
Dewdney JCH: Australian Health Services. Sydney, Wiley, 1972
Dienes CT: Judges, legislators and social change. Am Behav Sci 13:511, 1970
Dietrich C: The nurse and the law. Hospitals 10:34, 1936
Dingle J: The ills of man. Sci Am 229:77, 1974
Discussion on proposed legislation against midwives. Med Rec 53:210, 1898
Dock LL: A History of Nursing, vol. 3. New York, Putnam, 1912
Dock LL: State registration. Br J Nurs, February 1905, p 148
Dock LL: What we may expect from the law. Am J Nurs 1:8, 1900
Doubleday EM: Nursing homes registration bill. Nurs Times 23:1236, 1927
Draye MA, Pesznecker BL: Diagnostic scope and certainty: an analysis of family nurse practitioner practice. Nurse Pract 4:15, 1979
Driscoll VM: Liberating nursing practice. Nurs Outlook 20:24, 1972
Driscoll VM: Reflections on the birth of an idea. J of NY St Nurs Assoc 2:5, 1971
Dublin LI: The First One Thousand Midwifery Cases of the Frontier Nursing Service. New York, Metropolitan Life Insurance Company, 1932
Dublin TD: Foreign physicians: their impact on U.S. health care. Science 185:407, 1974
Durbin E, Zuckerman S: Legislation affects nursing practice. Nurs Admin Q 2:39, 1978
Durham vs. United States, 214 F. 2d 862, 874, Washington, D.C. Cir. (1954)
Eccard WT: Revolution in white: new approaches in treating nurses as professionals. Vanderbilt Law Rev 30:839, 1977
Eckstein H: Pressure Group Politics: The Case of the British Medical Association. London, Allen, 1960
Editorial: All those who nurse for hire! Am J Nurs 39:275, 1939
Education for Nurse-Midwifery: The Report of the Second Work Conference on Nurse-Midwifery Education. New York, Maternity Center Association, 1967
Educational preparation for nursing. Nurs Outlook 26:568, 1977
Ehrenreich B, English D: Witches, Midwives and Nurses. Old Westbury, N.Y., Feminist Press, 1973
Engel G: The birth of an occupation: perspectives of physician's assistants. Presented at the American Sociological Association Meeting, 1976
Ennis B, Siegel L: The Rights of Mental Patients: The Basic ACLU Guide to a Mental Patient's Rights, 1973
Epstein CF: Woman's Place. Options and Limits in Professional Careers. Berkeley, University of California Press, 1970
Evang K: Health Services in Norway. Olso, Hammerstad, 1969
Eve RC: Licensing of midwives. Charlotte (NC) Med J 6:990, 1895
Executive board initiates child health manpower training program in a major effort to improve pediatric care. Newsl Am Acad Pediatr 20:14, 1969
The expanded role of the nurse: a joint statement of CNA/CMA. Canadian Nurse, May 1977, p 23

Farrisey RM: How the pediatric nurse associate movement began. In Child Health Care in the '70's. Eastern Regional Workshop on Pediatric Nurse Associate Programs, American Nurses' Association. Boston, American Academy of Pediatrics, 1972
Fein R. The Doctor Shortage: An Economic Diagnosis. Washington, Brookings Institute 1967
Fein R: An economist's view: medical manpower a continuing crisis. JAMA 201:171, 1976
Fenwick EG: The organization and registration of nurses. Nurs Rec, April 12, 1902, p 284
Fenwick EG: State registration of trained nurses. Nineteenth Century 67:1049, 1910
Fenwick EG: The nursing profession and the board of trade. Br J Nurs, January 22, 1916, p 73; January 29, 1916, p 73
Fenwick EG: The nurses' registration act. Br J Nurs, January 10, 1920, p 20
Ferguson MC: Nursing at the crossroads; which way to turn, a look at the model of the nurse practitioner. J Adv Nurs 1:237, 1976
Fish MS: Nursing vis-a-vis medicine. A proposal for legislation. In American Nurses' Association: Licensure and Credentialing: Proceedings of the ANA Conference for Members and Professional Employees of State Boards of Nursing and ANA Advisory Council. Detroit, American Nurses' Association, 1974
Flexner A: Medical education in the United States and Canada. Carnegie Found Advanc Teach Bull 4, 1910
Fogotson EH: Licensure, accreditation and certification as assurance of high quality health care. Paper presented at National Health Forum Meeting, Los Angeles, March 1968
Fogotson EH, Bradley CR, Ballenger M: Health service for the poor—the manpower problem: innovations and the law. Wisc Law Rev 1970:756, 1970
Fogotson EH, Roemer R, Newman RW, Cook JL: Licensure of other medical personnel. In Report of the National Advisory Commission on Health Manpower, vol. 2., Washington, U.S. Government Printing Office, 1967
Forman AM, Cooper EM: Legislation and nurse-midwifery practice in USA. J Nurse-Midwif 21:iii, 1976
Forman AM: Patterns of Legislation and Practice of Nurse-Midwifery in the USA. New York, American College of Nurse-Midwives, 1974
Freidman AP: Chronic Recurring Headache. East Hanover, N.J., Sandoz, 1973
Freidman WG: Law in a Changing Society. New York, Columbia University Press, 1964
Freidson, E: Professional Dominance: The Social Structure of Medical Care. New York, Atherton Press, 1970
Freidson E: The future of professionalization. In Stacey M (ed): Health and the Division of Labor. New York, Prodist, 1977
Gamer M: The ideology of professionalism. Nurs Outlook 27:108, 1979
Gans HJ: The Levittowners. New York, Pantheon, 1967
Georgopoulas BS, Christman L: The clinical nurse specialist: a role model. In Reihl JP, McVay JW (eds): The Clinical Nurse Specialist: Interpretations. New York, Appleton, 1973
Goffman E: The Presentation of Self in Everday Life. Garden City, N.Y.: Doubleday Anchor, 1959
Goldberg G, Grady M, Budd M: Applicability of protocol management of chronic disease to an aged population. Cambridge, Massachusetts Institute of Technology, Beth Israel Hospital, July 1970
Goodspeed HE: The independent practitioner—can it survive? J Psychiatr Nurs 14:33, 1976
Goodstine L, Streiff K, Bragg F: Evaluation of aide triage of ambulatory patients. Cambridge, Massachusetts Insitute of Technology, Beth Israel Hospital, Ambulatory Care Project 20, April 1971
Greely DM: American foreign medical graduates. J Med Educ 41:641, 1966

Green K: Occupational Licensing and the Supply of Nonprofessional Manpower. U.S. Department of Labor Manpower Research Monograph no. 11. Washington, U.S. Government Printing Office, 1969
Greenfield S, Friedland G, Seifers S, et al: Protocol management of dysuria, frequency and vaginal discharge. Annals Internal Medicine 81:452–57, 1974
Greenfield S, Bragg F, McCraith D et al: An upper respiratory complaint protocol for physician-extenders. Archives Internal Medicine 133:294–99, 1974
Greenfield S et al: Nurse protocol management of low back pain. West J Med 123:350, 1975
Greenridge J, Zimmern A, Kohnke M: Community nurse practitioners—a partnership. Nurs Outlook 21:228, 1973
Griggs vs. Duke Power Company, 401 U.S. 424 (1971)
Guidelines on short term continuing education programs for pediatric nurse associates. Am J Nurs 71:509, 1971
Hall V: Statutory Regulation of the Scope of Nursing Practice: A Critical Survey. Chicago, National Joint Practice Commission, 1975
Harrison G, Harrison JH: The Nurse and the Law. Philadelphia, Davis, 1945
Hastings JEF: Federal-provincial insurance for hospital and physician's care in Canada. Int J Health Serv 1.398, 1971
Hays JS: The psychiatric nurse as sociotherapist. Am J Nurs 62:64, 1962
Health Care Financing Administration, HEW: Rural health clinics: conditions for certification. Fed Reg 43:5373, 1978
Hemelt MD, Mackert ME: Dynamics of Law in Nursing and Health Care. Reston, Va., Reston, 1978
Hedrick V: A national survey: educating for the expanded role. Nurse Pract 3:13, 1978
Hershey N: Legal Aspects of Nursing. New York, American Nurses' Association, 1962
Hershey N: Nurses' medical practice problems, part I. Am J Nurs 62:3, 1962
Hershey N: An alternative to mandatory licensure of health professionals. Hosp Prog 50:71, 1969
Hershey N: Legal issues in nursing practice. In Spaulding EK, Notter LE (eds): Professional Nursing: Foundations, Perspectives and Relationships. Philadelphia, Lippincott, 1970
Hershey N: Expanded roles for professional nurses. J Nurs Admin 3:30, 1973
Hershey N: Nursing practice acts and professional delusion. J Nurs Admin 4:36, 1974
Herzog EL: The underutilization of nurse practitioners in ambulatory care. Nurse Pract 2:26, 1976
Hicks EJ: New nurse practice act: close up and its workings; what new law will mean to physician, hospital administrator and nurse. NY St J Med 38:1098, 1938
History and development of official examination of nurses and social hygiene workers. Rev. Philanthrop 50:81, 1930
Hoebel EA: Man in the Primitive World. New York, McGraw-Hill, 1958
Hoekelman RA: Evaluating the pediatric nurse associate. In Child Health Care in the '70's: Eastern Regional Workshop on Pediatric Nurse Associate Programs, American Nurses' Association and American Academy of Pediatrics, Boston, 1972
Holder AR: Medical Malpractice Law. New York, John Wiley, 1975
Holland S: Manifesto against state registration. Br J Nurs, March 1904, p 246
Holmes OW Jr: The Common Law. Boston, Little, Brown, 1881
Hospital liable for nurses' failure to report questioned patient care. Citation 36:1, 1977
Hudak CM, Lohr TL, Gallo BM: Critical care nursing: what makes it special. In Hudak GM, Lohr TL, Gallo BM (eds): Critical Care Nursing. New York, Lippincott, 1977
Hughes C et al: Twenty Thousand Nurses Tell Their Story. Philadelphia, Lippincott, 1958
Hutchison D: Certification: new impetus to continuing education. Contin Educ Nurs, September/October 1973, p 3

Illinois nurses say state nursing act is being violated. Am J Nurs 78:185, 1978
The impact of title VI on health facilities. George Washington Law Rev 36:980, 1968
Independence of nursing function affirmed by New York legislature. Am J Nurs 7:1901, 1971
Informed consent, parts I, II, II. JAMA 214:1181, 1383, 1611; 1970
Institutional licensure opposed by NCSNNE. Am J Nurs 72:701, 1973
International Council of Nurses, Florence Nightingale International Foundation: Report of an International Seminar on Nursing Legislation Warsaw, 1970. Basel, Karger, 1971
Iverson M: Our nursing laws. Train Nurs Hosp Rev 9:78, 1918
Jacobsen M: Nursing laws and what every nurse should know about them. Am J Nurs 40:1221, 1940
Jacox A, Norris C (eds): Organizing for Independent Nursing Practice. New York, Appleton, 1977
Jamieson EM, Sewell M: Trends in Nursing History. Philadelphia, Saunders, 1944
Johnson DE: A philosophy of nursing. Nurs Outlook 7:198, 1957
Judge rules PA orders not legal until countersigned. Am J Nurs 78:1143, 1978
Kerher BH, Intriligator MD: Malpractice and the employment of allied health personnel. Med Care 8:876, 1975
Kelly LY: Nursing practice acts. American Journal of Nursing 74:1310–19, July, 1974
Kelly LY: Credentialing of health care personnel. Nurs Outlook 25:562, 1977
Kelly LY: End paper: the revolt of the nurses. Nurs Outlook 26:661, 1978
Kinlein ML: Independent nurse practitioner. Nurs Outlook 20:22, 1972
Kinkela GG, Kinkela RV: Licensure: what's it all about? J Nurs Admin 4:18, 1974
Kinkela GG, Kinkela RV: Laws for leaders, institutional licensure: cure-all or chaos? J Nurs Admin, May–June 1974, p 16
Kinlein ML: Independent Nursing Practice with Clients. Philadelphia, Lippincott, 1977
Kissam PC: Physician assistant and nurse practitioner laws: a study of health law reform. Kansas Law Rev 24:1, 1975
Kissam PC: Physician's assistants and nurse practitioners: law for expanded medical delegation. In Bliss AA, Cohen ED (eds): The New Health Professionals, Germantown, Md., Aspen Systems Corporation, 1977
Kobrin FE: The American midwife controversy: a crisis of professionalization. Bull Hist Med 40:350, 1966
Komaroff AT, Winickoff RN: Common Acute Illnesses: A Problem Oriented Textbook with Protocols. Boston, Little, Brown, 1977
Komaroff A, Black W, Flatley M, et al: Protocols for physician assistants: management of diabetes and hypertension. N Engl J Med 290:307, 1974
Kortright JL: Should midwives be registered? NY J Gynecol Obstet 3:197, 1893
Kozlow D (ed): National Disease and Therapeutic Index, Specialty Profile. Ambler, Pa., Lea, 1970
Kreuter FR: What is good nursing care? Nurs Outlook 5:302, 1957
Lego S: Nurse psychotherapists: how are we different. Perspect Psychiatr Care 11:144, 1973
Leininger M: An open health care system model. Nurs Outlook 21:171, 1973
Leitch C, Mitchell ES: A state-by-state report: the legal accomodation of nurses practicing expanded roles. Nurse Pract 2:19, 1977
Lesnik MJ, Anderson BE: Legal Aspects of Nursing. Philadelphia, Lippincott, 1947
Lewin K: Group decision and social change. In Maccoby E et al (eds): Readings in Social Psychology. New York, Holt, Rinehart and Winston, 1958
Lewis CE, Resnick BA: Nurse clinics and progressive ambulatory patient care. N Engl J Med 277:1236, 1967
Lewis C: The team is in the doctor's bag. Paper presented at the meeting of the National League for Nursing, Detroit, May 1969

Lewis EP: The right to inform. Nurs Outlook 25:561, 1977
Litoff JB: American Midwives: 1860 to the Present. Westport, Ct., Greenwood Press, 1978
Lloyd JJ: Arguments for state regulation of health professions. Hosp Prog 51:71, 1970
Lombardi T, Hoffman GN: Medical Malpractice Insurance: A Legislator's View. Syracuse, Syracuse University Press, 1978
Longest VB: Expanded roles for Veterans Administration nurses. Am J Nurs 73:2087, 1973
Lubic RW: Myths about nurse-midwifery. Am J Nurs 74:268, 1974
Lynaugh JE, Bates B: Physical diagnosis: a skill for all nurses? Am J Nurs 74:58, 1974
Mabbot JM: The regulation of midwives in New York. Am J Obstet Dis Wom Child 60:516, 1907
Macket R et al: Physician's assistants as facilitators of clinical competence in a neurosciences course. J Med Educ 51:428, 1976
Magaw A: Observations on 1092 cases of anesthesia from January 1, 1899 to January 1, 1900. Tr Nurs Hosp Rev 31:150, 1903
Magaw A: A review of over 14,000 surgical anesthetics. Surg Gynecol Obstet 3:795, 1906
Maister M: The control of nursing homes and midwives; legal aspects and education. S Afr J R San Inst 59:118, 1938
Major regulations provisions: rural health clinic services bill. Fed Reg 43:8259, 1978
Mandelbaum JL: Malpractice roulette: pediatric nurse practitioner risk. Pediatr Nurs 3:30, 1977
March JG, Simon HA: Organizations. New York, Wiley, 1958
Marshall HE: Mary Adelaide Nutting: Pioneer of Modern Nursing. Baltimore, Johns Hopkins Press, 1972
Massachusetts Nurses' Association: Position statement on the physicians' assistant. Boston, March 1971
Mauksch IG: The nurse practitioner movement—where does it go from here? Am J Public Health 68:1074, 1978
Mauksch IG, Rogers M: Nursing is coming of age through the practitioner movement. Am J Nurs 75:1834, 1975
McAdams D: Institution-based licensure system may help solve the licensure dilemma. Hosp Prog 50:52, 1969
McAtee P, Zurfluh P, Andrews P: Certification: a progress report. Pediatr Nurs 3:26, 1977
McGivern D: Baccalaureate preparation of the nurse practitioner. Nurs Outlook 22:94, 1974
Meglen MC, Burst HV: Nurse-midwives make a difference. Nurs Outlook 22:386, 1974
Merton R: Social Theory and Social Structure, revised and enlarged ed. Glencoe, Ill.: Free Press, 1975
Miike LH: Institutional licensure: an experimental model, not a solution. Med Care 12:214, 1974
Miike L, Cohen H: Developments in Health Manpower Licensure and Related Health Personnel Credentialing. Washington, DHEW 74-3101, June, 1973
Millard RM: The new accountability. Nurs Outlook 23:496, 1975
Miller C: Nurses and the Law. Danville, Ill., Interstate Printers and Publishers, 1970
Miller J et al: Use of physicians assistants in thoracic and cardiovascular surgery in the community hospital. Am Surg 44:162, 1977
Mills EW, Dale J: Florence Nightingale and state registration. Int Nurs Rev 11:31, 1964
Montag M, Gotkin LG: Community College Education for Nursing. New York, McGraw-Hill, 1959

Morgan D: The future expanded role of the nurse. Can Hosp 39:75, 1962
Muller vs. United States Steel Corp., 509 F.2d 293 (10th Cir. 1975)
Murchison I, Nichols TS, Hanson R: Legal Accountability in the Nursing Process. St. Louis, Mosby, 1978
Murchison I, Nichols TS: Legal Foundations of Nursing Practice. London, Collier-Macmillan, 1970
Murray VV: Nursing in Ontario. Toronto, Committee on the Healing Arts, 1970
Nagel S: The Legal Process from a Behavioral Perspective. Homewood, Ill., Dorsey Press, 1969
National Academy of Sciences: Allied Health Personnel: A Report on Their Use in the Non-Military Health Care Program. Washington, NAS, 1969
National Center for Health Statistics, U.S. Department of Health, Education and Welfare: State Licensing of Health Occupation, Public Health Service Publication No. 1758, Washington, U.S. Government Printing Office, 1968
National Commission for the Study of Nursing and Nursing Education: An Abstract for Action. New York, McGraw-Hill, 1970
National Committee on Accrediting: Staff Working Papers, Part I: Accreditation of Health Educational Programs. Washington, 1972
National Committee on Accrediting: Study of Accreditation of Selected Health Education Programs. Washington, 1972
National Health Council: Credentialing of Health Manpower—Conference Report. New York, NHC, 1978
National New Health Practitioner Program: Profile, 1976–1977. Washington, Association of Physician Assistant Programs, 1977
New Massachusetts law restores autonomy to board of nursing. Am J Nurs 76:831, 1976
New York, State of: A bill for the registration of nurses of New York State. Br J Nurs, March 28, 1903, p 252
New York State Nurses' Association: Resolution on Entry into Professional Practice. Albany, NYSNA, 1974
New York State Nurses' Association: Statement on the physicians' associate and specialist's assistant. Albany, January 1972
New Zealand: the hospital nurses registration act. Nurs Rec, November 23, 1901, p 416
Noonan B: Eight years in a medical nurse clinic. Am J Nurs 72:1128, 1972
North Carolina, State of: An act to provide for the registration of trained nurses. Br J Nursing, April 18, 1903, p 314
Nova Scotia Council of Health: Health Care in Nova Scotia, A New Direction for the Seventies. 73–76, 1972
Nuckolls KB: Who decides what the nurse can do? Nurs Outlook 22:626, 1974
Nurse anesthetists. JAMA 211:1591, 1970
The nurse as a therapist vs. her role in the medical model; Psychiatric nurse vs. mental health worker. Perspect Psychiatr Care 6:271, 288; 1968
Nurse practitioners fight moves to restrict their practice. Am J Nurs 78:1285, 1978
Nurses' Board of Western Australia: Policy on the role of the nurse. Aust Nurs J 3:43, 1973
Nursing and mid-wifery. S Afr Nurs J 16:11, 1950
Nursing in Canada: from pioneering history to a modern federation. Int Nurs Rev 15:1, 1968
Nursing legislation, 1939: what the state nurses' association accomplished. Am J Nurs 39:974, 1939
Nuttall R, Scheuch E, Gordon C: On the structure of influence. In Clark T (ed): Community Structure and Decision Making: Comparative Analyses. San Francisco, Chandler, 1968

Olden, Jean: ANA certification: recognition of excellence. Assoc Op Room Nurs J March 1974, p 675
Olsen L: The expanded role of the nurse in maternity practice. Nurs Clin N Am 9:459, 1974
Osler W: Aequanimitas. Philadelphia, Blakeston, 1942
O'Sullivan J: Law for Nurses and Allied Health Professionals in Australia. Sydney, Law Book Co, 1977
Palmer SF: The effect of state registration upon training schools. Am J Nurs 5:656, 1905
Patterns of Legislation and the Practice of Nurse-Midwifery in the United States. New York, American College of Nurse-Midwives, 1974
Penka WJ: History of the Kansas nurse practice act, 1913–1973. Kans Nurs 48:3, 1973
Perry B: Physician's assistant: an overview of an emerging health profession. Med Care 12:982, 1977
Pesznecker BL, Draye MA: Family nurse practitioners in primary care: a study of practice and patients. Am J Public Health 68:977, 1978
Peterson P: Should institutional licensure replace individual licensure? Am J Nurs 74:446, 1974
Plessy vs. Ferguson, 163 U.S. 537 (1896)
Poole E: Nurses on Horseback. New York, Macmillan, 1933
Poole H: The reasons for the state registration of trained nurses. Nus Rec, August 1900, p. 131
Positions, conclusions and recommendations from the study of credentialing in nursing: a new approach. Nurs Outlook 27:263, 1979
Poynter FNL: The Evolution of Medical Practice in Britain. London, Pitman, 1961
Proof of competency for Michigan nurses is required by 1984. Am J Nurs 78:2001, 1978
Rachels J: Active and passive euthanasia. N Engl J Med 292:78, 1975
Rae J: Life of Adam Smith (orig 1895). New York, A. M. Kelley, 1965
Rafferty R, Carner J: Nursing Consultants, Inc.— a corporation. Nurs Outlook 21:232, 1973
Rakel E: Primary care—whose responsibility. J Fam Pract 2:429, 1975
Ratcliffe R: The Good Samaritan and the Law. Garden City, N.Y., Doubleday Anchor, 1966
Rebirth of the midwife. Life 71:50-55, November 19, 1971
Redman E: The Dance of Legislation. New York, Simon and Schuster, 1973
Regenie S: Dateline: New York State, 1973. J Nurse-Midwif 18:19, 1973
Regenie SJ: The new definition of nursing in relation to nurse-midwifery. J NY St Nurs Assoc 4:16, 1973
Regional review. Nurs Pract 3:6, 1978
Report of convention. Am J Nurs 74:1272, 1974
Report on Licensure and Related Personnel Credentialing. DHEW Publication Number HSM 72-11. Washington, U.S. Government Printing Office, 1971
Riehl JP, McVay JW (eds): The Clinical Nurse Specialist: Interpretations. New York, Appleton, 1973
Roberts MM: American Nursing: History and Interpretation. New York, Macmillan, 1961
Robinson A, Kinlein ML: Independent nurse-practitioner. RN 35:40, 1972 January, 1972
Robinson V: White Caps: The Story of Nursing. Philadelphia, Lippincott, 1946
Rockefeller Foundation: Laws Governing the Practice of Midwifery (1904-1930). New York: Rockefeller Foundation, 1931
Rogers ME: Reveille in Nursing. Philadelphia, Davis, 1964
Rogers ME: Nursing: to be or not to be? Nurs Outlook 20:42, 1972
Roemer MI: Primary care and physician extenders in affluent countries. Int J Health Serv 7:545, 1977

Roemer MI, Roemer R: Health Manpower in the Changing Australian Health Services Scene. DHEW Publication HRA 76-58. Washington, Health Resources Administration, U.S. Department of Health, Education and Welfare, 1976
Roemer MI, Roemer R: Health Manpower in the Socialist Health Care System of Poland. DHEW Publication HRA 77–85. Washington, Health Resources Administration, U.S. Department of Health, Education and Welfare, 1977
Roemer MI, Roemer R: Health Manpower Policies in the Belgian Health Care System. DHEW Publication HRA 77-38. Washington, Health Resources Administration, U.S. Department of Health, Education and Welfare, 1977
Roemer MI, Roemer R: Health Manpower under National Health Insurance—The Canadian Experience. DHEW Publication HRA 77-37. Washington, Health Resources Administration, U.S. Department of Health, Education and Welfare, 1977
Roemer MI, Roemer R: Manpower in the Health Care System of Norway. DHEW Publication HRA 77-39. Washington, Health Resources Administration, U.S. Department of Health, Education, and Welfare, 1977
Roemer R: Legal systems regulating health personnel: a comparative analysis. Milbank Mem Fund Q 46:279, 1968
Roemer R: Licensing and regulation of medical and medical-related practitioners in health service teams. Med Care 9:42, 1971
Roemer R: The nurse practitioner in family planning services: law and practice. Fam Plan Populat Rep 6:28, 1977
Rooks JB, Fischman SH, Kaplan E, et al: Nurse-Midwifery in the United States 1976–77. Washington, American College of Nurse-Midwifes, 1978
Roon LM: The history of nursing legislation in the British Commonwealth, 1891–1939. PhD diss., Radcliffe College, 1952
Rosenberg C, Smith-Rosenberg C (eds): The Male Mid-wife and the Female Doctor: The Gynecology Controversy in Nineteenth-Century America. New York, Arno Press, 1974
Rosinski E: Social classes of medical students. JAMA 193:89, 1965
Ross HL, Campbell D, Glass G: Determination of the social effects of a legal reform. Am Behav Sci 13:494, 1970
Rothman DA, Rothman NL: The Professional Nurse and the Law. Boston, Little, Brown, 1977
Rouslin S: On certification of the clinical specialists in psychiatric nursing, editorial. Perspect Psychiatr Care 10:59, 1972
Royal Australian Nursing Federation, National Florence Nightingale Committee of Australia: Survey Report on the Wastage of General Trained Nurses from Nursing in Australia, 1967
Runyan J: The Memphis chronic disease control program: comparisons in outcomes and the nurse's expanded role. JAMA 213:264, 1975
Rural health bill signed: payments to NP's authorized. Am J Nurs 78:8, 1978
Russel RO: Freedom to Die: Moral and Legal Aspects of Euthanasia. New York, Human Sciences Press, 1977
Russell RO: Moral and legal aspects of euthanasia. Humanist 34:22, 1974
Ryan J, Gearhart MK, Simons S: From personal responsibility to professional accountability in psychiatric nursing. J Psychiatr Nurs 15:19, 1977
Sackett DL et al; The Burlington randomized trial of the nurse practitioner: health outcomes of patients. Ann Int Med 80:137, 1974
Sadler AM: Legal and related barriers to increased utilization of new health practitioners. Ala J Med Sci 2:223, 1974
Sadler AM: New health practitioner education: problems and issues. J Med Educ 50:67, 1975

Sadler AM, Sadler BL: Recent developments in the law relating to physicians' assistants. Vanderbilt Law Rev 24:1205, 1971
Sadler AM, Sadler B, Bliss A: The Physician's Assistant: Today and Tomorrow. New Haven, Yale University Press, 1975
Sadler BL: Licensure for the physicians assistant. In Lippart VW, Purcell EF (eds): Intermediate-Level Health Practitioners. New York, Josiah Macy Foundation, 1973
Sarner H: The Nurse and the Law. Philadelphia, Saunders, 1968
Schachtel BP: The pediatric nurse practitioner: origins and challenges. Med Care 16:1019, 1978
Schmahl JA: The psychiatric nurse and psychotherapy. Nurs Outlook 10:460, 1962
Schneller E: The Physician's Assistant. Lexington, Mass., Health, 1978
Schonfeld H, Heston J, Falk I: Number of physicians required for primary medical care. N Engl J Med 286:571, 1972
Schorr TM: Where the action is. Am J Nurs 72:671, 1972
Schutt BG: Frontier's family nurses. Am J Nursing 72:903, 1972
Schutt BG: Spot check on primary care nursing. Am J Nurs 72:1996, 1972
Schwartz W, Gorry G, Kassirer J, et al: Decision analysis and clinical judgement. Am J Med 55:459-72, 1973
Seacat M, Schlachter L: Expanded nursing role in prenatal and infant care. Am J Nurs 68:822, 1968
Seymer LR: A General History of Nursing. New York, Macmillan, 1933
Shannon ML: Nurses in American history. Our first four licensure laws. Am J Nurs 75:1327, 1975
Shannon ML: The origin and development of professional licensure examinations in nursing: From a state-constructed examination to the state board test pool examination. PhD diss., Columbia University, 1972
Sheward V: A new Long Island concept: independent nurse. Newsday, August 13, 1973
Shoemaker MT: History of nurse mid-wifery in the United States. MS thesis, Catholic University of America, 1947
Shryock RH: Medical Licensing in America 1645-1695. Baltimore, Johns Hopkins Press, 1967
Siegal E, Bryson S: Redefinition of the role of the public health nurse in child health supervision. Am J Public Health. 53:1015, 1972
Sierra Vista Hospital vs. California Superior Court. 56 Cal Rptr 387 (1967)
Sigerist HE: The history of medical licensure. In: Roemer M (ed): Henry E. Sigerist on the Sociology of Medicine. 1960
Sigerist HE: The history of medical licensure. JAMA 104:1060, 1935
Silver H, Ford L: The pediatric nurse practitioner at Colorado. Am J Nurs 67:1143, 1967
Silver H, Ford L, Stearly S: A program to increase health care for children: the pediatric nurse practitioner program. Pediatrics 39:756, 1967
Sledge vs. J.P. Stevens Company, 10 E.P.D. 9110, 585, E.D. (North Carolina 1975)
Slome C et al: Effectiveness of certified nurse-midwives: a prospective evaluative study. Am J Obstet Gynecol 124:177, 1976
Smoyak S: Specialization in nursing: from then to now. Nurs Outlook 24:676, 1976
Smalkowski MF: A year later: an independent practitioner looks back. J Psychiatr Nurs, August 1976, p. 35
Smith HL: Two lines of authority: the hospital's dilemma. In Jaco EG (ed): Patients, Physicians and Illness. Glencoe, Ill., Free Press, 1958
Society for the State Registration of Trained Nurses: Deputation to the prime minister in support of state registration. Br J Nurs, May 1909, p 406
Society for the State Registration of Trained Nurses: Meeting to discuss the college of nursing conference on state registration. Br J Nurs, April 1916, p 316

Sonntay VK: Neurosurgery and the physician assistant. Surg Neurol 8:207, 1977
Sorkin A: Health Manpower. An Economic Perspective. Lexington, Mass., Lexington Books, 1977
Spitzer W et al: Nurse practitioners in primary care III. The Southern Canadian randomized trial. Can Med Assoc J 108:1005, 1973
Spitzer W et al: The Burlington randomized trial of the nurse practitioner. N Engl J Med 290:5, 1974
Stachyra M: Nurses, psychotherapy and the law. Perspect Psychiatr Care 7:200, 1969
Stachyra M: Self-regulation through certification. Perspect Psychiatr Care 11:48, 1973
The state board test pool examination. Am J Nurs 52:613, 1952
State Licensing of Health Occupations. National Center for Health Statistics Public Health Service Publication 1758, Washington, U.S. Government Printing Office, 1967
The status of continuing education: voluntary and mandatory. Am J Nurs 77:410, 1977
Statutory status of six professions. Res Bull Nat Educ Assoc 16:184, 1938
Stead EA Jr: Training and use of paramedical personnel. N Engl J Med 277:800, 1967
Steele G: The midwife problem and its legal control. Maryland Med J 48:1, 1905
Stein L: The doctor-nurse game. Arch Gen Psychiatry 16:699, 1967
Stenger FE: Historical review of the nurse practice act and Susan B. Cook's contributions to nursing. Weather Vane 44:7, 1975
Steward PL, Cantor MG: Varieties of Work Experience: The Social Control of Occupational Groups and Roles. New York, Wiley and Sons, 1974
Stevenson N: Curriculum development in practical nurse education. Am J Nurs 64:81, 1964
St. Geme JW; et al: A curricular experiment with the nurse pediatrist. Am J Dis Child 122:195, 1971
Stoeckle JD, Noonan B, Farrisey RM, Sweatt A: Medical nursing clinic for the chronically ill. Am J Nurs 63:87, 1973
Strauss A et al: The hospital and its negotiated order. In Friedson E (ed): The Hospital in Modern Society. New York, Free Press of Glencoe, 1963
Streiff CJ: Nursing and the Law, 2nd ed. Rockville, Md. Aspen System Corp., 1975
Studdiford WE: Attempts at regulation of midwife practice. Am J Obstet Dis Women Child 63:898, 1911
Sullivan J, Dachelet CZ, Stultz HA, and Henry M: The rural nurse practitioner: a challenge and a response. Am J Public Health 68:972, 1968
Sultz HA; and Kinyon L: Longitudinal Study of Nurse Practitioners Phase I. HEW Division of Nursing, Bureau of Health Manpower, HRA 76-43, 1976
Sultz HA, Henry MO, Sullivan JA: Nurse practitioner: USA. Lexington, Mass., Heath, 1979
Tarasoff vs. Regents of University of California. 17 Cal. 3d 425, 441, fn. 13 131 Cal. Rptr. 14, 555 P. 2nd. 334, 1976
Tarasoff vs. Regents of California, 81 Cal. App. 3d 614, 1978
Terris M: False starts and lesser alternatives. Bull NY Acad Med 53:129, 1977
Terry CE: The mother, the midwife and the law. Delineator 92:12, 1916
Thatcher VS: A History of Anesthesia: With Emphasis on the Nurse Specialist. Philadelphia, Lippincott, 1952
Tirpak H: The frontier nursing services. Fifty years in the mountains. Nurs Outlook 23:308, 1975
Trained attendants and practical nurses. Am J Nurs 44:7, 1944
The Training and Responsibilities of the Midwife. New York, Josiah Macy, Foundation, 1967

Trandel-Korenchuk DM, Trandel-Korenchuk KM: How state laws recognize advanced nursing practice. Nurs Outlook 26:713, 1978

Tucker R, Wetterau B: Credentialing health personnel by licensed hospitals: The report of a study of institutional licensure. Chicago, Rush-Presbyterian-St. Luke's Medical Center, 1975

Ujhely GB: The nurse as psychotherapist: what are the issues? Perspect Psychiatr Care 11:155, 1973.

US Department of Health, Education and Welfare; Report of the National Advisory Commission on Health Manpower, vol. 1. Washington: U.S. Government Printing Office, 1967.

US Department of Health, Education and Welfare: Report of the National Advisory Commission Health Manpower, vol. 2. Washington: U.S. Government Printing Office, 1968

US Department of Health, Education and Welfare: Report on Licensure and Related Health Personnel Credentialing, HSM 72-11, Washington, DHEW, 1971

US Department of Health, Education and Welfare, Secretary's Committee to Study Extended Roles for Nurses: Extending the Scope of Nursing Practice. Washington: U.S. Government Printing Office, 1971

US Department of Health, Education and Welfare: Health Resources Statistics, Health Manpower and Health Facilities. Washington, DHEW, 1971–72

US Department of Health, Education and Welfare: Developments in Health Manpower Licensure, HRA 74-3000. Washington, DHEW, 1973

US Department of Health, Education and Welfare, National Center for Health Statistics: Health Resources Statistics, Health Manpower and Health Facilities. Washington: U.S. Government Printing Office, 1976

US Department of Health, Education and Welfare: Credentialing Health Manpower, 05 77-50057. Washington, DHEW, 1977

Utter vs. United Hospital Center Inc. 236 S.E. 2d 213 (West Virginia Supreme Court of Appeals, 1977)

Van Langendonck J: The European experience in social health insurance. Soc Sec Bull, July 1973

Van Massenhove G: The statute and the evolution of the profession. Nursing (Brussels) 44:1, 1972

Waller CE: The social security act in its relation to public health. Am J Public Health 25:1186, 1935

Weiler PG: Health manpower dialectic-physician, nurse, physician assistant. Am J Public Health 65:858, 1975

Weisl BAG: The nurse-midwife and the New York city health code. West J Surg, Obstet Gynecol 71:266, 1963

Wertz RW, Wertz DC: Lying-In: A History of Childbirth in America. New York, Schocken, 1979

West RM: Legislation and nursing growth, statutory control since 1903. Trained Nurse 80:700, 1928

West RM: History of Nursing in Pennsylvania. Pennsylvania State Nurses' Association, 1933

Whitaker JG: The issue of mandatory continuing education. Nurs Clin N Am 9:475, 1974

White MS: Competence and Commitment: The Making of a Nurse Practitioner. San Francisco, University of California, School of Nursing, 1978

Williams BN: Malpractice. How good is your insurance protection. Am J Nurs 76:81, 1976

Willian MK: An historical perspective: the pediatric nurse associate. Pediatr Nurs 5:2, 1979

Willian MK: Reimbursement: an issue of conflicts. Pediatr Nurs 4:61, 1978
Willig SH: The Nurses' Guide to the Law. New York, McGraw-Hill, 1970
Woodham-Smith C: Florence Nightingale, 1820–1910. New York, McGraw-Hill, 1951
Zahourek R, Leone D, Lang F: Creative Health Services. St. Louis, Mosby, 1976
Zaslove MS, Underleider JT, Fuller M: The importance of the psychiatric nurse: views of physicians, patients and nurses. Am J Psychiatr 125:482, 1968
Zimmerman A: Taft-Hartley amended: implications for nursing. Am J Nurs 75:284, 1975

Index

A

Abortion, as crime, 3
Absolute standard of care, 78
Adversary system, 6
Albano, Edwin, 59
Alderson-Broaddus College, physician's assistant program of, 171
Alma-Ata conference, 153
American Academy of Family Practice, 59
American Academy of Pediatrics, 40, 176
American Association of Operating Room Nurses, 117, 206, 207
American College of Nurse Midwives, 204
American Hospital Association, 112, 174, 207
  Ameriplan, 113
  Special Committee on Licensure, 113
American Journal of Nursing, 24, 25, 26
American Medical Association, 19, 113, 174, 176
  founding of, 18
  and physician's assistants, 172
American Nurses' Association, 28, 174, 176
  "Code for Nurses," 83–84
  Congress for Nursing Practice, 164
  Council of Advanced Practitioners of Psychiatric and Mental Health Nursing, 166
  and credentialing, 122
  definition of nursing, 23, 30, 31, 51
  Division on Psychiatric Mental Health Nursing Practice, 164
  entry-into-practice resolutions, 38, 205, 206, 211–12
  founding of, 24

American Nurses' Association *(cont.)*
  and individual licensure, 117
  and nurse associates, 40
  standards of, 61
Animal bites, reportable, 76
Apprenticeship system, 24, 31, 37, 115, 144
Arbitrary imprisonment, 79
Arizona, medical practice act of, 61, 62
Assault, 68, 73
Associate in Arts degree, 37, 38
Attendants, 29, 50. *See also* Nursing assistants
Attorney, 6
Australia
  health care in, 142, 143
  nursing functions in, 144–46

B

Baccalaureate degrees and programs, 37, 38, 146
Barber v. *Reiking*, 32
Battery, 68, 72, 73, 75
Beatty, Richard L., 126, 127
Belgium
  health care in, 143
  nursing functions in, 149
Benne, Kenneth D., 36
Bennett Amendment, 136, 137
Bergmann, Barbara, 128
Beth Israel Hospital, Boston, 179, 194
Biomedical revolution, 141, 142
Birnbaum, Max, 36
Black, W. L., 189
Boards of medicine, 18, 19, 175

229

Boards of medicine *(cont.)*
  and role expansion, 55, 57
Boards of nursing, 27, 43
  and incompetency, 122
  membership of, 27, 28, 33, 48–50, 63, 122
  and role expansion, 55, 57, 61
Buckeye Nurses' Association, 207
Bullough, Bonnie, 127, 153
Bush nurses, 146
Business organizations of nurses, types of, 158–60

C

Cady, Lois, 128
California
  continuing education in, 209
  definition of registered nurse in, 60
  Good Samaritan statute in, 75
  institutional licensing in, 119
  nurse practice act of, 61, 89, 167, 180
  protocols in, 61, 180
  and statutory law, 9
California Nurses' Association, 31, 32
Calnen, Terrence, 165
Canada
  health care in, 142, 143
  nursing functions in, 146–48
Cardiopulmonary resuscitation, 32, 75
Career mobility, 38–39, 122, 206
Carnegie Commission on Higher Education, 110
Carnegie Foundation for Advancement of Teaching, 18
Certification, 61, 122, 166
  national system of, 118
  of specialized nurses, 203–5
Character, defamation of, 68, 77, 79
Child abuse, reporting, 77
Child Abuse and Treatment Act, 77
Christiensen v. *State of Iowa*, 136, 137
Chronic illness, and role expansion, 41, 148
Church groups, nursing by, 50

Civil law, 7, 9–10, 12–13
Civil Rights Act (1965), 135–36
Clinical nurse specialist, 164
  certification of, 203, 205
  and education, 39
  as force for role expansion, 40–41
  in mental health, 164–68
Code states, 9
College nursing programs, 31, 37, 38, 146
Colorado
  medical practice act of, 61, 128
  nurse practice act of, 128
  physician's assistant licensing in, 62
Colorado Child Health Assistant law, 175
Colorado, University of, physician's assistant program of, 171
Common law, 3, 7–9, 12
Commonwealth Fund, 110
Community health nurse
  in Australia, 145–46
  in Canada, 147
Competency measurement, 122
Comprehensive Health Manpower Training Act, 171
Confidentiality, 78–79
Connecticut
  medical practice act of, 62
  nursing board of, 120
Consciousness, lapses of, reporting, 76
Consent, 73–75
Conservatorship, 79
Consumers
  and health care, 162
  on nursing boards, 33, 48, 49, 50, 63, 122
Continuing education, 38, 122
  in Australia, 144
  mandatory, 101–2, 209–10
Cooper v. *National Motor Bearing Company*, 32–33
Coronary care units, 32, 40–41
Council on Medical Education, 172
Courts, 6, 11–13
Credentialing, 207–8
Criminal acts, reporting, 76
Criminal law, 9, 10, 11–12

D

Dahl, R. A., 94, 95
Darling v. Charleston Community Hospital, 2–8
Dartmouth Promis Laboratory, 179
Dean, Winston, 175
Decision making, by nurses, 43, 44
Defibrillators, use of, by nurses, 32
Delaware, nurse practice act of, 51
Delegatory provisions, 61–62, 63, 174–75
Demographic changes, and role expansion, 41
Denver, Colorado, sex discrimination case in, 125–37
Diagnosis, by nurses, 52, 53, 54
  authorization of, 33, 55, 57–58, 60, 61–62, 160
  exclusion of, 30–31, 33, 44, 50–51, 52, 151
Diagnosis, nursing, differentiated from medical, 58
Depositions, 67, 68
Dock, Lavinia, 25, 26
Domestic servants, nursing by, 50
Drug users, 81
Drugs
  and consent, 74
  cumulative effects of, 82
  handling of, 82
  interactions, 82
  and known drug users, 81
  prohibition on prescribing, 82
  and protocols, 180
Duke University, physician's assistant program of, 171

E

Education, nursing, 24–26, 28, 31, 48. *See also* Apprenticeship system; Continuing education; Entry-into-practice resolutions; Graduate education; Inservice training
  in Australia, 144, 145–46

Education, nursing *(cont.)*
  in Belgium, 149
  in Canada, 146, 147, 148
  credentialing, 207–8
  as force in role expansion, 36–39
  in Norway, 149
  of nurse practitioner, 177, 205
  of practical nurse, 206, 207
Education, physician, 16–18, 21, 39, 52
Education, physician's assistant, 171, 172, 173, 177
Edwards, Charles, 121
Emancipated minors, 73–74
Emergencies, 50
  and consent, 73
  and Good Samaritan statutes, 75–76
  and physician's orders, 81
Employment patterns
  of nurses, 24, 29, 257–60. *See also* Private practice
  of physician's assistants, 173–74
England
  licensure in, 26
  nursing education in, 25–26
  physicians in, 16–17
Entry-into-practice resolutions, 38, 205–7, 211–12
Epstein, C. F., 88, 93, 95
Equal Pay Act (1964), 135, 136
Equivalency examinations, 122
Examinations
  equivalency, 122
  national pool, 31
  for physician's assistants, 172
  proficiency, 122
  state board, 31, 48, 114

F

False imprisonment, 72
Family practice, 20, 21, 38, 39
  in Norway, 150
Federal courts, 11. *See also* Supreme Court
Federal employees, nursing by, 50

232 Index

Feldsher, 150–51
Feminist movement, 156–57
Fenwick, Ethel Gordon Bedford, 26
First aid, 75
Flexner, Abraham, 18
Flexner report, 18, 39
Florida
 continuing education in, 209
 medical practice act of, 61
Florida Nurses' Association, 176
Fogotson, Edward, 113
Friends, nursing by, 50

G

Gans, H. J., 95
Goffman, E., 95
Good Samaritan statutes, 75–76
Gordon, C., 88
Graduate education, 38–39, 164, 165, 205
 in Australia, 145
 in Poland, 150
Graham, Edith, 204
Gratuitous services, 50
Griggs v. *Duke Power Company,* 136

H

Hawaii Nursing, Medical and Hospital Association, 32
Health care, 109
 costs of, 39
 difficulty of entry into, 156
 financing of, 113, 141, 142–43, 161. *See also* Medicaid; Medicare
 as human right, 141–42
Health, Education and Welfare, U. S. Department of, 62, 110
 Bureau of Health Manpower Education, 117–18
 and licensure, 120–22
Health personnel. *See also specific title*
 certification of, 118
 licensing of, 118, 119–20, 121

Health insurance. *See* Health care, financing of
Health Professions Educational Assistance Act (1976), 152
Heimlich maneuver, 75
Herbert, Sidney, 43
Hershey, Nathan, 111, 112
"Hershey model," 111
Hoebel, E. A., 5
Holmes, Oliver Wendel, Jr., 8
Hospital Educational and Research Foundation of Pennsylvania, 118–19
Hospital schools of nursing, 24, 37, 38
 in Australia, 144
 in Canada, 146
Hospitals. *See also* Licensure, institutional
 leaving, against medical advice, 82–83
 liability of, 70–71, 78
 policies of, 71
 and private practice, 161–62

I

Idaho
 as code state, 9
 nurse practice act of, 33, 55
 protocols in, 61
 standard procedures in, 180
 standards of performance in, 180
Illinois
 Board of Opinions, 55
 Department of Registration and Education, 120
Illinois Hospital Association, 113
Illinois Nurses' Association, 118
Imprisonment
 arbitrary, 79
 false, 72
Incident report, 82
Individual licensure. *See* Licensure, individual
Infectious diseases, reporting, 76
Insanity, 7–8
Inservice training, 115
Institute of Public Administration, 118

Institutional licensure. *See* Licensure, institutional
Intensive care units, 32, 144
Intravenous fluids, starting, by nurses, 31

J

Job descriptions and classification, 111, 115
Job-worth analysis, 126–27
Joint Commission on Accreditation of Hospitals, 112, 115
Joint practice commissions, 32
Judges, 5
Jurisdictions, movement between, 31, 48, 114, 116, 117
Jury, 6, 67, 68

K

Kansas
  continuing education in, 209
  medical practice act of, 61
Karmel Committee, 145
Killing, 3, 4
Kinlein, M. Lucille, 156

L

Law, 3–13
  changing, 6–7, 8, 87–88
  civil, 7, 9–10, 12–13
  common, 3, 7–9, 12
  criminal, 9, 10, 11–12
  definition of, 3
  enforcement, 4
  functions of, 5
  history of, 4–7
  ignoring, 88
  Mosaic, 4, 5
  and physician's assistants, 174–75
  as restraining force in role expansion, 44–45
  statutory, 8–9, 10

Lay midwives, 204
Lego, Suzanne, 165
Lemmons, Mary, 127, 133
Lemmons case, 126, 127, 128, 129, 131, 134, 135, 137
Lewin, Kurt, 36, 37
Lewis, Charles, 156
Licensure by endorsement, 114
Licensure, individual, 109–10, 111, 113–14, 117, 118, 122
Licensure, institutional, 109–23, 174
  concepts of, 110–113
Licensure, medical, 14–15, 26, 77
Licensure, nursing, 20, 205
  first phase of, 23, 24–28, 203
  for practice of psychotherapy, 167
  second phase of, 23, 28–33, 203
  third phase of, 23, 33, 47–63, 203
Licensure, and physician's assistant, 174–75
Litoff, J., 204
Lloyd, J. J., 112
Lobbying, 27, 28, 90

M

McAdams, D., 112
McNaughten case, 7
Magaw, Alice, 204
Maine, medical practice act of, 61
Malpractice insurance, 10, 67, 209
Malpractice suits, 10, 67–84 *passim*, 159, 209
March, J. G., 96n
Maryland, physician supervision in, 63
Massachusetts
  continuing education in, 209
  licensing in, 119–20
Massachusetts Nurses' Association, 120
Master's degree, 38–39. *See also* Graduate education
Medex program, 171
Medibank, 142
Medicaid, 152, 161, 170
Medical licensure. *See* Licensure, medical
Medical monopoly, 14–21, 42, 172

Medical practice acts, 61–62, 63, 128, 174
　delegatory provisions of, 61–62, 63,
　　174–75
Medical records, 81–84
Medical societies, 17. *See also specific
　　name*
Medical staff review, 112
Medicare, 141, 152, 161, 170
Medication. *See* Drugs
Medicine, unlicensed practice of, 77–78
Mental health, clinical nurse specialists in,
　　164–68
Mental patients, 72, 79
Merton, R., 96n
Michigan Heart Association, 32
Middle Ages, 15–16
Miike, Lawrence, 111
Millis Commission, 39
Minnesota
　continuing education in, 209
　physician supervision in, 63
Minority groups, 152–53
Minors
　and consent, 73
　emancipated, 73–74
Mississippi, boards of nursing and health
　　of, 55
Model Penal Code, 8
Montag, Mildred, 38
Montana, as code state, 9
Mosaic law, 4, 5
Muller v. United States Steel Corporation,
　　137

N

National Advisory Commission on Health
　　Manpower, 113
National Association of Pediatric Nurse
　　Associates and Practitioners
　　(NAPNAP), 61
National Association for Practical Nurse
　　Education and Service, 117
National Board of Medical Examiners, 172
National Commission of the Certification
　　of Physician's Assistants, 172

National Commission for the Study of
　　Nursing and Nursing Education, 32,
　　117
National Federation of Licensed Practical
　　Nurses, 117
National League for Nursing, 24, 31, 174
　Council of Baccalaureate and Higher
　　Degrees, 38, 205, 206
　and individual licensure, 117
National League for Nursing Education, 28
National Organization of Public Health
　　Nurses, 28
National pool examinations, 31
Nebraska
　boards of nursing and medicine, 55, 57
　continuing education in, 209
Negligence, 3, 10, 32–33, 68–69, 72–73,
　　81, 82, 158. *See also* Malpractice
　　suits; Standard of care; *specific case*
　definition of, 69
　standard of care as criterion for deter-
　　mining, 69–70
New Jersey
　certification for clinical nurse specialist
　　in mental health in, 166
　nurse registration act of, 26, 27
　scope of practice in, 59
New Jersey Hospital Association, 112
New York
　Board of Regents, 120
　nurse practice act of, 28, 33
　nurse registration act of, 26, 27
　nursing diagnosis in, 57–58, 60
　scope of practice in, 23, 29
New York State Nurses' Association,
　and entry-into-practice resolutions, 205,
　　206, 207
New Zealand, first nurse registration act in,
　　25
Nightingale, Florence, 24, 25, 26, 42–43,
　　67, 83, 127, 128
North Carolina
　nurse practice act of, 51
　nurse registration act of, 26–27
North Dakota, as code state, 9
Norway
　health care in, 143

Norway *(cont.)*
  nursing fuctions in, 149–50
Nurse(s). *See also* Nursing; Practical nurse(s)
  consultation of, with physician, 58
  definition of, 60
  education of. *See* Education, nursing
  employment patterns of, 24, 29, 157–60
  informal power of, 20
  in private practice, 156–62, 165–67
  role expansion of. *See* Role expansion
  salaries of, 125–37 *passim*
  scope of function of, 29, 30, 58–59, 77–78, 144, 145
  status of, 156, 157. *See also* Sex discrimination; Sex stereotyping
Nurse anesthetists, 55
  certification of, 203, 204, 205
  in Norway, 149
  regulations for, 61
Nurse clinicians. *See* Clinical nurse specialist
Nurse-midwives, 55
  certification of, 203, 204, 205
  in Norway, 149–50
  regulations for, 61
Nurse-physician relationship, 42, 43–44, 157
Nurse practice acts, 44, 122, 141, 203. *See also* Nurse registration acts
  of California, 61, 89, 167, 180
  of Colorado, 128
  of Delaware, 51
  history of, 23, 28–33
  of Idaho, 33, 55
  of New York, 23, 33
  of North Carolina, 51
  of Tennessee, 33, 51
  of South Dakota, 33
  of Virginia, 51
  of Washington, 61, 100–8
Nurse practitioners, 151
  in Canada, 147–48
  certification of, 61, 203, 204, 205
  definition of, 55
  education of, 177, 205
  as force for role expansion, 39, 41

Nurse practitioners *(cont.)*
  and licensure, 119
  as physician substitute, 152–53
  and physician's assistants, 170–171, 175–177
  in private practice, 160
  and protocols, 181
  in rural areas, 161, 170
  and scope of function, 58–59
Nurse registration acts, 24–28. *See also* Nurse practice acts
Nursemaids, nursing by, 50
Nurses' Associated Alumnae, 24, 25, 26
Nurses' Association of the American College of Obstetricians and Gynecologists, 117
Nursing. *See also* Nurse(s)
  in Australia, 144–46
  in Belgium, 149
  in Canada, 146–48
  definition of, 29–30, 102, 103–5, 141
  hierarchical structure of, 28, 29, 50, 164
  in Norway, 149–50
  in Poland, 150–51
  role, expansion of. *See* Role expansion
  team, 29
Nursing assistants, 28, 50. *See also* Attendents
Nursing notes, 82–83
Nuttall, R., 88

O

Occupational injuries, reporting, 76
Ohio Nurses' Association, 207
Oklahoma
  as code state, 9
  medical practice act of, 61
Ophthalmia neonatorum, reporting, 76
Orders, 81–82, 176
Oregon, continuing education in, 209
Organizations, 88–94. *See also* Business organizations of nurses, types of; *specific name*
  information base of, and power, 89–90

Organizations *(cont.)*
  personal attributes of members of, and power, 93–94
  physical resources of, and power, 91–93
  professional expertise of, and power, 90–91
  size of, and power, 89
Osler, William, 15
Outpost nurses, 148

P

Palmer, Sophia, 24, 26
Patient
  contact of, with nonward personnel, 71
  as danger, 78–79
  mental, 72, 79
  noncompliant, 82
  rights of, 72, 73, 80–81
  as risk, 71–72
Patient records, 81–84
Patient's Bill of Rights, 80–81
Peer evaluation, 122
Pennsylvania, licensing in, 118–19
Pesticide poisoning, reporting, 76
Phenylketonuria, reporting, 76
Physician(s). *See also* Medical monopoly
  board certification of, 19
  competence of, 18–19
  delegation of medical acts by, 61–62, 63, 174–75
  education of, 16–18, 21, 39, 52
  foreign, 21
  income of, 39
  office employees of, nursing by, 50
  in Norway, 150
  in Poland, 150–51
  power of, 19, 20
  primary care, 29, 41, 151–52
  role of, 156
Physician extenders, 59. *See also* Nurse practitioners; Physician's assistants
Physician-nurse relationship, 42, 43–44, 157
Physician's assistants, 61
  current patterns concerning, 173–74

Physician's assistants *(cont.)*
  education of, 171, 172, 173, 177
  fear of competition from, 59
  as force for role expansion, 39–40
  history of, 171–72
  and the law, 62, 174–75
  and nurse practitioner, 170–71, 175–77
  salaries of, 173
Poland
  health care in, 143
  nursing functions in, 150–51
Political performance, 95–99
Political process, 87, 94–99
Poverty
  and use of nurse practitioners, 152, 170
  and use of physician's assistants, 170, 171
Power. *See also* Medical monopoly
  absent, 88
  analysis of, 88–94
  manifest, 88
  of nurses, informal, 20
  of physicians, 19, 20
  potential, 89
  reputational, 88
Practical nurse(s), 28
  definition of, 30
  education of, 206, 207
  licensure of, 29, 48
  and state boards, 50
  status of. *See* Nursing, hierarchical structure of
Precedents, 9
Prescriptions, signing of, 181. *See also* Drugs
Primary care physicians, 39, 41, 151–52
Privacy, invasion of, 68, 77, 78, 79–80
Private duty nurses, 24, 29
Private practice, 156–62, 165–67
Product liability, 69–70, 71
Professional associations, 61, 112, 120. *See also specific name*
Proficiency examinations, 122
Protocols, 61
  adapting, 181, 201
  concept of, 186–88
  construction of, 179–84, 188–94

Protocols (cont.)
  definition of, 186
  and the law, 201-2
  for presenting complaints, 182, 187
  for managing diagnosed illnesses, 182
  types of, 182
  validation of, 194-200, 202
Psychosocial diagnosis, 58
Psychosocial functions, 31, 170, 176
Psychotherapy, 165-68 passim
Public health nurses, in Norway, 150

R

Redman, E., 95
Registered nurse. See also Nurse(s)
  definition of, 51
  title of, 28, 29
Regulatory law, 10, 174, 175
Relicensure, 122
Relocation, of nurses, 31, 48, 114, 116, 117
Reporting statutes, 76-77, 78, 80
Res ipsa loquitur, 68-69
Respondeat superior, 70, 72, 83, 161
Restraint, 72
Robb, Isabel Hampton, 25, 26
Roemer, R., 112
Role expansion, 31-32, 33, 141-53 passim, 157
  and court decisions, 208-9
  forces restraining, 36, 42-44
  forces stimulating, 36-41
  facilitating, 51-63
  and medical monopoly, 19-20, 21
Rural areas, 152, 161, 170, 172, 181
Rural Health Clinic Services Act (1977), 152, 170

S

Salaries
  of nurses, 41, 125-37 passim
  of physicians, 39
  of physician's assistants, 173

Sarner, Harvey, 32
Scheuch, E., 88
Schmahl, J. A., 165
Sex discrimination, 24, 42-44, 93.
  in Denver, 125-37 passim
Sex stereotyping, 128, 129, 133, 134, 135, 136, 156-57, 170
Sigerest, Henry, 15
Silver, Henry, 40
Simon, H. A., 96n
Sledge v. J. P. Stevens Company, 137
Smith, Adam, 15
Social Security Act, 170
South Carolina Board of Nursing, 48
South Dakota
  as code state, 9
  nurse practice act, 33
Stachyra, Marcia, 166
Standard of care
  absolute, 78
  as criterion for determining negligence, 69-72
  in emergencies, 75
Stanford University, physician's assistant program of, 171
Stare decisis, 9
State courts, 11
Statutes, reporting, 76-77, 78, 80
Statutory law, 8-9, 10
Stead, Eugene, 171
Stein, Leonard, 43
Strikes, nurses', 19-92
Student nurses, 50
Supreme Court, 9, 11

T

Team nursing, 29
Tennessee
  Board of Nursing, 180
  nurse practice act of, 33, 51
  protocols in, 61, 180
Testimony, 67-68, 69, 77
Torts, 10, 72-75
Treatment, by nurses,
  alteration of, 180

238 Index

Treatment, by nurses *(cont.)*
    authorization of, 33, 55, 57, 61–62, 160
    exclusion of, 30–31, 33, 44, 50–51, 150
Trial, 68

U

Ujhely, Gertrude B., 165, 166
Uncertainty absorption points, 96*n*
Urinary tract infection/vaginitis protocol, 189–200
Utter v. *United Hospital Center, Incorporated,* 208–9

V

Vena punctures, 31
Virginia
    nurse practice act of, 51

Virginia *(cont.)*
    nurse registration act of, 26
    regulation of attendants in, 29
Vocational nurse. *See* Practical nurse(s)

W

Warnings, 78–79
Washington
    certification in, 205
    nurse practice act of, 61, 100–8
    protocols in, 180
Washington State Nurses' Association, 176
Weapons, dangerous, reporting, 76
Willard Commission, 39
Winner, Fred M., 134–35, 136
Wisconsin, licensing in, 120
Wisconsin Nurses' Association, 157
Work-related injuries, reporting, 76
Wyoming, protocols in, 61

DATE DUE			
JUL 7 1982			
SEP 04 1985			